AMERICA'S BEST
HOTELS, RESTAURANTS & SPAS
2008 FOUR AND FIVE STAR WINNERS

Acknowledgements

We gratefully acknowledge the help of our representatives for their efficient and perceptive inspections of the lodging and dining establishments listed; the establishments' proprietors for their cooperation in showing their facilities and providing information about them; and the many users of previous editions who have taken the time to share their experiences.

The information contained herein is derived from a variety of third-party sources. Although every effort has been made to verify the information obtained from such sources, the publisher assumes no responsibility for inconsistencies or inaccuracies in the data or liability for any damages of any type arising from errors or omissions.

Neither the editors nor the publisher assume responsibility for the services provided by any business listed in this guide or for any loss, damage or disruption in your travel for any reason.

ISBN: 978-0841-60726-2
10 9 8 7 6 5 4 3 2 1

Manufactured in Canada
Book Design by Karine Gallet

CONTENTS

Mobil's Four-Star and Five-Star Winners 2008

Celebrating 50 years

Because time is precious and the travel industry is ever-changing, having accurate, reliable travel information at your fingertips is essential. Mobil Travel Guide has provided invaluable insight to travelers for 50 years, and we are committed to continuing this service into the future.

The Mobil Corporation (known as Exxon Mobil Corporation since a 1999 merger) began producing the Mobil Travel Guide books in 1958 following the introduction of the U.S. interstate highway system in 1956. The first edition covered only five Southwestern states. Since then, our books have become the premier travel guides in North America, covering all 50 states and Canada.

Since its founding, Mobil Travel Guide has served as an advocate for travelers seeking knowledge about hotels, restaurants and places to visit. Based on an objective process, we make recommendations to our customers that we believe will enhance the quality and value of their travel experiences. Our trusted Mobil One- to Five-Star rating system is the oldest and most respected lodging and restaurant inspection and rating program in North America. Most hoteliers, restaurateurs and industry observers favorably regard the rigor of our inspection program and understand the prestige and benefits that come with receiving a Mobil Star rating.

The Mobil Travel Guide process of rating each establishment includes:
* ★ Unannouced facility inspections
* ★ Incognito service evaluations
* ★ A review of unsolicited comments from the general public
* ★ Senior management oversight

For each property, more than 450 attributes, including cleanliness, physical facilities and employee attitude and courtesy, are measured and evaluated to produce a mathematically derived score, which is then blended with the other elements to form an overall score. These scores form the basis that we use to assign our Mobil One- to Five-Star ratings.

This process focuses on guest expectations, guest experience and consistency of service, not just physical facilities and amenities. It's fundamentally a rating system that rewards those properties that continually strive for and achieve excellence each year. The very best properties are consistently raising the bar for those that wish to compete with them.

Only facilities that meet Mobil Travel Guide's standards earn the privilege of being listed in the guide. Deteriorating, poorly managed establishments are deleted. A Mobil Travel Guide listing constitutes a positive quality recommendation. Every listing is an accolade, a recognition of achievement.

We do not charge establishments for inclusion in our guides. We have no relationship with any of the businesses and attractions we list and act only as a consumer advocate. We do the investigative legwork so that you won't have to.

Restaurants and hotels—particularly small chains and stand-alone establishments—change management or even go out of business with surprising quickness. Although we make every effort to continuously update information, we recommend that you call ahead to make sure the place you've selected is still open.

We hope that your travels are enjoyable and that our books help you get the most out of every trip you take. If any aspect of your accommodation, dining, spa or sightseeing experience motivates you to comment, please contact us. Mobil Travel Guide, 200 W. Madison St., Suite 3950, Chicago, IL 60606, or send an e-mail to info@mobiltravelguide.com

Happy travels.

WELCOME

Few accolades are more coveted in the hospitality industry than Mobil's Four- and Five-Star Awards. *America's Best Hotels, Restaurants & Spas* gathers together in one volume the exceptional properties that achieved this status. In this book are the very best establishments the United States has to offer—places that provide not just a comfortable room for the night or superb food in lovely surroundings, but exquisite establishments where every detail is attended to. Trained professionals carefully evaluate all Mobil Four- and Five-Star lodgings, restaurants and spas each year. No Mobil Four- or Five-Star winner rests on its laurels; each must earn the award every year.

HOW TO USE THIS BOOK

HOTELS

FIVE STAR HOTELS

A Mobil Five-Star lodging provides consistently superlative service in an exceptionally distinctive luxury environment, with expanded services. Attention to detail is evident throughout the hotel, resort, or inn, from bed linens to staff uniforms.

FOUR STAR HOTELS

A Mobil Four-Star lodging provides a luxury experience with expanded amenities in a distinctive environment. Services may include, but are not limited to, automatic turndown service, 24-hour room service and valet parking.

For every property, we also provide pricing information. The pricing categories break down as follows:

$ = Up to $150
$$ = $151-$250
$$$ = $251-$350
$$$$ = $351 and up

All prices quoted are accurate at the time of publication, however prices cannot be guaranteed.

RESTAURANTS

FIVE STAR RESTAURANT

A Mobil Five-Star restaurant offers one of the few flawless dining experiences in the country. These establishments consistently provide their guests with exceptional food, superlative service, elegant décor and exquisite presentations of each detail surrounding a meal.

FOUR STAR RESTAURANT

A Mobil Four-Star restaurant provides professional service, distinctive presentations and wonderful food.

Each restaurant listing gives the cuisine type, street address, phone and website, meals served, days of operation (if not open daily year-round) and pricing category. Information about appropriate attire is provided, although it's always a good idea to call ahead and ask if you're unsure; the meaning of "casual" or "business casual" varies widely in different parts of the country. We also indicate whether the restaurant has a bar, whether a children's menu is offered and whether outdoor seating is available. If reservations are recommended, we note that fact in the listing. When valet parking is available, it is noted in the description. Because menu prices can fluctuate, we list a pricing category rather than specific prices. The pricing categories are defined as follows, per diner, and assume that you order an appetizer or dessert, an entrée and one drink:

$ = $15 and under
$$ = $16-35
$$$ = $36-85
$$$$ = $86 and up

All prices quoted are accurate at the time of publication, however prices cannot be guaranteed.

SPAS

Mobil Travel Guide is pleased to announce its newest category, hotel and resort spas. Until now, hotel and resort spas have not been formally rated or inspected by any organization. Every spa selected for inclusion in this book underwent a rigorous inspection process similar to the one Mobil Travel Guide has been applying to lodgings and restaurants for five decades. After researching more than 300 spas and performing exhaustive incognito inspections of more than 200 properties, we narrowed our list to the best spas in the United States and Canada.

Mobil Travel Guide's spa ratings are based on objective evaluations of more than 450 attributes. Approximately half of these criteria assess basic expectations, such as staff courtesy, the technical proficiency and skill of the employees and whether the facility is maintained properly and hygienically. Several standards address issues that impact a guest's physical comfort and convenience, as well as the staff's ability to impart a sense of personalized service and anticipate clients' needs. Additional criteria measure the spa's ability to create a completely calming ambience.

FIVE STAR SPA

The Mobil Five-Star spa provides consistently superlative service in an exceptionally distinctive luxury environment with extensive amenities. The staff at a Mobil Five-Star spa provides extraordinary service beyond the traditional spa experience, allowing guests to achieve the highest level of relaxation and pampering. A Mobil Five-Star spa offers an extensive array of treatments, often incorporating international themes and products. Attention to detail is evident throughout the spa, from arrival to departure.

The Mobil Four-Star spa provides a luxurious experience with expanded amenities in an elegant and serene environment. Throughout the spa facility, guests experience personalized service. Amenities might include, but are not limited to, single-sex relaxation rooms where guests wait for their treatments, plunge pools and whirlpools in both men's and women's locker rooms, and an array of treatments, including a selection of massages, body therapies, facials and a variety of salon services.

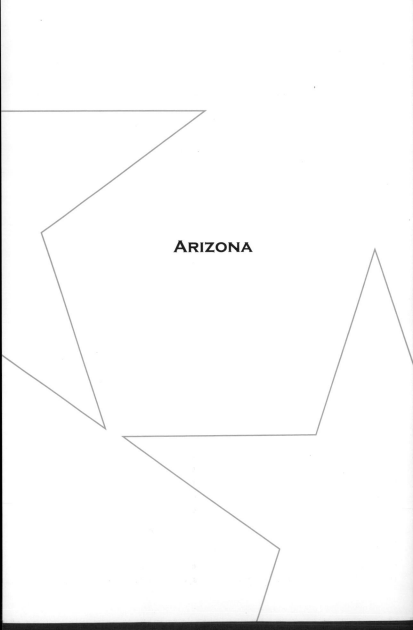

ARIZONA

ARIZONA

Carefree/Paradise Valley

THE BOULDERS RESORT AND GOLDEN DOOR SPA ★ ★ ★ ★

34631 N. Tom Darlington Dr., Carefree, 480-488-9009, 866-397-6520;
www.theboulders.com

Located in the foothills of the Sonoran Desert just north of Scottsdale, the Boulders Resort and Golden Door Spa blends perfectly with the surrounding rock outcroppings, ancient boulders and saguaro cactus plants. The adobe casitas are distinguished by overstuffed leather chairs, exposed beams and Mexican tiles, while one-, two- and three-bedroom Pueblo Villas are ideal for families or for those on longer visits. The resort boasts a first-rate tennis facility and an 18-hole championship golf course. There's also rock climbing, hiking and tours of Native-American cave dwellings and ruins. Guided hikes after dark using night vision equipment are especially fun. The Golden Door Spa, an outpost of the famous California retreat, is divine. Look for superb facials, an array of massages and relaxing body wraps at this on-site spa.

199 rooms. Pets accepted, some restrictions; fee. High-speed Internet access. Five restaurants, three bars. Children's activity center. Fitness center, fitness classes, spa. Three outdoor pools, whirlpool. Golf, 36 holes. Tennis. Business center. $$$$

Scottsdale

FOUR SEASONS RESORT SCOTTSDALE AT TROON NORTH ★ ★ ★ ★

10600 E. Crescent Moon Dr., Scottsdale, 480-515-5700, 800-819-5053;
www.fourseasons.com

Located on a 40-acre nature preserve, this beautiful resort features rooms spread across 25 Southwestern-style casita buildings, with views of the stunning desert. Amenities include down duvets, CD players and baths stocked with luxury products and soaking tubs. Spring for a suite if you can—you'll get a plunge pool, alfresco garden shower and indoor kiva fireplace. A veritable mecca for golfers, the resort grants priority tee times at Troon North's two courses, considered among the best in the world. The spa offers everything from desert nectar facials to moonlight massages performed in the privacy of your room's balcony or terrace. There are also salon services like manicures and pedicures and a fitness center with cutting edge equipment and a movement studio. Three restaurants reflect the resort's casual elegance and serve cuisine that references the

Southwestern setting (think kiva-oven roasted pizza with carne asada, roasted peppers and jalapeño jack cheese).

210 rooms. High-speed Internet access. Restaurant, bar. Children's activity center. Fitness Center, Spa. Pets accepted. Pool. Golf. Tennis. $$$$

THE PHOENICIAN ★ ★ ★ ★

6000 E. Camelback Rd., Scottsdale, 480-941-8200, 800-888-8234;
www.thephoenician.com

This world-class resort, located at the base of Camelback Mountain, is ultra-luxurious. Everywhere you look you see crystal, rich fabrics and leather-topped furniture. The rooms and suites feature imported Irish linens and oversized bathrooms with Italian marble. But for all of this luxury, there is no attitude at this gracious resort. Someone is always around to help—to steer you toward one of the nine pools or one of a number of recreational opportunities, including desert hikes. For an even more luxurious experience, you can opt to stay in the Canyon Suites within the Phoenician which offer sprawling, opulent rooms, each with a separate pool and private cabana. Guests are assigned to ambassadors who arrange everything from in-room aromatherapy baths to chauffered trips into town in the resort Mercedes. The resort's golf courses and full-service spa serve as primary temptations.

647 rooms. Wireless Internet access. Restaurant, bar. Children's activity center. Fitness center. Spa. Airport transportation available. Pets accepted. Pool. Golf. Tennis. Business center. $$$

Phoenix

THE RITZ-CARLTON, PHOENIX ★ ★ ★ ★

2401 E. Camelback, Phoenix, 602-468-0700, 800-241-3333;
www.ritzcarlton.com

This hotel is located smack in the middle of the Camelback Corridor, the exclusive shopping, dining and financial district of Phoenix. The classically decorated rooms have views of the skyline or the Squaw Peak Mountain Range—and of course, there's the famed Ritz-Carlton level of service. Concierges will offer tips on everything from the area's best golf courses to the tastiest cocktail to sip in the lobby lounge. You'll find modern takes on French classics like steak au poivre with crispy frites at the hotel's festive Bistro 24. The outdoor pool sparkles and the sundeck area is cooled with hydro-misters.

281 rooms. Wireless Internet access. Restaurant, two bars. Airport transportation available. Fitness center. Pool. Business Center. $$$

Chandler

KAI ★ ★ ★ ★

5594 W. Wild Horse Pass Blvd., Chandler, 602-385-5726;
www.wildhorsepassresort.com
Lodged in the Sheraton Wild Horse Pass Resort, this sophisticated eatery showcases locally grown produce. Executive chef Michael O'Dowd and Native American chef de cuisine Jack Strong prepare a menu of dishes that showcase ingredients grown by the local Gila River Indian community, including chiles and seeds that thrive in the area. A surprisingly rich Arizona-made olive oil is used in recipes that merge contemporary tastes and time-honored Native American techniques. (Kai means "seed" in Pima.) The results include lobster tail, corn and avocado atop fry bread, and rack of lamb with fresh mole sauce. Desserts like cheesecake take on a new meaning when prepared with unique ingredients such as goat's milk, mesquite meal crust and hibiscus syrup.

Southwestern menu. Dinner. Closed Sunday-Monday. Bar. Business casual attire. Outdoor seating. $$$

Tucson

THE VENTANA ROOM ★ ★ ★ ★

7000 N. Resort Dr., Tucson, 520 615-5494; www.ventanaroom.com
Located in the Loews Ventana Canyon Resort, the Ventana Room is the place to go for panoramic views of the city lights and mountain ranges. The contemporary American cuisine features wild cuts of game, as well as steaks and seafood. A three-, four- or five-course prix fixe menu is available, with offerings such as Alaskan black cod with braised fennel and carmelized pancetta or Australian wagyu beef tenderloin with pomegranate port reduction. The substantial wine list includes bottles from around the world. Those who want to check out the action in the kitchen can reserve the chef's table, which offers seating for six and a chance to sample a specially prepared menu.

French menu. Dinner. Closed Sunday-Monday; also mid-August-mid-September. Bar. Business casual attire. Reservations recommended. Valet parking. $$$$

Phoenix

ALVADORA SPA AT ROYAL PALMS ★ ★ ★ ★

5200 E. Camelback Rd., Phoenix, 602-977-6400, 800-672-6011;
www.royalpalmsresortandspa.com

Inspired by the region's native flowers, herbs and oils, this Mediterranean-style spa brings the outdoors in through its open-air design and plant-inspired therapies. The healing properties of water are a focal point here, whether you're soaking in a bath of grape seeds and herbs or floating in the Watsu pool. Indulge in the Fango mud wrap, a traditional therapy that uses volcanic mud from Italy's northern regions to purify and cleanse skin. The vino therapy facial uses grape leaf extract for intense moisturizing. Enjoy yoga, tai chi, meditation and mat Pilates classes in the 24-hour fitness center.

Scottsdale

THE CENTRE FOR WELL BEING ★ ★ ★ ★

6000 E. Camelback Rd., Scottsdale, 480-941-8200, 800-843-2392;
www.centreforwellbeing.com

This spa, which is located at the Phoenician resort, is always changing and updating—which means services here are on the cutting edge. There is everything from jin shin jyutsu, which utilizes a series of holding techniques to alleviate tension blocked in the body, to a neuromuscular treatment that offers spot relief for injuries (say, if you overdid it playing golf). Tweak your workout routine by scheduling a fitness consultation with one of the staff experts, or simply indulge in a traditional massage. Of course, you'll want to go home looking as great as you feel, and for that there's no shortage of wraps, facials and scrubs. Even the state-of-the-art gym is inticing.

SPA AT FOUR SEASONS RESORT SCOTTSDALE AT TROON NORTH ★ ★ ★ ★

10600 E. Crescent Moon Dr., Scottsdale, 480-513-5145, 888-207-9696;
www.fourseasons.com

You're guaranteed to relax at this 12,000-square-foot spa that includes a full-service salon and fitness center. The resort's signature moonlight massage is the perfect way to end the day. Or try the "head over heels" treatment, an indulgent session of reflexology performed by two technicians and followed up with a rejuvenating facial and relaxing hand massage. You'll also find hot stone massages and facials that feature local, seasonal ingredients, including saguaro blossom, the state flower, as well as the more common green tea and honey. The salon goes beyond traditional services to include such treats as scalp massages and nourishing hair treatments. Half-day and full-day packages are available. $$

WILLOW STREAM SPA, THE SPA AT THE FAIRMONT SCOTTSDALE PRINCESS ★ ★ ★ ★

7575 E. Princess Dr., Scottsdale, 480-585-2732, 800-908-9540; www.fairmont.com

The facilities at the Fairmont Scottsdale Princess are superb—from championship golf courses to award-winning restaurants—and the spa is no exception. The mission here is to help you find more energy, and many of the treatments make use of the Havasupai Waterfall (inspired by the oasis of waterfalls in the Grand Canyon) located on the spa's first floor. The Havasupai Body Oasis treatment, for example, combines warm eucalyptus and herbal baths with the healing power of the waterfalls. Other treatments also reflect local surroundings. The Desert Purification features a body mask of cornmeal, clay and oats. An Ayate cloth (made from the cactus plant) is then used to exfoliate skin. Or simply recharge with a facial, massage or spa pedicure.

Paradise Valley

THE SANCTUARY SPA AT SANCTUARY ON CAMELBACK MOUNTAIN ★ ★ ★ ★

5700 E. McDonald Dr., Paradise Valley, 480-607-2330, 800-245-2051; www.sanctuaryoncamelback.com

Originally designed as a tennis club in the 1950s by Frank Lloyd Wright protégé Hiram Hudson Benedict, the resort was completely renovated in 2001. The understated elegance first defined by Benedict is still here. The resort's spa was expanded and seems to include practically every treatment under the sun, from standard facials to acupuncture and numerology. The spa menu offers several Asian-inspired treatments including Thai massage and shiatsu. The resort retains its commitment to the championship tennis courts that defined it from the start, but the grounds are also ideal for yoga and meditation. Guided desert hikes are available.

Tucson

THE SPA AT OMNI TUCSON NATIONAL ★ ★ ★ ★

2727 West Club Dr., Tucson, 520-575-7559; www.tucsonnational.com

The Spa at Omni Tucson National has a tranquil and picturesque location in the foothills of the Santa Catalina Mountains. Whether you have half an hour or an entire day, this spa has something to offer. In 25 minutes, the tension reliever massage works its magic where you are most knotted up, while the business facial cleanses, tones, exfoliates and hydrates in just under 30 minutes. Other facials include aromatherapy, deep-cleansing, anti-aging and deluxe hydration. Body masks smooth rough skin with a variety of ingredients, including seaweed, desert rose clay, rich mud from the Dead Sea, shea butter and aspara, a plant that grows by the beach and is recognized for its calming properties.

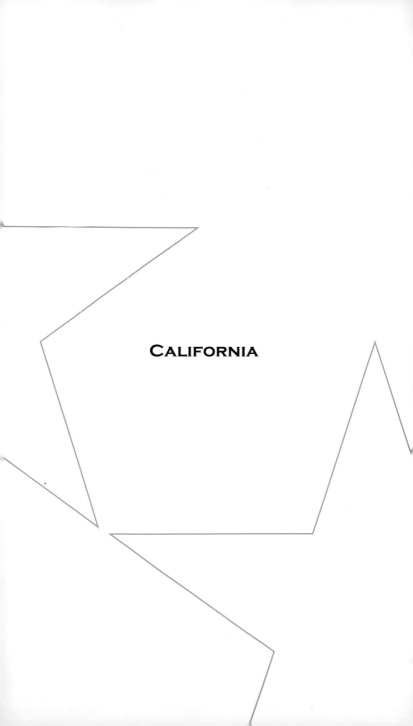

California

CALIFORNIA

Oakhurst

CHATEAU DU SUREAU ★ ★ ★ ★ ★

48688 Victoria Lane, Oakhurst, 559-683-6860; www.chateausureau.com

Foodies have been flocking to the Elderberry House restaurant since 1984 for its haute cuisine. The restaurant did so well that owner Erna Kubin-Clanin opened an inn to accommodate her guests. Tucked away in the heart of the Sierra Nevada forest, this charming Provençal castle features quaint balconies and a dramatic round fieldstone tower. The grounds are planted with manicured topiaries and the stucco walls are dotted with Elderberry bushes that cover the castle's rolling hills. Inside, chambermaids in black with white linen aprons deliver baskets of goodies and tea. There is no front desk and no check-in formalities. The 10 unique bedrooms, nearly all of which have fireplaces, include canopy and sleigh beds, cathedral ceilings and views of the Sierra Nevada Mountains.

12 rooms. Closed two weeks in January. Complimentary full breakfast. Restaurant, bar. Spa. $$$$

San Francisco

FOUR SEASONS HOTEL SAN FRANCISCO ★ ★ ★ ★ ★

757 Market St., San Francisco, 415-633-3000, 800-819-5053; www.fourseasons.com

Occupying several levels of a residential tower, this showpiece of contemporary design is two blocks from Union Square's shopping and just around the bend from the Museum of Modern Art. In its sophisticated guest rooms and suites, considered the largest in the city, floor-to-ceiling windows frame unparalleled views of Market Street, Yerba Buena Gardens or San Francisco Bay. King-sized beds adorn every room and the warm cream color scheme and spacious marble-lined bathrooms with deep soaking tubs and separate glass-enclosed showers promote a sense of effortless luxury throughout. Service here is polished and professional, from the delivery of cocktails in the Seasons Bar and Lounge to turndown each night. The Sports Club/LA adjacent to the hotel offers cutting-edge classes and is home to Splash, the city's premier day spa.

277 rooms. High-speed Internet access. Restaurant, bar. Fitness center, spa. Whirlpool. $$$$

THE RITZ-CARLTON, SAN FRANCISCO ★ ★ ★ ★ ★

600 Stockton St., San Francisco, 415-296-7465, 800-241-3333;
www.ritzcarlton.com

Housed in a 1909 historic landmark on Nob Hill, this refined hotel sets the standard in elegance. The space is filled with a museum-quality collection of European and American artwork and the guest rooms and suites are no less sumptuous. Club level accommodations include separate concierge service, and lovely food and beverage offerings which are updated five times each day, from breakfast to late-night sweets. The award-winning Dining Room is ideal for special occasions with its distinguished setting and artful Japanese-influenced French cuisine. Other venues include the Terrace, for Mediterranean specialties, and the Lobby Lounge and Bar, home to the largest single malt scotch collection in the United States.

336 rooms. Pets accepted, some restrictions; fee. High-speed Internet access. Two restaurants, bar. Fitness center, spa. Indoor pool, whirlpool. Business center. $$$$

ST. REGIS HOTEL, SAN FRANCISCO ★ ★ ★ ★ ★

125 Third St., San Francisco, 415-284-4000; www.stregis.com

One of San Francisco's newest luxury hotels, this outpost of the luxe St. Regis brand is located in an historic building in the vibrant SoMA neighborhood close to the San Francisco Museum of Modern Art. Rooms are generously sized and decorated in a clean, modern style most interior designers would clamor to claim as their own. Caramel-colored, leather-covered walls make the rooms cozy, while the oversized beds are a perfect spot to cuddle up for a snooze. The staff attends to large and small requests with equal confidence, and can offer tips on where to find the best shops, restaurants and more in the surrounding neighborhood. Bathrooms are clad in marble and feature rainfall showerheads, petite LCD televisions for catching up on the morning news and Remède amenities. The flagship restaurant, Ame, was conceived by Hiro Sone and Lissa Doumani of St. Helena's Terra restaurant, and features a New American menu with an emphasis on seafood.

260 rooms. High-speed Internet access. Restaurant, bar. Fitness center, spa. Indoor pool, whirlpool. Business center. $$$$

Avalon

THE INN ON MOUNT ADA ★ ★ ★ ★

398 Wrigley Rd., Avalon, California 90704, 310-510-2030, 800-608-7669, fax 310-510-2237, www.innonmtada.com

Located in Catalina Island's sole city of Avalon, the Inn on Mount Ada was previously William Wrigley Jr.'s private mansion (named for his wife Ada). Completed in the early 1920s, Wrigley's white palace, with its recognizable red conical roof, now hosts visitors who book one of the six luxurious rooms, each with a magnificent harbor or ocean view and plenty of antiques. Start the day with complimentary breakfast and then cruise the island on personal golf carts.

6 rooms. Children over 14 years only. Restaurant. $$$$

Big Sur

POST RANCH INN ★ ★ ★ ★

Hwy. 1, Big Sur, 831-667-2200, 800-527-2200; www.postranchinn.com

Perched on a cliff overlooking Big Sur's rugged coastline, this inn is an ideal romantic getaway. Designed to blend with the Santa Lucia Mountains, the buildings resemble sophisticated tree houses. Each of the 30 guest rooms has an incredible ocean or mountain view from the floor-to-ceiling windows, king-size bed, wood-burning fireplace, indoor spa tub, private deck and digital music system. The wet- and mini-bars are filled with complimentary snacks, juices and half-bottles of red and white wine. What you won't find: TVs or alarm clocks. Wake up when you want to and head to the spa. The Sierra Mar restaurant serves superb California cuisine and has an extensive wine list.

No children allowed. Complimentary breakfast. Restaurant, bar. Fitness center, spa. Whirlpool. $$$$

Calistoga

CALISTOGA RANCH ★ ★ ★ ★

580 Lommel Rd., Calistoga, 707-254-2800, 800-942-4220; www.calistogaranch.com

The 46 private guest lodges at this posh resort in the hills offer a quiet retreat after a day spent exploring local vineyards. Each cedar-shingle bungalow has a fireplace, indoor/outdoor showers, duvet-topped bed, soaking tub and a large deck. The on-site restaurant features American cuisine that embraces organic ingredients from the farmers in Napa Valley, and wines are paired with seasonal tasting menus created by chef Eric Webster. Guests can participate in a host of complimentary activities, from yoga classes to origami workshops. Culinary events include cooking demonstrations led by instructors from the nearby branch of the Culinary Institute of America, and tasting excursions to nearby wineries. The Bathhouse spa offers a luxurious retreat with soaking pools that overlook the oaks.

46 rooms. Restaurant. Spa. $$$$

Carmel Valley

BERNARDUS LODGE ★ ★ ★ ★

415 Carmel Valley Rd., Carmel Valley, 831-658-3400, 888-648-9463; www.bernardus.com

Long considered one of the finest winemaking estates in California, Bernardus Lodge has a scenic Central Valley location and luxurious guest rooms, which include feather beds, cozy fireplaces and oversized bathtubs for two. Upon arrival, guests are immediately greeted with a vintage wine and cheese welcome spread. The refined yet casual décor features richly upholstered furnishing, plank flooring and exposed ceiling beams. Each room is appointed with antique armoires and impressive French doors that lead onto a private garden patio or balcony. The spa offers a wide variety of treatments and the meditation garden is an ideal spot to enjoy the picturesque Tuscan hillside. The lodge's formal restaurant, Marinus, is an epicurean's delight serving up succulent dishes such as pancetta-wrapped venison and Dungeness crab cannelloni.

57 rooms. Wireless Internet access. Two restaurants, bar. Fitness center. Spa. Outdoor pool, whirlpool. Tennis. Airport transportation available. Business center. $$$$

Half Moon Bay

THE RITZ-CARLTON, HALF MOON BAY ★ ★ ★ ★

1 Miramontes Point Rd., Half Moon Bay, 650-712-7000; www.ritzcarlton.com

From its cliff-top setting to its shingled architecture, this hotel looks like a slice of Scotland on the northern California coast. But while the windswept dunes and emerald links hint of a foreign land, this exquisite resort—only 30 miles from San Francisco—has a decidedly West Coast flavor. The guest rooms and suites are the essence of relaxed sophistication and high style, with soft colors, floral or striped fabrics and nautical artwork. Golfers will develop a soft spot for the resort's 36 oceanfront holes, while others can go horseback riding on the secluded beach or play volleyball, basketball or croquet. There's also an oceanfront yoga studio and candlelit Roman mineral baths. Pets are welcome in the resort's guesthouses, but beware: they're likely to be spoiled with dog bones served on silver trays.

261 rooms. Pets accepted, some restrictions; fee. High-speed Internet access. Two restaurants, two bars. Children's activity center. Indoor pool, children's pool, whirlpool. Airport transportation available. $$$$

Palo Alto

FOUR SEASONS HOTEL SILICON VALLEY AT EAST PALO ALTO ★ ★ ★ ★

2050 University Ave., East Palo Alto, 650-566-1200; www.fourseasons.com
Built in 2006, this 10-story, 190,000-square-foot luxury palace's contemporary rooms have marble bathrooms with deep-soaking tubs, separate glass-enclosed showers, flat-screen TVs, DVD/CD players and floor-to-ceiling windows. Work out in the state-of-the-art fitness center—exercise machines have their own audiovisual monitors and wireless headsets—or pick up a map of nearby jogging and biking trails. The full-service spa has seven treatment rooms. The hotel's contemporary dining room, Quattro serves up Italian-influenced California cuisine.

200 rooms. Wireless Internet access. Restaurant, bar. Fitness center, spa. Outdoor pool, whirlpool. Business center. $$$$

Pebble Beach

CASA PALMERO AT PEBBLE BEACH ★ ★ ★ ★

1518 Cypress Dr., Pebble Beach, 831-622-6650, 800-654-9300;
www.pebblebeach.com
This grand Mediterranean-style estate overlooks the first and second fairways of Pebble Beach. The extensive grounds are a profusion of trellised walkways, manicured gardens and trickling adobe fountains. Guest rooms echo the resort's sophistication with their overstuffed furniture, sun-soaked patios and neutral tones. Complimentary refreshments are offered every evening in the bar and lounge, and the library boasts an exhaustive collection of classics. Enjoy the serene pool area or take advantage of the larger Pebble Beach complex's four restaurants, shops, private tennis club, spa and of course, world-renowned golf.

24 rooms. Complimentary full breakfast. High-speed Internet access. Bar. Spa. Airport transportation available. $$$$

THE INN AT SPANISH BAY ★ ★ ★ ★

2700 Seventeen Mile Dr., Pebble Beach, 831-647-7500, 800-654-9300;
www.pebblebeach.com
Direct access to the revered links at Pebble Beach makes this inn popular with golfers, while the splendid natural setting overlooking the Pacific Ocean and Spanish Bay has universal appeal. Views of the Del Monte Forest, golf course and ocean are striking, especially when enjoyed from the privacy of a traditionally decorated guest room or suite. A gallery of

shops showcases fine sportswear and resort apparel along with tennis and golf equipment. From an expertly staffed tennis and fitness facility to the outdoor pool, the amenities are top-notch. Four distinctive dining establishments provide an array of food offerings.

269 rooms. High-speed Internet access. Three restaurants, three bars. Fitness center, spa. Beach. Whirlpool. Airport transportation available. Business center. $$$$

THE LODGE AT PEBBLE BEACH ★ ★ ★

1700 Seventeen Mile Dr., Pebble Beach, 831-624-3811, 800-654-9300;
www.pebblebeach.com
Distinguished by its impressive architecture and spectacular oceanside setting, this is the jewel in the crown of the world-class Pebble Beach resort. The traditionally-styled rooms are spacious, and most include a fireplace and patio or balcony with views of flowering gardens or oceanside fairways. Spa rooms have a private garden with outdoor whirlpool spas. Unwind by the pool or play tennis in the resort's state-of-the-art facility. The four restaurants also offer a variety of elegant settings, and run the gamut from casual American fare and succulent seafood to updated, lightened versions of French classics. The spa celebrates the diversity of natural resources indigenous to the Monterey Peninsula in its treatments and therapies.

161 rooms. High-speed Internet access. Four restaurants, four bars. Fitness center, spa. Beach. Children's pool, whirlpool. Airport transportation available. $$$$

San Francisco

MANDARIN ORIENTAL SAN FRANCISCO ★ ★ ★

222 Sansome St., San Francisco, 415-276-9888, 800-622-0404;
www.mandarinoriental.com
This sleek hotel in the downtown business district occupies the top two levels of the city's third-tallest building and has incredible birds-eye views of the city and San Francisco Bay. Spacious guest rooms and suites incorporate Asian-influenced décor and furnishings, and feature plush Frette Egyptian linens and oversized, rose marble bathrooms. Executive desks and well-appointed work spaces, along with a modern full-service business center make this a popular choice for business travelers. The full-service fitness center offers yoga classes, new cardio machines and pampering massage services. You can dine on Pacific Rim cuisine at Silks or unwind with afternoon tea or cocktails at MO Bar.

158 rooms. Pets accepted, some restrictions; fee. Wireless Internet access. Two restaurants, bar. Fitness center. Business center. $$$$

San Martin

CORDEVALLE ★ ★ ★ ★

1 Cordevalle Club Dr., San Martin, California 95046, 408-695-4500,
888-767-3966, fax 408-695-4563, www.cordevalle.com
CordeValle sprawls over 1,700 acres in the foothills between San Jose and Monterey, attracting small business groups as well as golfers and those looking for a romantic weekend. The spacious, high-ceilinged bungalows overlook a rolling 18-hole Robert Trent Jones, Jr. golf course. Retreat to one of the 750-square foot bungalows where you'll find a wet bar, flat screen TV, whirlpool tub, fireplace and crisp, neutral-toned California contemporary décor. Each treatment room in the resort's spa has a private garden, and the on-site vineyard produces the wine and cheese that's placed in guest rooms as a welcome gift.

45 rooms. Check-in 3 p.m., check-out noon. Restaurant, bar. Fitness room. Outdoor pool, whirlpool. Golf. Tennis.

St. Helena

MEADOWOOD NAPA VALLEY ★ ★ ★ ★

900 Meadowood Lane, St. Helena, 707-963-3646, 800-458-8080;
www.meadowood.com
On 250 wine-country acres, Meadowood is large, but its staff is attentive—from the esteemed resident wine tutor to the guest services manager assigned to each arriving visitor. Enjoy a game of croquet, tennis or golf, or simply lounge by the pool. The suites, cottages and lodges blend classic country style and California sensibilities with their stone fireplaces, skylights, vaulted ceilings, private decks and luxurious bathrooms—not to mention plenty of modern amenities such as flat-screen TVs, DVD/CD players, coffee and tea pots and toasters. The Grill is available for casual dining under the shade of an umbrella, and the Restaurant turns out eager-to-please gastronomic delights.

85 rooms. Wireless Internet access. Two restaurants, three bars. Children's activity center. Fitness center. Spa. Children's pool, whirlpool. $$$$

FIVE STAR RESTAURANTS

San Francisco

THE DINING ROOM ★ ★ ★ ★ ★

600 Stockton St., San Francisco, 415-773-6168; www.ritzcarlton.com
This revered, formal restaurant sets the standard in elegant dining. The arrival of Champagne signals the opening of the meal, and a live harpist adds to the ambiance. The room is replete with authentic French windows, golden tones and pristine table linens and the atmosphere is

elite yet unpretentious. Executive chef Ron Siegel incorporates inventive Asian flavors into his modern French cuisine, developing decadent dishes such as lemon-cured Toro and lobster knuckle risotto with candy cap mushrooms. Choose from six- or eight-course tasting menus, or explore the numerous à la carte options. The sommelier will assist you in selecting wines to complement any menu choice. Be sure to indulge in the wonderful selection of farmhouse cheeses for dessert.

French/Japanese menu. Dinner. Closed Sunday-Monday. Bar. Children's menu. Business casual attire. Reservations recommended. Valet parking. $$$

Yountville

THE FRENCH LAUNDRY ★ ★ ★ ★ ★

6640 Washington St., Yountville, 707-944-2380; www.frenchlaundry.com

At this former French steam laundry, chef Thomas Keller has raised the standard for fine dining in America. While the country locale—a circa-1900 rock and timber cottage—makes diners feel at home, tables topped with Limoges china, crystal stemware and floor-length linens, set the tone for the nine-course French or vegetarian tasting menus that change daily but always rely on seasonal produce and organic meats. Dishes are small and prompt contemplation on the perfect marriage of fresh, pristine ingredients on each plate. The affable staff keeps the experience casual and comfortable, yet refined and memorable. Reservations are taken two months in advance, so be prepared if you're hoping to snag a table at this perennially outstanding American classic.

American/French menu. Dinner. Closed Monday; also two weeks in January and one week in late July-early August. Jackets required. Reservations recommended. $$$$

FOUR STAR RESTAURANTS

Big Sur

SIERRA MAR ★ ★ ★ ★

Hwy. 1, Big Sur, 831-667-2800; www.postranchinn.com

This acclaimed restaurant located in the Post Ranch Inn blends comfort with elegance from its cliff-top location. With spectacular sunset views of Big Sur and the Pacific Ocean, expect to be wooed by the simple splendor of chef Craig von Foerster's menu. Focusing on California cuisine with French and Mediterranean influences, the four-course prix fixe menu changes daily and utilizes seasonal organic products. The foie gras crème brulée is remarkable; lunch patrons shouldn't pass up the renowned Kobe beef burger. The restaurant also claims to have one of the most extensive wine cellars in North America.

California menu. Lunch, dinner. Bar. Casual attire. Reservations recommended. Valet parking. Outdoor seating. $$$$

Carmel Valley

MARINUS ★ ★ ★ ★

415 Carmel Valley Rd., Carmel Valley, 831-658-3595; www.bernardus.com
This warm, country inn-style restaurant located in the Bernardus Lodge has exposed-beam ceilings, earth-toned walls, vintage tapestries and a magnificent 12-foot-wide European limestone fireplace—plus a patio and surrounding gardens. Dishes use organic and fresh ingredients, and may include turbot with caramelized endive and celery root purée, and local spot prawns with crispy marinated vegetables and truffle vinaigrette. The impressive wine cellar stocks more than 1,000 selections.

California menu. Dinner. Business casual attire. Reservations recommended. Valet parking. $$$$

Los Gatos

MANRESA ★ ★ ★ ★

320 Village Lane, Los Gatos, 408-354-4330; www.manresarestaurant.com
This intimate restaurant is the showcase for chef David Kinch's inventive contemporary French cuisine with Spanish influences. The menu relies on local ingredients, many from the restaurant's own garden, and the dishes are consistently intricate and subtle. Be prepared to devote the majority of your evening to this epicurean affair, but the onslaught of exotic flavor combinations is undoubtedly worth it. The chef's tasting menus are particularly prized and include fresh ingredients from surrounding local farms. The exquisitely presented dishes are served in a provincial dining room decorated with warm burgundy tones and soft romantic lighting.

International menu. Dinner. Closed Monday. Bar. Business casual attire. Reservations recommended. $$$$

Oakhurst

ERNA'S ELDERBERRY HOUSE ★ ★ ★ ★

48688 Victoria Lane, Oakhurst, 559-683-6800; www.chateausureau.com
This restaurant offers a spectacular seasonal menu of California cuisine served in a setting decorated with antique French Provençal furnishings, brocade tapestries and original oil paintings. Since 1984, owner Erna Kubin-Clanin has guided the kitchen toward farm-raised meats and local produce. Prix fixe menus change daily and consist of six courses paired with three or four California or international wines. The 725-bottle wine list is overseen by Erna's daughter Renée and includes several rare cult California wines as well as many Austrian selections, in honor of Erna's birthplace.

California, French menu. Dinner. Closed first two weeks in January. Bar. Business casual attire. Reservations recommended. Valet parking. Outdoor seating. $$$$

Redwood City

THE VILLAGE PUB ★ ★ ★ ★

2967 Woodside Rd., Redwood City, 650-851-9888; www.thevillagepub.net
About 30 minutes from San Francisco and San Jose, this upscale pub emphasizes the use of local artisanal and organic ingredients, including produce cultivated at the restaurant's partner farm in the nearby Santa Cruz Mountains. The seasonal menus feature contemporary dishes like duck leg confit with turnips, cabbage and quince, and cauliflower and Meyer lemon risotto with crispy pancetta and capers. Diners craving more traditional pub fare will find burgers, steaks and fries as well. The ample wine list includes a number of reasonably priced selections along with half-bottles and a variety of by-the-glass options.

American menu. Lunch, dinner. Bar. Casual attire. Reservations recommended. $$$

Rutherford

AUBERGE DU SOLEIL RESTAURANT ★ ★ ★ ★

180 Rutherford Hill Rd., Rutherford, 707-963-1211, 800-348-5406;
www.aubergedusoleil.com
French-born San Francisco restaurateur Claude Rouas set out to create a Provence-like destination restaurant in northern California when he opened Auberge du Soleil in 1981. Diners liked it so much they demanded overnight accommodations—and received them four years later. The seasonal French-California menu features artisanal ingredients and products from local farms, spotlighted in dishes such as tomato risotto with wild shrimp, white corn soup with Maine crab and roasted lamb with potato gnocchi. Don't miss the local cheese selections for dessert. The six-course tasting menu comes with wines to match from the large, locally strong list. If you're touring the valley by car, consider a lunch stop where you can enjoy the views from the terrace.

California, French menu. Breakfast, lunch, dinner. Bar. Business casual attire. Reservations recommended. Valet parking. Outdoor seating. $$$$

San Francisco

AQUA ★ ★ ★ ★

252 California St., San Francisco, 415-956-9662; www.aqua-sf.com
This sophisticated dining spot, located in San Francisco's Financial District, consistently pulls in the power set with its upscale setting and sumptuous seafood, including Japanese hamachi and Alaskan black cod.

The butter-poached lobster comes with truffle bucattini carbonara, while the snapper is accented with Thai basil consommé and green curry. Chef Laurent Manrique's mastery of classic European cooking techniques is evident in his surprising, yet harmonious combinations of fresh seafood. A professional, amiable waitstaff keep courses moving with precision.

Seafood menu. Lunch, dinner. Bar. Business casual attire. Reservations recommended. Valet parking. $$$

CAMPTON PLACE RESTAURANT ★ ★ ★ ★

340 Stockton St., San Francisco, 415-955-5564, 866-332-1670;
www.camptonplace.com

Located in the historic Campton Place Hotel, this contemporary, comfortable dining room bathed in cream and dark chocolate hues offers an innovative menu of modern American fare with French and Mediterranean touches. Chef Peter Rudolph expertly prepares light and flavorful dishes using classical techniques and a bountiful selection of California's fresh ingredients. Choose from three-, four- or seven-course tasting menus and splurge on the thoughtful and extensive wine pairings. The service is smoothly choreographed and the Champagne cart at the outset of the meal sets the precedent. Cheese aficionados will rejoice at the sizable selection of farmhouse and artisanal cheeses served tableside.

American menu. Breakfast, lunch, dinner. Bar. Business casual attire. Reservations recommended. Valet parking. $$$

FLEUR DE LYS ★ ★ ★ ★

777 Sutter St., San Francisco, 415-673-7779; www.fleurdelyssf.com

The signature Californian-French fare may not be as dramatic as the brightly colored, tented main dining room, but it still demands your full attention. Regarded as one of the most romantic restaurants in the city, this gourmandizing enclave of grand bouquets and soft candlelight woos even the most skeptical palette. World-renowned chef-owner Hubert Keller's creative platters look and taste like art (think Hawaiian prawns on fennel confit, or filet mignon topped with sautéed foie gras). Every detail is accounted for and every dish is exquisite including parsnip blinis with dollops of caviar.

French menu. Dinner. Closed Sunday. Bar. Business casual attire. Reservations recommended. Valet parking. $$$$

GARY DANKO ★ ★ ★ ★

800 North Point St., San Francisco, 415-749-2060; www.garydanko.com

A seemingly endless expanse of blond wood illuminates this luxurious dining space, where guests feel the warmth as soon as they take their seats. Each of chef and owner Gary Danko's dishes relies upon pristine seasonal ingredients prepared with classic French techniques. Signature dishes include glazed oysters with osetra caviar and lettuce cream, and horseradish-crusted salmon with dilled cucumbers. The 1,200-bottle wine cellar offers an exceptional selection of grand vintages as well as coveted wines from small producers.

California, French menu. Dinner. Bar. Business casual attire. Reservations recommended. Valet parking. $$$$

LA FOLIE ★ ★ ★ ★

2316 Polk St., San Francisco, 415-776-5577; www.lafolie.com
At the Russian District's La Folie, chef-owner Roland Passot has a passion for food, folly and adventure. Order his Discovery Menu for a chef-led culinary journey composed of impeccably prepared dishes of French-Californian descent. (À la carte and vegetarian menus are also available.) Citrus lobster salad with shaved fresh hearts of palm and a trio of rabbit are Passot's signature creations. The impressive wine list spans the globe.

French menu. Dinner. Closed Sunday. Bar. Business casual attire. Reservations recommended. Valet parking. $$$$

MASA'S ★ ★ ★ ★

648 Bush St., San Francisco, 415-989-7154; www.masasrestaurant.com
Located in the Hotel Vintage Court, this opulent dining room is the perfect setting for its divine cuisine, a savvy blend of French technique, Asian innovation and richly flavorful ingredients. The prix fixe menu includes signature dishes like St. Peters fish with Japanese crosnes, edamame and tamari emulsion, and Liberty Valley duck breast with honey-roasted quince, duck leg confit and pomegranate sauce.

French menu. Dinner. Closed Sunday-Monday; also two weeks in January and week of July 4. Bar. Business casual attire. Reservations recommended. Valet parking. $$$$

SILKS ★ ★ ★ ★

222 Sansome St., San Francisco, 415-986-2020;
www.mandarinoriental.com/sanfrancisco
Duck inside this restaurant in the Mandarin Oriental to indulge in three or four-course prix fixe menus overseen by acclaimed Executive Chef Milan Drager and Chef de Cuisine Joel Huff. The Pacific Rim and West Coast signature choices include Tasmanian trout with preserved lemon, bone marrow risotto and English pea purée, as well as the chocolate marquise dominos with Frangelico gelée and white pepper sorbet.

American menu. Breakfast, lunch, dinner. Bar. Children's menu. Business casual attire. Reservations recommended. Valet parking. $$$

San Martin

CYRUS ★★★★

29 North St., Healdsburg, 707-433-3311; www.cyrusrestaurant.com
Located in the heart of Sonoma wine country, Cyrus is owned by chef Douglas Keane and mâitre'd Nick Peyton. The stylish dining room, with its arched vaulted ceilings, is the perfect setting for Keane's contemporary American cuisine, which is offered in a flexible prix fixe format of three to five dishes selected from any section of the menu. Each dish is flawlessly executed and the desserts by pastry chef Suzanne Popick are equally perfect. Bar manager Scott Beattie crafts his libations using seasonal fruits and flavorings.

Continental menu. Dinner. Bar. Business casual attire. Reservations recommended. $$$

St. Helena

TERRA ★★★★

1345 Railroad Ave., St. Helena, 707-963-8931; www.terrarestaurant.com
Chef and owner Hiro Sone has been wowing diners at Terra, his cozy, intimate Napa Valley restaurant, since 1988. Set one block off the main drag on Railroad Avenue in St. Helena, Terra is located in a charming old stone building, rustically finished with vintage red-tiled floors, exposed stone walls and wood-beamed ceilings. The food is spectacular—a successful blend of flavors from France, Asia and northern California. Signatures change with the seasons and include red wine-braised veal cheeks, lobster tortelloni and stone fruit tarte tatin. With gracious hospitality and warmth, the staff at Terra makes you feel like you're dining at home.

French menu, Italian menu. Dinner. Closed Tuesday; also two weeks in early January. Business casual attire. Reservations recommended. $$$

FOUR STAR SPAS

Big Sur

POST RANCH SPA ★★★★

Hwy. 1, Big Sur, 831-667-2200, 800-527-2200; www.postranchinn.com
This spa focuses on nature-based therapies, from the wildflower facial with organic plants and Big Sur flowers, to the skin-renewing Hungarian herbal body wrap, which blends organic herbs (including sage, ivy, cinnamon and paprika) with a thermal mud body masque. Several treatments also draw from Native American rituals, including the Big Sur jade stone therapy, which uses jade collected from nearby beaches and basalt river rocks to massage sore muscles, and then cooled marble to release inflammation.

Private hikes, meditation sessions, yoga and couples massage instruction are also available.

Calistoga

THE BATHHOUSE ★ ★ ★

580 Lommel Rd., Calistoga, 707-254-2820; www.calistogaranch.com
The northern California town of Calistoga is famous for its natural hot springs and mineral clay baths. The Bathhouse at Calistoga Ranch was opened in 2004 by the group behind sister property Auberge du Soleil and features five treatment rooms, inspired by the native landscape and designed with organic elements such as copper, stone, wood and water. Four of the treatment rooms feature large terraces with soaking tubs and showers, and all are tailor-made for treatments involving a bath: buttermilk baths, mud baths or thermal mineral pool soaks. The spa draws water from the local hot springs and uses Napa Valley ingredients, including honey, grapeseed and bay laurel, in many of the treatments. The mud wrap promises to boost immunity. Morning yoga takes place in the resort's wine cave.

Carmel Valley

THE SPA AT BERNARDUS LODGE ★ ★ ★ ★

415 Carmel Valley Rd., Carmel Valley, 831-658-3400, 888-648-9463; www.bernardus.com
This spa has seven treatment rooms, an open-air "warming pool" and a meditation garden with bubbling fountains. Indigenous herbs, flowers, essential oils and healing waters are incorporated into the spa's treatments. Couples can opt for the vineyard romance treatment, which includes a harvest crush body exfoliation, lavender grape seed bath, warm grape seed oil massage and a tea service of grape seed herbal tea. In keeping with the winery theme, the chardonnay facial is an 80-minute, hydrating treatment that incorporates chardonnay grape seeds, which are loaded with antioxidents.

Half Moon Bay

THE RITZ-CARLTON SPA, HALF-MOON BAY ★ ★ ★ ★

1 Miramontes Point Rd., Half Moon Bay, 650-712-7040, 800-241-3333; www.ritzcarlton.com
Golfers will be taken in by the 36-hole oceanfront course at this resort, but its 16,000-square-foot spa is equally impressive. Wind down with a co-ed, candlelit Roman mineral bath, or lounge in the oceanfront Jacuzzi. The signature pumpkin body peel delivers the nourishing benefits of this

local treat. The well-equipped fitness center overlooks the ocean and the gazebo lawn, which also includes a heated yoga studio.

Napa

THE SPA AT THE CARNEROS INN ★ ★ ★ ★

4048 Sonoma Hwy., Napa, 707-299-4900; www.carnerosinn.com
Napa Valley's Carneros Inn takes the country farmhouse and turns it on its head with clean lines and simple sophistication, and the sun-filled, mood-lifting spa perfectly complements the resort's laid-back attitude. The themed treatment menu draws from the harvests, farms, cellars, minerals and creeks of the Carneros Valley. Therapies include honeydew exfoliations, paprika facials, goat butter massages, grape seed and guava body scrubs, and lemongrass and ginger sea mineral body wraps. For those guests who prefer to remain within the confines of their private cottages, the spa presents a menu of in-room treatments, including organic garden wraps and couples' massages.

Oakhurst

SPA DU SUREAU ★ ★ ★ ★

48688 Victoria Lane, Oakhurst, 559-683-6860; www.chateausureau.com
Decorated throughout in charming Art Deco style, there are only three treatment rooms (all with iPod docks) and one wet room at this petite spa. The standout is the decadent double treatment room with its black marble fireplace, two massage tables separated by translucent drapes, lounge chairs and Jacuzzi. The spa also features a Hydrostorm shower system—one of only a handful in the country—that uses aroma and color therapy aquatics. The treatment menu spotlights traditional European Kur baths, which include marine hydrotherapy and mineral rich baths, and use only top-notch ingredients, such as moor mud from the Czech Republic, which is touted for its high concentration of vitamins and minerals.

Pebble Beach

THE SPA AT PEBBLE BEACH ★ ★ ★ ★

1700 Seventeen Mile Dr., Pebble Beach, 831-624-7615, 888-565-7615;
www.pebblebeach.com
Blending California's Spanish-colonial heritage with Pebble Beach's gloriously rugged natural setting, the Spa at Pebble Beach epitomizes an oasis within an oasis. Nestled in the heart of Del Monte Forest, the grounds of the 22,000 square-foot spa are a profusion of landscaped floral gardens and trickling terra cotta fountains. Treatments take advantage of the surrounding environment by incorporating the calming properties of both earth and water, such as the Red Flower Ritual, which

combines flower oils, fruit essences and the rich minerals of the sea into a relaxing massage and body scrub.

Rutherford

THE AUBERGE SPA ★ ★ ★ ★

180 Rutherford Hill Rd., Rutherford, 707-963-1211; www.aubergedusoleil.com
The glorious Napa Valley surroundings have inspired this spa's philosophy, with vineyard, garden and valley themes dominating the treatment menu. Nutrient-rich grapeseed and locally grown herbs and flowers are the foundation for the vineyard's massages, body treatments and facials. Seasonal treatments are also a highlight of a visit to this spa, where a rosemary renewal massage is featured in spring, a luscious peaches and cream body mask in summer, a harvest-inspired cleanse or body glaze in fall and a peppermint and eucalyptus body treatment in winter.

San Martin

THE SPA AT CORDEVALLE ★ ★ ★ ★

1 Cordevalle Club Dr., San Martin, 408-695-4500, 888-767-3966; www.cordevalle.com
This top-notch facility treats its guests to luxurious amenities, elegant interiors and a full-service menu. Classic contemporary is the reigning style at this spa, where earth tones and sandstone fireplaces create a serene atmosphere. The services blend European traditions with modern philosophies, and most of the treatments use locally grown herbs, flowers and even grapes from the hillsides just outside the window. Several therapies have been created specifically with the golfer's needs in mind. The restful pace found here is perhaps best enjoyed from the private gardens accompanying each treatment room.

San Francisco

REMÈDE SPA AT THE ST. REGIS HOTEL SAN FRANCISCO ★ ★ ★ ★

125 Third St., San Francisco, 415-284-4000; www.stregis.com
Stark white and incredibly chic, the reception area at this spa is an appropriate introduction to the progressive treatments that fuel its reputation. Guests are invited to indulge in Champagne, artisan cheeses, and decadent truffles while they wait for their treatments. Ten treatment rooms and a 50-foot indoor pool are among the 9,000-square-foot facility's amenities. The treatments focus on vitamin-and antioxidant-rich treatments that nourish and replenish the skin. The spa uses Laboratoire Remède skincare products, specially formulated to combat wrinkles and tighten skin. Facial treatments are customized to quench thirsty skin, smooth lines or exfoliate as needed.

St. Helena

THE SPA AT MEADOWOOD ★ ★ ★ ★

900 Meadowood Lane, St. Helena, 800-458-8080;
www.meadowood.com/wellness/

Massages delivered fireside, a rejuvenating facial with organic ingredients, a relaxing yoga class. These are just some of the pampering, incredibly indulgent services available at this Wine Country spa. Signature treatments include the Meadowood Harvest Wrap, which begins with a tea tree exfoliant and ends with your body swaddled in warm towels and blankets while you soak in the benefits of a hydrating body masque. Those short on time can opt for the 30-minute foot relief, which includes just enough pressure-point relieving massage to invigorate you for another day of wine tasting.

SOUTHERN CALIFORNIA

FIVE STAR HOTELS

Beverly Hills

THE BEVERLY HILLS HOTEL ★ ★ ★ ★ ★

9641 Sunset Blvd., Beverly Hills, 310-276-2251, 888-897-2804;
www.beverlyhillshotel.com

Deliciously pink, this iconic hotel oozes Hollywood glamour. It has long been a hideaway for stars, who like to stay in the bungalows tucked away along the lush garden paths. The hotel maintains the allure of 1940s Hollywood in both its public and its private rooms, which are decorated in soothing sage, yellow and beige tones and are furnished with canopied beds. Fireplaces add a romantic touch and terraces and balconies focus attention on the gardens. A variety of dining venues, such as the classic Polo Lounge and the recently opened Sunset Bar, still attract producers and stars, but visitors in the know head for the pool where the scene is best viewed from a fantastic private cabana.

204 rooms. Pets accepted; some restrictions; fee. Wireless Internet access. Restaurant, bar. $$$$

THE PENINSULA BEVERLY HILLS ★ ★ ★ ★ ★

9882 S. Santa Monica Blvd., Beverly Hills, 310-551-2888;
www.beverlyhills.peninsula.com

This French Renaissance-style hotel is designed to resemble a luxurious private residence (one you'll never want to leave). The antique-filled guest rooms feature oversized marble tubs and state-of-the-art electronic systems that allow visitors to control the environment with the touch of a button. The meticulous gardens, rooftop pool and relaxing spa make the space feel like home. Even pets are pampered with doggie beds (including turndown) and their own room service menu. The dining here is exceptional, from the delicious West Coast cuisine of the Belvedere to the wonderful afternoon tea of the Living Room. The flexible check-in/check-out policy is particularly convenient: whenever a guest checks in, they have 24 hours before check-out.

194 rooms. Pets accepted; some restrictions; fee. Wireless Internet access. Two restaurants, bar. $$$$

RAFFLES L'ERMITAGE BEVERLY HILLS ★ ★ ★ ★ ★
9291 Burton Way, Beverly Hills, 310-278-3344, 800-768-9009; www.raffles-lermitagehotel.com
This hotel maintains a sanctuary-like ambience in the heart of Beverly Hills with its stylish and serene Asian-inspired contemporary décor. The spacious rooms are equipped with state-of-the-art technology including 40-inch flat-screen TVs, Bose stereos and computer-controlled lighting and climate. Crowds flock to JAAN's for sumptuous French dishes infused with Indochine flavors. The Writer's Bar (named for the scripts that adorn the walls) is a nice spot to sip cocktails. The rooftop pool provides guests with a view of the prestigious neighborhood and the Amrita spa offers Ayuverdic techniques. Pets are not only welcome here, they get their own beds, snacks and toys and private dog walkers are available.

119 rooms. Wireless Internet access. Restaurant, bar. Fitness center. Spa. Outdoor pool, whirlpool. $$$$

Dana Point

ST. REGIS RESORT, MONARCH BEACH ★ ★ ★ ★ ★
1 Monarch Beach Resort, Dana Point, 949-234-3200, 800-722-1543; www.stregismb.com
Even seasoned travelers will swoon over the luscious, secluded setting and the Tuscan-inspired design of this resort which is tucked away on 200 acres high above the Pacific Ocean. Elegant marble floors, plush carpets and massive sofas grace the public areas. The oversized guest rooms have dramatic contemporary décor with wood shutters, marble bathrooms, private balconies, goose down comforters and 300-thread count sheets. The resort has an 18-hole championship golf course, award-winning spa, beach club (with surfing lessons) and nature trails. In between, dine at one of the six ocean-view restaurants.

400 rooms. Pets accepted. High-speed Internet access. Six restaurants, three bars. Fitness center. Spa. Beach. Pool. Golf. Tennis. Business center. $$$$

Los Angeles

HOTEL BEL-AIR ★ ★ ★ ★ ★

701 Stone Canyon Rd., Los Angeles, 310-472-1211, 888-897-2804;
www.hotelbelair.com
Amenities are plentiful at this timeless hotel situated close to the action
of Los Angeles, yet far enough to transport guests to a romantic world
dotted with intimate courtyards, fountains and the Bel-Air's signature
Swan Lake. Guest rooms offer French and Italian furnishings, private
sun-soaked terraces, Alicante marble and one-of-a-kind touches that are
only found in the finest hotels. Privacy is guaranteed with rooms spread
throughout the 12-acre grounds, and guests can take advantage of the
well-equipped fitness center or the luxurious pool in confident seclusion.
Gourmands will enjoy the in-kitchen dining experience of Table One as
well as the enchanting garden setting of the Terrace.

91 rooms. Pets accepted, some restrictions; fee. Wireless Internet access.
Restaurant, bar. Fitness center. Pool. Business center. $$$$

FOUR STAR HOTELS

Beverly Hills

THE BEVERLY HILTON ★ ★ ★ ★

9876 Wilshire Blvd., 310-274-7777; www.beverlyhilton.com
This celebrated hotel perched at the corner of Wilshire and Santa Monica
Boulevards has been completely renovated. Even with the sparkling new
interiors and amenities, there's still a touch of Old Hollywood. Black and
white photos of celebrities can be found throughout the hotel and the
carpeting in the lobby is, of course, red. After a long day of shopping, make
an appointment at the new Star Spa or take a dip in the Olympic-sized
pool. Then, stop by the lounge for a cocktail (and to spy on celebrities).
There's also the famous Polynesian-themed Trader Vic's Lounge, now
located poolside. The hotel's Circa 55 restaurant offers a California twist
on breakfast, lunch and dinner.

570 rooms. Pets accepted, some restrictions; fee. Wireless Internet access.
Two restaurants, two bars. $$$

BEVERLY WILSHIRE, A FOUR SEASONS HOTEL ★ ★ ★ ★

9500 Wilshire Blvd., Beverly Hills, 310-275-5200, 800-819-5053;
www.fourseasons.com
It doesn't get any better than this prestigious address at the intersection of
Rodeo Drive and Wilshire Boulevard. Bridging old and new, this Italian
Renaissance-style hotel is a happy marriage of two distinctive sensibilities.
The guest rooms of the Beverly Wing have contemporary décor, while
the Wilshire Wing's rooms appeal to guests with an eye for classic design.

As with any Four Seasons hotel, the service is exemplary. A very British afternoon tea is served at the Lobby Lounge, and the convivial bar is a perfect place to sit back and watch the glamorous parade of this star-studded city.

399 rooms. Pets accepted, some restrictions. Complimentary continental breakfast. High-speed Internet access. Two restaurants, two bars. Spa. Fitness center. Pool. Business center. $$$

FOUR SEASONS HOTEL LOS ANGELES AT BEVERLY HILLS ★ ★ ★ ★

300 S. Doheny Dr., Beverly Hills, 310-273-2222, 800-819-5053;
www.fourseasons.com
Located on a quiet, palm-lined street just a mile from the exclusive boutiques of Rodeo Drive and Robertson Boulevard, this hotel is a wonderful retreat. Guest rooms include Frette linens and oversized marble bathrooms with Bulgari toiletries. The rooftop pool is surrounded by lush gardens and is dotted with private cabanas. Don't miss the marvelous sunset massage from a candlelit cabana. Complimentary limousine rides to shopping and restaurants are available.

285 rooms. Pets accepted, some restrictions. Wireless Internet access. Three restaurants, bar. Spa. Fitness center. Pool. Business center. $$$$

Carlsbad

FOUR SEASONS RESORT AVIARA, NORTH SAN DIEGO ★ ★ ★ ★

7100 Four Seasons Point, Carlsbad, 760-603-6800, 800-819-5053;
www.fourseasons.com/aviara
Avid golfers come to play the 18-hole golf course designed by Arnold Palmer. But that's just one reason to come to this splendid resort on 200 lush acres overlooking the Batiquitos Lagoon, the Pacific Ocean and a nature preserve that's home to a variety of wildlife. The architecture pays homage to the region's history with its Spanish colonial design, and guest rooms feel luxurious and homey, with sumptuous sitting areas, sliding French doors that open up to private patios or balconies, and marble bathrooms with deep soaking tubs. Dining choices range from Italian to California cuisine and the lively wine bar boasts dramatic floor-to-ceiling windows offering views of the Pacific.

349 rooms. Two restaurants, bar. Children's activity center. Fitness center. Spa. Pets accepted. Pool. Golf. Tennis. Business center. $$$$

Dana Point

THE RITZ-CARLTON, LAGUNA NIGUEL ★ ★ ★ ★

1 Ritz-Carlton Dr., Dana Point, 949-240-2000, 800-241-3333;
www.ritzcarlton.com

Situated atop a 150-foot bluff overlooking the ocean, this Mediterranean-style villa is a first-class haven. Guest rooms have been decorated in a palette of cream and soft blue to reflect the beach setting and have ocean, pool or garden views. The resort has three restaurants, including the unique wine tasting room ENO, which offers an extensive menu of wines, cheeses and chocolates from around the globe. Surfing lessons are available at the beach, and the spa is fabulous with its contemporary California-glam décor and full menu of luxe treatments. Golfers come to play several spectacular courses nearby.

393 rooms. Wireless Internet access. Three restaurants, bar. Pets accepted. Fitness center. Pool. Tennis. Business center. $$$$

Laguna Beach

MONTAGE LAGUNA BEACH ★ ★ ★ ★

30801 S. Coast Hwy., Laguna Beach, 949-715-6000, 877-782-9821;
www.montagelagunabeach.com

Reigning over Laguna Beach from its rugged clifftop location, this stylish getaway blends arts and crafts style with the luxury of a full-service resort. Rooms, suites and bungalows feature 400-thread-count linens and marble bathrooms with a large shower and tub, and private balconies or patios with ocean views. Dining at Montage takes sophisticated California cuisine to a new level, particularly at the romantically cozy oceanfront bungalow restaurant, the Studio. There you'll find seasonal options like pan-seared John Dory with fennel, carmelized cauliflower and madras curry. The full-range spa has more than 20 treatment rooms and the poolside cabanas are decked out with flat-screen TVs and DVD/CD players.

262 rooms. Wireless Internet access. Three restaurants, four bars. Fitness center. Pool. Beach. Pets accepted. $$$$

RANCHO VALENCIA RESORT & SPA ★ ★ ★ ★

5921 Valencia Circle, Rancho Santa Fe, 858-756-1123, 800-548-3664;
www.ranchovalencia.com

Located in the canyon of Rancho Santa Fe on 40 manicured acres of rolling hills, this relaxing retreat is just minutes from the charming boutiques and cafés of La Jolla. If you're looking for something secluded, this is it. The resort is made up of 20 pink casitas, which house only 49 suites, each featuring fireplaces with hand-painted tiles, beamed ceilings and private garden patios and large bathrooms, some with Jacuzzi bathtubs and steam showers. There's also an award-winning tennis program, relaxing spa and guests have privileges at local golf courses. An outstanding restaurant makes for a perfect stay.

49 rooms, all suites. Pets accepted; fee. High-speed Internet access. Restaurant, bar. Fitness center. $$$$

La Jolla

LODGE AT TORREY PINES ★ ★ ★ ★

11480 N. Torrey Pines Rd., La Jolla, 858-453-4420; www.lodgetorreypines.com
The Lodge sits on a rocky cliff overlooking the Pacific Ocean and is surrounded by protected forest and unspoiled beaches. The view is gorgeous, but many are drawn by another aspect of the location: the lodge neighbors the 18th hole of the Torrey Pines Golf Course, one of the most acclaimed courses in the world. Tee times are guaranteed for guests who want to try their hand at the championship course. The resort itself is a celebration of the American Craftsman period, from its stained glass and handcrafted woodwork to its Stickley-style furnishings. The warm guest rooms boast custom-designed furniture, modern amenities and spectacular views of the golf course or the central courtyard.

170 rooms. High-speed Internet access. Two restaurants, two bars. Fitness center, spa. Tennis. Airport transportation available. $$$

Montecito

SAN YSIDRO RANCH, A ROSEWOOD RESORT ★ ★ ★ ★

900 San Ysidro Lane, Montecito, 805-969-5046, 800-368-6788;
www.sanysidroranch.com
John and Jackie Kennedy spent part of their honeymoon on this 550-acre resort, tucked away in the foothills of Montecito. Lushly planted acres are filled with fragrant flowers and plants, and stunning vistas of the Pacific Ocean and the Channel Islands can be seen in the distance. The bungalows, with their cozy blend of overstuffed chintz armchairs, oriental rugs and vaulted, wood-clad ceilings, provide luxuries like wood-burning fireplaces and Frette linens. Gifted cuisine is a hallmark of this resort, and the two restaurants provide charming settings for the imaginative food.

40 rooms. High-speed Internet access. Restaurant, bar. Pets accepted. Pool. Tennis. $$$$

Newport Beach

THE ISLAND HOTEL, NEWPORT BEACH ★ ★ ★ ★

690 Newport Center Dr., Newport Beach, 866-554-4620; www.theislandhotel.com
This 20-story tower is angled toward the Pacific Ocean and is only minutes from the beach. Guest rooms are spacious and comfortable with marble

bathrooms, luxurious Italian linens and well-appointed work spaces. The private balconies and furnished patios offer exceptional views of the Pacific Ocean and Newport Harbor. You may never want to leave the pool with its lush landscaping, 17-foot fireplace for chilly evenings and dataports and telephone jacks to stay in touch. Overlooking the nearby islands of Balboa, Lido and Catalina, this Newport Beach gem is only minutes from upscale shopping and golf facilities.

295 rooms. High-speed Internet access. Two restaurants, bar. Fitness center. Spa. Airport transportation available. Pets accepted. $$$

San Diego

U.S. GRANT HOTEL ★ ★ ★ ★

326 Broadway, San Diego, 866-837-4270, 800-237-5029; www.usgrant.net
This nearly 100-year-old hotel, which was opened in 1910 by Ulysses S. Grant, Jr. and his wife Fannie, recently underwent a multi-million dollar renovation that restored the polish to the historic, grand building. The opulent new interiors blend updated Art Deco furniture and decorative objects seamlessly with the belle époque bones of the hotel. Rooms feature original French art, custom imported wool carpets and marble bathrooms. The staff tends to guests' desires with old-world aplomb. Spa treatments, from hot stone to deep tissue massage, are available in-room through a local spa.

317 rooms. Restaurant, bar. Fitness center. $$$$

Santa Barbara

BACARA RESORT & SPA ★ ★ ★ ★

8301 Hollister Ave., Santa Barbara, 805-968-0100, 877-422-4245; www.bacararesort.com
With its spectacular setting overlooking the Pacific and dash of old-time Hollywood glamour, this resort is a jetsetter's fantasy. The luxurious rooms include Frette linens and private balconies. Service is attentive enough to make anyone feel like a celebrity. There are three infinity-edge pools on the grounds with 26 private cabanas. And the spa has everything to help guests relax and feel pampered, from citrus-avocado body polishes to earth crystal therapies. There's also golf, tennis, yoga, meditation and delicious California cuisine in the restaurant.

360 rooms. Restaurant, bar. Children's activity center. Pets accepted. Pool. Golf. Tennis. Business center. $$$$

FOUR SEASONS RESORT THE BILTMORE SANTA BARBARA ★ ★ ★ ★

1260 Channel Dr., Santa Barbara, 805-969-2261; www.fourseasons.com
Situated on 20 lush acres on the Pacific Ocean, the resort pays tribute to

the region's Spanish colonial history with its red-tiled roof, arches and hacienda-style main building. The guest rooms, located both in the main building and in separate cottages, feature a relaxed Spanish-colonial décor and include down pillows and luxe bathrobes. Crisp white cabanas line the sparkling pool. Besides offering a full menu of massages, facials and body wraps, the world-class spa incorporates botanicals from the gardens into its treatments. Dinner at the oceanfront Bella Vista restaurant is a special treat, particularly if you get a table close to one of the outdoor firepits.

211 rooms. High-speed Internet access. Two restaurants, bar. Spa. Pets accepted. Pool. Tennis. Business center. $$$$

Westlake Village

FOUR SEASONS HOTEL LOS ANGELES, WESTLAKE VILLAGE ★ ★ ★ ★

2 Dole Dr., Westlake Village, 818-575-3000, 800-819-5053;
www.fourseasons.com

Set on expansive, landscaped grounds, this hotel in suburban Los Angeles offers a tranquil escape from the city. Connected to the California Longevity and Health Institute, a premier medical spa, the hotel provides serenity-seeking Angelenos a place to rest up and rejuvenate in style. Rooms are traditionally decorated with classic touches like mahogany furniture, chintz-covered sofas and marble bathrooms. The on-site Onyx restaurant serves light, healthful Asian cuisine.

269 rooms. Pool. Spa. $$$$

FOUR STAR RESTAURANTS

Beverly Hills

THE BELVEDERE ★ ★ ★ ★

9882 S. Santa Monica Blvd., Beverly Hills, 310-788-2306;
www.beverlyhills.peninsula.com

The Belvedere may be the best hotel restaurant in the country. The spacious dining room, located in the Peninsula hotel, is dressed in cream tones, with tables topped with Villeroy & Boch china and pewter vases filled with fresh seasonal flowers. A pianist performs nightly and completes the elegant setting. Guests can also dine on the stunning sun-soaked patio, which is landscaped with beautiful greenery and flowers. The cuisine is a lively combination of heartland staples and global-accented fare. Diners are encouraged to create their own tasting menu with small bites including the famed macaroni and cheese.

Modern American menu. Lunch, dinner, brunch. Bar. Children's menu. Business casual attire. Reservations recommended. Valet parking. Outdoor seating. $$$$

Dana Point

STONEHILL TAVERN ★ ★ ★ ★

1 Monarch Beach Resort, Dana Point, 949-234-3318;
www.michaelmina.net/stonehill

Famed San Francisco chef-turned-restaurateur Michael Mina's urban bistro is located at the site of his first restaurant at the St. Regis Monarch Beach Resort. The space that formerly housed Mina's seafood restaurant, Aqua, has been transformed into a sleek, intimate spot by acclaimed interior designer Tony Chi with comfortable couches, glass-enclosed booths and a large terrace. The menu includes Mina's signature appetizer trios—three different preparations of one ingredient, such as tuna, lobster or duck, as well as twists on American classics (think fried chicken with mascarpone polenta and a root beer float for dessert). An impressive wine program focuses on boutique California producers, but also includes a diverse selection from Austria and Burgundy.

American menu. Dinner. Closed Monday-Tuesday. Bar. Business casual attire. Reservations recommended. Valet parking. Outdoor seating. $$$$

Laguna Beach

STUDIO ★ ★ ★ ★

30801 S. Coast Hwy., Laguna Beach, 949-715-6000;
www.studiolagunabeach.com

Housed in a cozy arts and crafts cottage overlooking the ocean, this restaurant at Montage Resort is a study in understated elegance. The menu is the creation of award-winning chef James Boyce and features contemporary California cuisine made with the freshest local ingredients. Settle in for a supper made up of dishes like pan-seared John Dory with baby fennel, cipollini onions and caramelized cauliflower, or vinegar-braised short ribs with butter-roasted asparagus. The wine cellar features more than 1,800 bottles with plenty of California selections and wines available by the glass.

California menu. Dinner. Closed Monday. $$$

La Jolla

A.R. VALENTIEN ★ ★ ★ ★

11480 N. Torrey Pines Rd., La Jolla, 858-453-4220; www. lodgetorreypines.com

La Jolla's Lodge at Torrey Pines may be best known for its golf, but its much-lauded restaurant, A.R. Valentien, gives the sport a run for its money. Named after a Craftsman-style California artist, the dining room is a showcase of stained glass lighting and Mission-style furnishings with large windows overlooking the 18th hole. Chef Jeff Jackson delivers stand-out traditional American cooking focusing on the quality of the ingredients. Settle in and sample dishes like local swordfish with toasted orzo, clams, roasted peppers and tapenade crostini. The outstanding wares of West Coast producers dot the superlative cheese list, so be sure to save room for a taste.

American menu. Dinner. Reservations recommended. $$$

THE DINING ROOM AT JACK'S ★ ★ ★ ★

7863 Girard Ave., La Jolla, 858-465-8111; www.jackslajolla.com
Part of a cluster of restaurants and lounges all under one roof in downtown La Jolla (Jack's Grille and Jack's Ocean Room are the other two dining outlets and there are multiple lounges), the Dining Room is undoubtedly the star of the group. Chef Tony DiSalvo gives San Diegoans some of the best food in the area. The menu looks traditional at first, but look again—dishes include lobster with Kaffir lime juice and sticks of Fuji apple, or spice-crusted black sea bass with Japanese eggplant. The room is crisp and elegant, with tall banquettes to snuggle up in as well as white-linen topped tables for lingering over decadent desserts like chocolate caramel custard.

Seafood menu. Dinner. Reservations recommended. $$$

Los Angeles

ORTOLAN ★ ★ ★ ★

8338 W. Third St., Los Angeles, 323-653-3300; www.ortolanrestaurant.com
French chef Christophe Émé, formerly of L'Orangerie, has ventured out on his own with Ortolan (named for a small songbird) and created an exquisite menu that blends classic French style with contemporary elements. Signature dishes include crispy langoustines with basil, chickpeas and minestrone, and roasted squab breast and leg with a gratin of macaroni and tapenade salad. The modernized provincial atmosphere, with cream-colored booths and banquettes, floor-to-ceiling velvet drapes, crystal chandeliers and antique mirrors, is equally dazzling.

French menu. Dinner. Closed Sunday. Bar. Business casual attire. Valet parking. $$$

PATINA ★ ★ ★ ★

141 S. Grand Ave., Los Angeles, 213-972-3331; www.patinagroup.com/patina
Celebrity chef Joachim Splichal's French-California cooking, interpreted here by executive chef Theo Schoenegger, celebrates local and regionally sourced foods in dishes such as foie gras with Ranier cherry jam, salmon with heirloom tomatoes, and olive-oil poached squab with truffles from Umbria. The polished dining room, with walnut-paneled walls and curved ceilings, echoes the hall itself, prepping concertgoers for events. Make a night of it by reserving the kitchen table and indulging in a six-

course market tasting menu. The bar serves nibbles and drinks after performances, and a lunch menu caters to tourists visiting the hall, as well as the downtown business crowd.

California menu. Lunch, dinner. Bar. Business casual attire. Reservations recommended. Valet parking. Outdoor seating. $$$

THE RESTAURANT AT HOTEL BEL-AIR ★ ★ ★ ★

701 Stone Canyon Rd., Los Angeles, 310-472-1211; www.hotelbelair.com
The constantly changing menu at this restaurant in the Hotel Bel-Air continues to be a superior draw for diners looking for a fresh, innovative meal. Those who want a close look at the pure brilliance of the restaurant's cooking staff can reserve Table One, an exclusive dining room adjacent to the kitchen where chef Douglas Dodd personally leads guests through a seven-course meal. The main Mediterranean-style dining room is decorated in butter cream tones with a Venetian chandelier, and the Tuscan-inspired terrace has a heated terra cotta floor and outdoor fireplace to keep diners warm on cool nights.

California menu, French menu. Breakfast, lunch, dinner, brunch, afternoon tea. Bar. Children's menu. Business casual attire. Reservations recommended. Valet parking. Outdoor seating. $$$$

SONA ★ ★ ★ ★

401 N. La Cienega Blvd., Los Angeles, 310-659-7708; www.sonarestaurant.com
Since it opened in 2002, Sona has received numerous accolades. Owner/ executive chef David Myers and pastry chef, Ramon Perez, turn out refined plates, and the seasonally-inspired menu incorporates organic and free-range artisanal products. Signature dishes include Maine lobster risotto, Elysian Fields lamb and any one of the adventurous desserts. Wine is a passion at Sona, where more than 21,000 bottles are stocked in temperature-controlled cellars (the restaurant even uses a special detergent-free high-temperature dishwasher for the glassware to make sure the taste of the wine remains pure). This restaurant is perfection down to the little details, including Izabel Lam china and Riedel stemware.

French menu. Dinner. Closed Sunday-Monday. Bar. Business casual attire. Reservations recommended. Valet parking. $$$

San Diego

LAUREL ★ ★ ★ ★

505 Laurel St., San Diego, 619-239-2222; www.laurelrestaurant.com
Make a grand entrance down a sweeping, wrought-iron staircase into this sleek and sexy 3,200-square-foot dining room. The décor, a glamorous update of traditional colonial that pairs houndstooth chairs with deconstructed crystal chandeliers and acid-green tufted banquettes, is as eye-catching as the stylish crowd that gathers around the bar each evening

to sip cocktails such as sparkling cosmopolitans (which are spiked with Champagne). The food is rustic, contemporary and French; signature dishes include salmon with white asparagus and paella loaded with local seafood such as rock shrimp and mussels. The restaurant's stellar wine list emphasizes the Rhône region of France. Laurel also hosts some of the best live jazz musicians in town, making the bar a lively spot to unwind and make new friends.

French, Mediterranean menu. Dinner. Bar. Casual attire. Valet parking. $$$

Santa Barbara

MIRÓ AT BACARA RESORT ★ ★ ★ ★

8301 Hollister Ave., Santa Barbara, 805-968-1800, 877-422-4245; www.bacararesort.com

Santa Barbara's luxurious Bacara Resort is home to the delightful Miró Restaurant. Joan Miró-style artwork, deep red dining chairs, a contemporary carpet and fantastic views of the Pacific Ocean set the scene, while the chef creates masterful renditions of traditional Spanish cooking such as oak-grilled lamb chops with aged Sherry and pan-roasted lobster with oven-roasted tomatoes. The 12,000-bottle wine cellar has something to match each meal. For a more casual alternative, the Miró Bar and Lounge features homemade sangria and tapas.

Mediterranean menu. Dinner. $$$

Santa Monica

MELISSE ★ ★ ★ ★

1104 Wilshire Blvd., Santa Monica, 310-395-0881; www.melisse.com

Classic French technique is the basis for the creative contemporary American menu at Melisse, an elegant, Provençal-style dining room. Warmed with fresh flower arrangements and paintings of rural French landscapes, the room at Melisse is lovely and intimate with tabletops set with fine linens and beautiful hand-painted china. Chef/owner Josiah Citrin creates intricate dishes from stunning, seasonal ingredients procured from regional farmers. His notable creations served in four-, five-, seven- or eight-course menus include lobster bolognese with black truffles, sweet corn ravioli, Dover sole roasted on the bone (and filleted tableside) and dry-aged Cote de Boeuf for two, also carved tableside.

French menu. Dinner. Bar. Casual attire. Reservations recommended. $$$$

Laguna Beach

SPA MONTAGE AT MONTAGE RESORT ★ ★ ★ ★ ★

30801 S. Coast Hwy., Laguna Beach, 949-715-6000, 866-271-6953; www.spamontage.com

Spa Montage is a stunning facility that takes advantage of its superior beachfront setting. An indoor-outdoor structure and floor-to-ceiling windows framing 160-degree views alleviate any guilt guests may feel for opting to stay in for a bit of pampering on a sunny day. The spa's holistic, get-back-to-nature approach is evident in its design, as well as in the products it uses. Custom-mixed lotions and oils blend natural ingredients, including eucalyptus, lavender, orange blossoms and citrus. Wrap up in one of the spa's cashmere robes and try any number of therapies, from a California citrus polish to an algae cellulite massage. Hungry spa-goers can find a cozy spot by the lap pool, where healthy snacks and meals are available from the Mosaic Grille.

Beverly Hills

THE BEVERLY HILLS HOTEL SPA BY LA PRAIRIE ★ ★ ★ ★

9641 Sunset Blvd., Beverly Hills, 310-887-2505; www.beverlyhills.com

The Clinic La Prairie in Montreux, Switzerland is among the world's leading spas, and its anti-aging treatments are considered revolutionary. The staff at this spa uses the same therapies while providing guests with white-glove treatment in its plush surroundings. La Prairie's commitment to anti-aging is perhaps best experienced through one of the spa's many decadent facials. The Caviar Firming Facial is an extravagant treat, using a concentration of caviar extracts and alpha hydroxy acids to lift and polish skin. The Intensive De-Aging facial uses a cellular complex and glycolic acid blend to reduce the appearance of fine lines. Massages and nail services are available at the spa, in a poolside cabana or in the privacy of a guest room.

THE SPA AT BEVERLY WILSHIRE ★ ★ ★ ★

9500 Wilshire Blvd., Beverly Hills, 310-275-5200, 800-545-4000; www.fourseasons.com

This spa is instantly inviting. The entrance features subtle lighting and rich mahogany walls accented with pictures of the spa's signature Gerber daisy, while a curving sauna anchors the entire facility. Choose from a cart overflowing with fruits and snacks as you lounge on long beds in the tranquility lounge. In addition to the nine treatment rooms, you can enjoy an aromatherapy crystal steam room and showers that automatically adjust to certain temperatures and fragrances. A variety of facials and body wraps tout the healing benefits of volcanic mud or warm marine algae, while the massages work out tension. After a spell in the sauna, cool off with chilled aromatherapy-scented face towels.

THE PENINSULA SPA, BEVERLY HILLS ★ ★ ★

9882 S. Santa Monica Blvd., Beverly Hills, 310-712-5288, 800-462-7899; www.beverlyhills.peninsula.com

The staff at the Peninsula knows how to help guests relax, and the technicians manning the hotel spa are no exception. Try the exclusive Shiffa precious gem treatment, which uses massage oils containing ruby, emeralds, sapphires and diamonds. The signature pedicure includes foot reflexology, a flowering herbal foot bath, a massage with Jasmine oil and a warming mask and paraffin treatment. The red carpet facial involves a crystalline gemstone mask to help remove fine lines and a cactus extract to lift and tighten skin. It also includes a hand microdermabrasion treatment with glycolic peppermint cream. There are several treatments for men, and the facility includes a well-equipped fitness center as well as a 60-foot rooftop lap pool lined with private cabanas.

Dana Point

THE RITZ-CARLTON SPA, LAGUNA NIGUEL ★ ★ ★

1 Ritz-Carlton Dr , Dana Point, 949 240-2000, 800-241-3333; www.ritzcarlton.com

Eleven treatment rooms, a full service beauty salon, a circular manicure and pedicure station and a modern fitness center are available to guests at the Ritz-Carlton Spa. Choose from holistic treatments that incorporate ancient practices as well as the latest skin treatments, massages and exfoliations. Collagen infusion facials and California citrus body polishes stand out among the spa's signature treatments. There are also seasonal treatments such as a summer chocolate sugar scrub pedicure. Treatments are rooted in the sea's purifying elements: rich minerals, sea salt or nutrient-rich algae and water.

SPA GAUCIN ★ ★ ★

1 Monarch Beach Resort, Dana Point, 949-234-3200, 800-722-1543; www.stregismonarchbeach.com

Spa Gaucin at the St. Regis is the picture of elegance with dark woods, Asian-style accents and three-story waterfalls. The warm cream interior accentuates specially commissioned artwork throughout the space and the 25 treatment rooms offer state-of-the-art amenities (including gas fireplaces to cozy up to). The spa menu includes everything from Thai massage to vitamin C facials to the signature pear body polish. Try the

Solace Mineral Trio, a hydrating treatment utilizing grapeseed body exfoliation and a volcanic clay wrap, or the Dermal Quench facial to ward off jetlag. There's also an extensive offering of beauty treatments from tanning to microdermabrasion.

La Jolla

THE SPA AT TORREY PINES ★★★★

11480 N. Torrey Pines Rd., La Jolla, 858-453-4420, 800-656-0087;
http://spatorreypines.com
This spa at the Lodge at Torrey Pines has an oceanfront setting and surrounding forest that influence many of the treatments. There are numerous water treatments, including balneotherapy, a seawater bath in a hydrotherapy tub. Body scrubs use coastal sage and pine for exfoliation. Several facials combat aging, including a Champagne facial that uses yeast extracts. The spa also has a list of rituals on the menu, which blend body treatments with massage. The Aromasoul Ritual, for instance, uses Chinese massage techniques to increase the flow of energy and replenish vitality. Before or after a treatment, spend some time relaxing in the men's or women's lounge, both of which are decorated with a soothing blend of arts and crafts style and Asian accents and include a fireplace (for ladies) and television (for men).

Los Angeles

THE FOUR SEASONS SPA, LOS ANGELES AT BEVERLY HILLS ★★★★

300 S. Doheny Dr., Los Angeles, 310-786-2222, 800-819-5053;
www.fourseasons.com
Book this luxurious spa's private poolside cabana for the California Sunset massage, a soothing treatment that feels even more relaxing when had alfresco. The Punta Mita massage is another signature treatment, combining tequila and sage. Body scrubs use an array of products, including chamomile and Turkish salt to exfoliate and polish skin. The Thermal Mineral Kur begins with a moor mud wrap, followed by a bath filled with mineral crystals from Hungary's renowned Sarvar Springs, before finishing with a soothing massage. The spa's divine facials cleanse, refresh and revive with a variety of options, including a fruit and pumpkin enzyme peel.

Newport Beach

THE SPA AT THE ISLAND HOTEL ★ ★ ★ ★

690 Newport Center Dr., Newport Beach, 949-759-0808, 866-554-4620; www.theislandhotel.com

Slip away to the Spa at the Island Hotel for a muscle-relieving massage or detoxifying volcanic clay treatment that is said to reenergize the body from head to toe. Spacious and modern, the spa's elegant touches—granite floors, silver tea pitchers and a calming water wall—instantly set a tranquil and tasteful tone. The spa's signature rituals use elements from India, Bali and the Hawaiian Islands. The Island Tropical Splendor, for instance, is a full-body scrub blending fresh coconut, rice and vetiver—a perennial grass native to India known for its medicinal and aromatic properties.

Ojai

SPA OJAI ★ ★ ★ ★

905 Country Club Rd., Ojai, 805-646-1111, 888-697-8780; www.ojairesort.com

Golfers, hikers and couples on romantic getaways all come to this sophisticated 31,000-square-foot sanctuary of health and well-being for a spa experience like no other. Spa Ojai features signature services such as Kuyam—a treatment that combines the therapeutic effects of cleansing mud, dry heat, inhalation therapy and guided meditation. This communal experience (kuyam means "a place to rest together") accommodates up to eight men or women. There's also an extensive array of facial, skin and body treatments, as well as a variety of art classes in the adjacent studio.

San Diego

SPA AT FOUR SEASONS RESORT AVIARA, NORTH SAN DIEGO ★ ★ ★ ★

7100 Four Seasons Point, Carlsbad, 760-603-6800, 800-819-5053; www.fourseasons.com/aviara

This newly renovated 15,000-square-foot spa has both indoor and outdoor treatment rooms and a solarium lounge equipped with a fireplace and plenty of comfortable lounging chairs. Pamper your skin with an avocado body wrap and customized facials designed to sooth, quench or rejuvenate stressed skin. The spa offers 11 different kinds of massages, including water shiatsu (watsu) treatments which involve massage and stretching while you float in a heated pool. More adventurous spa-goers can sample from the menu of Aryurvedic treatments based on ancient Eastern beauty rituals. The on-site José Eber Salon provides hair, nail and makeup services.

Santa Barbara

BACARA SPA ★ ★ ★ ★

8301 Hollister Ave., Santa Barbara, 805-968-1800, 877-422-4245;
www.bacararesort.com
With the Pacific Ocean on one side and the Santa Ynez Mountains on the other, Bacara is all about location. A fitness center, a saline-filled pool and secluded nooks for sunbathing flank more than 30 treatment rooms and indoor and outdoor massage stations. The spa offers an intriguing selection of global healing regimens, and an Eastern Origin menu, which features options such as reiki and shiatsu massage. The rugged terrain of the Santa Ynez Mountains is the perfect place for a rigorous walk, run or hike. Clay tennis courts, pools almost too pretty to swim in and yoga on the beach are just a few of the other fitness options.

SPA AT FOUR SEASONS RESORT SANTA BARBARA ★ ★ ★ ★

1260 Channel Dr., Santa Barbara, 805-969-2261, 800-819-5053;
www.fourseasons.com
Pure luxury sums up the look and feel of this oceanfront spa, whose design echoes the Spanish colonial style of the Four Seasons Resort in which it's located. Treatments rooms are more residential than spa-like, with kiva fireplaces, plush treatment tables and mission-style furniture. The signature avocado citrus wrap combines fruit extracts with sea salts and clay to hydrate and heal. The caviar facial is another signature therapy, and the Thai coconut scrub uses coconut and rice and includes a Thai foot massage. Or try a JAMU massage, which combines Chinese, Hindu and European techniques of acupressure, long strokes and rolling motions. Hair and styling services, manicures, pedicures and makeup are also available.

Westlake Village

THE SPA AT FOUR SEASONS LOS ANGELES, WESTLAKE VILLAGE ★ ★ ★ ★

2 Dole Dr., Westlake Village, 818-575-3000; www.fourseasons.com
A 40,000 square-foot space with Asian-influenced décor, this spa is a tranquil spot for top-notch pampering. Treatments take their cue from Asian traditions, with everything from shiatsu to reiki making an appearance on the spa menu. Couples can opt for a traditional massage in the outdoor spa cabanas, which include a private plunge pool. Or book a spa suite for your treatment, which features a fireplace and plunge pool. A nutritionist is on hand to help with diet consultations, and personal trainers can recommend a new workout plan.

Colorado

Colorado

Colorado Springs

THE BROADMOOR ★ ★ ★ ★

1 Lake Ave., Colorado Springs, 719-634-7711; www.broadmoor.com

Located at the foot of the Rocky Mountains and surrounded by beautiful Cheyenne Lake, the Broadmoor has been one of America's favorite resorts since 1918. This all-season paradise is close to Colorado Springs, yet feels a million miles away. The opulent accommodations include rooms with views of the mountains or lake. Activities range from tennis at the tennis club to playing the links at three championship golf courses, paddleboating on the lake and horseback riding. Kids will love the "mountain" waterslide. And the world-class spa incorporates indigenous botanicals and pure spring water. The resort includes 15 restaurants, cafés and lounges, and several shops.

700 rooms, all suites. Pets accepted. High-speed Internet access. Restaurants, bars. Spa. Airport transportation available. Pool. Golf. Tennis. Business center. $$$

Aspen

THE LITTLE NELL ★ ★ ★ ★ ★

675 E. Durant Ave., Aspen, 970-920-4600; www.thelittlenell.com

Tucked away at the base of a mountain, the Little Nell provides a perfect location either to hit the slopes or roam the streets in search of Aspen's latest fashions. The rooms and suites are heavenly cocoons with fireplaces, overstuffed furniture and luxurious bathrooms. Some suites feature vaulted ceilings showcasing glorious mountainside views, while others overlook the charming former mining town. The gracious staff fulfills any request, from last minute dinner reservations to taking your dog for a walk around town while you soak in the outdoor pool and Jacuzzi. Enjoy the well-equipped fitness center and take advantage of the services of the ski concierges, who will assist with equipment storage and purchasing lift tickets. Montagna restaurant is one of the most popular spots in town with its inventive reinterpretation of American cuisine.

92 rooms. Pets accepted. Closed late April-mid-May. High-speed Internet access. Three restaurants, two bars. Airport transportation available. Pool. Business center. $$$$

Denver

THE BROWN PALACE HOTEL ★ ★ ★ ★

321 17th St., Denver, 303-297-3511, 800-321-2599; www.brownpalace.com
Denver's most celebrated and historic hotel, the Brown Palace has hosted presidents, royalty and celebrities since 1892. The elegant lobby features a magnificent stained-glass ceiling that tops off six levels of cast-iron balconies. The luxurious guest rooms have two styles—Victorian or Art Deco. The award-winning Palace Arms restaurant features signature favorites like rack of lamb and pan-roasted veal. Cigar aficionados take to the library-like ambience of the Churchill Bar. Afternoon tea is accompanied by live harp music. And Ellyngton's Sunday brunch is legendary. After a busy day of exploring nearby attractions like the 16th Street Mall and the Museum of Natural History, the full-service spa is the perfect place to unwind with a deep tissue massage, body treatment or facial.

241 rooms. Pets accepted. Wireless Internet access. Three restaurants, bar. Spa. $$$

Aspen

THE ST. REGIS ASPEN ★ ★ ★ ★

315 E. Dean St., Aspen, 970-920-3300, 888-454-9005;
www.stregis.com/aspen
Located at the base of Aspen Mountain between the gondola and lift, this hotel's upscale Western atmosphere is the perfect respite from skiing, shopping or warm weather activities such as fly-fishing and white water rafting. The outdoor pool and accompanying lounge are ideal for whiling away warm afternoons, or you can relax in the lavish spa. Rooms are richly decorated in muted colors with bursts of color and oversized leather furniture. (Expect complimentary water bottle service and a humidifier at turndown.) The Club Floor offers its own concierge and five complimentary meals throughout the day. Olives Aspen serves Mediterranean-inspired cuisine from renowned chef Todd English, and Whiskey Rocks is a popular gathering place.

253 rooms. Closed late October-mid-November. High-speed Internet access. Restaurant, two bars. Airport transportation available. $$$$

Avon

THE RITZ-CARLTON BACHELOR GULCH ★ ★ ★ ★

130 Daybreak Ridge, Avon, 970-748-6200;www.ritzcarlton.com
Rugged meets refined at this resort, located at the base of the mountain

at Beaver Creek. From the 10-gallon-hat-clad doorman who greets you to the rustic great room, this resort captures the spirit of the Old West in an elegant setting. The rooms and suites are comfortable and stylish, with leather chairs, dark wood furniture and wood beamed ceilings. Iron chandeliers and twig furnishings adorn the public spaces. This family-friendly resort offers an abundance of activities, including fly fishing, a horseshoe pit, two children's play areas, an outdoor pool, golf and, of course, skiing.

237 rooms. Pets accepted. Wireless Internet access. Two restaurants, bar. Spa. Ski in/ski out. Golf. Tennis. Business center. $$$$

FOUR STAR RESTAURANTS

Aspen

MONTAGNA ★ ★ ★ ★

675 E. Durant Ave., Aspen, 970-920-4600; www.thelittlenell.com
Located in the Little Nell hotel, Montagna is one of the top dining spots in Aspen. With its buttery walls, iron chandeliers and deep picture windows, the restaurant has the feeling of a chic Swiss chalet. The menu is outstanding (from the milk-fed veal chop with chanterelles, radishes and balsamic to the fresh rigatoni with lamb sausage), and the sommelier oversees a 15,000-bottle wine cellar. The superb brunch features sweet dishes like lemon soufflé pancakes with fresh raspberry syrup as well as savory offerings such as huevos rancheros with homemade salsa and ancho chile sauce.

American menu. Dinner, lunch, breakfast. Sunday brunch. Closed late April-mid-May. Bar. Children's menu. Casual attire. Valet parking. Outdoor seating. $$$$

Beaver Creek

MIRABELLE AT BEAVER CREEK ★ ★ ★ ★

55 Village Rd., Beaver Creek, 970-949-7728; www.mirabelle1.com
Love is in the air at this charming 19th-century cottage in the mountains. Each of the spacious, bright rooms is cozy and warm, while the porch, lined with colorful potted flowers, is the perfect spot to dine on warm evenings. The food is just as magical. The kitchen offers sophisticated French food prepared with a modern sensibility. Signature dishes include Colorado lamb chops and roasted elk medallions with fruit compote. The house-made ice cream is the perfect finish.

French menu. Dinner. Closed Sunday; also May, November. Bar. Children's menu. Casual attire. Outdoor seating. $$$

Boulder

FLAGSTAFF HOUSE RESTAURANT ★ ★ ★ ★

1138 Flagstaff Rd., Boulder, 303-442-4640; www.flagstaffhouse.com

From its location on Flagstaff Mountain, this is easily one of the most amazing spots to watch the sunset, and the food rivals the spectacular setting. The upscale and inspired menu changes daily, with plates like beef wellington dressed up with black truffle sauce and Hawaiian ono with ginger, scallions and soft-shell crabs. The wine list is massive (the restaurant has a 20,000-bottle wine cellar), so enlist the assistance of the attentive sommelier for guidance. The restaurant is owned by the Monette family, which means you'll be treated to refined service and homegrown hospitality, making dining here a delight from start to finish. Try to arrive early for a pre-dinner cocktail at the handsome mahogany bar.

American menu. Dinner. Bar. Business casual attire. Reservations recommended. Valet parking. Outdoor seating. $$$$

Colorado Springs

PENROSE ROOM ★ ★ ★ ★

1 Lake Ave., Colorado Springs, 719-577-5733, 800-634-7711;
www.broadmoor.com

This recently renovated restaurant offers a spectacular dining experience set against the magnificent views of Colorado Springs and Cheyenne Mountain. Chef Bertrand Bouquin serves up contemporary, continental cuisine featuring the influences of Italy, Spain, Africa and France. The menu changes often and features prix fixe meals of three, four and seven courses. Favorite appetizers include pistachio-laden warm goat cheese salad, five herb ravioli and chilled Peekytoe crab with cherry relish salad. Entrées include roasted loin of Colorado lamb with purple mustard and slowly cooked halibut in black olive oil. After dinner, enjoy live music and dancing.

French menu. Dinner. Closed Sunday. Bar. Children's menu. Jacket required. Reservations recommended. Valet parking. $$$$

Denver

RESTAURANT KEVIN TAYLOR ★ ★ ★ ★

1106 14th St., Denver, 303-640-1012; www.ktrg.net

Located inside the stylish Hotel Teatro, across from the Denver Center for Performing Arts, this 70-seat restaurant brings French style to downtown Denver. Vaulted ceilings are offset with Versailles mirrors and alabaster chandeliers. Chairs are covered in green- and yellow-striped silk fabric, and tables are topped with yellow Frette linens, Bernardaud china and Christofle silver. Chef Kevin Taylor earns applause for his unpretentious contemporary cuisine. Start with seared Grade A French foie gras, and then try one of the signature dishes such as butter-poached Atlantic salmon, pancetta-roasted pork loin, and Colorado lamb sirloin. Top it off with a killer dessert like caramelized pineapple Napoleon. The restaurant features seasonal menus that change every two months, plus four- and five-course tasting menus and a prix fixe pre-theater menu. There are also 900 vintages here—ask for a private table in the wine cellar.

American, French menu. Dinner. Closed Sunday. Bar. Business casual attire. Reservations recommended. Valet parking. $$$

FOUR STAR SPAS

Avon

THE BACHELOR GULCH SPA AT RITZ CARLTON ★ ★ ★ ★

130 Daybreak Ridge, Avon, 970-343-1138, 800-576-5582;
www.ritzcarlton.com

The Bachelor Gulch Spa captures the essence of its alpine surroundings with polished rock, stout wood and flowing water in its interiors. The rock grotto with a lazy river hot tub is a defining feature, and the Fitness centers have majestic mountain views. The beauty of the outdoors also extends to the exceptional treatments which utilize ingredients indigenous to the region, including Alpine berries, Douglas fir and blue spruce sap. After a rigorous day on the slopes, there are also plenty of massage options, from the Roaring Rapids, which uses hydrotherapy, or the Four-Hands, where two therapists work out knots.

Colorado Springs

THE SPA AT THE BROADMOOR ★ ★ ★ ★

1 Lake Ave., Colorado Springs, 719-577-5770, 866-686-3965;
www.broadmoor.com

With the beautiful scenery of the Rocky Mountains as a backdrop, the Spa at the Broadmoor already has an advantage over other luxury spas. But even without these surroundings, an experience at this two-level lakefront spa is pure bliss. With Venetian chandeliers, earth tones and an overall feeling of serenity, the treatment rooms perfectly set the scene for the spa's luxurious massage therapies and skin treatments. If your Rocky Mountain adventures have left you with aching muscles, a variety of massage therapies will make you feel like new again, while facial therapies such as the calming chamomile facial will get skin glowing. The Junior Ice Cream manicure and pedicure is reserved for young guests.

Denver

THE SPA AT THE BROWN PALACE ★ ★ ★ ★ ★

321 17th St., Denver, 303-312-8940, 800-321-2599; www.brownpalace.com
An artesian well has supplied the Brown Palace Hotel since it opened in
1892. The soothing natural rock waterfall at the spa's entrance speaks
to this history. Five special soaks, which draw from the well located 750
feet beneath the hotel, are available. You can book the couples suite for
lunch and a private soak. There's also a dual reclining hydrotherapy tub.
The signature massage incorporates Swedish, reflexology and deep tissue
massage with lemongrass sage essential oils.

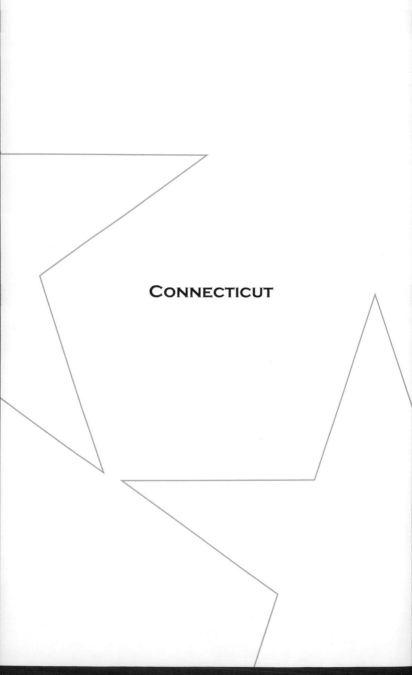

Connecticut

CONNECTICUT

Washington

MAYFLOWER INN ★ ★ ★ ★ ★

118 Woodbury Rd., Washington, 860-868-9466; www.mayflowerinn.com
This country inn, located less than two hours from New York City, evokes the feeling and quiet elegance of an English countryside hotel. It's set on 28 acres of rolling hills, streams and lush gardens. Guest rooms and suites are swathed in luxurious fabrics and feature four-poster, canopied beds, 18th- and 19th-century art, and modern touches like flat-screen TVs. The inn's dining room has a seasonal menu that makes good use of fresh, local ingredients with dishes such as organic Atlantic salmon with fresh veggies. The tap room has a more casual menu with classics like Vermont cheddar-topped burgers and lemon-rosemary chicken. The sprawling spa is a tranquil retreat where every detail is attended to.

24 rooms. Children over 12 years only. Wireless Internet access. Restaurant, bar. $$$$

Washington

THE MAYFLOWER SPA ★ ★ ★ ★

118 Woodbury Rd., Washington, 860-868-9466; www.mayflowerinn.com
The 20,000-square-foot Mayflower Spa, opened in 2006, features the same classic design, elegant furnishings and quiet luxury of its namesake inn. The three-, four- or five-day women-only program (there are also specialty weeks for couples and men) accomodates 28 guests. Those who come for the full spa experience receive a pre-arrival consultation to create a schedule of pampering services and fitness and nutrition classes. Guests are provided with everything from yoga mats to MP3 players to loungewear. The spa has an indoor heated pool and mosaic-domed whirlpool, as well as private yoga and Pilates studios. The extensive list of fitness classes provide a quandry for the indecisive—everything from kickboxing to ballet is on the menu.

WASHINGTON, DISTRICT OF COLUMBIA

WASHINGTON, DISTRICT OF COLUMBIA

Washington, D.C.

FOUR SEASONS HOTEL, WASHINGTON, D.C. ★ ★ ★ ★ ★

2800 Pennsylvania Ave. N.W.,Washington, D.C., 202-342-0444,
800-332-3442; www.fourseasons.com

This Four Seasons, located in Washington's historic Georgetown neighborhood, delivers a refined, residential experience that extends from your first step in the modern, sophisticated lobby to lights out in one of the luxuriously-appointed guest rooms. Yoga classes, a lap pool and cutting-edge equipment are found in the fitness center, while the seven spa treatment rooms are a quiet spot for indulging in signature services like the cherry blossom Champagne body wrap. The hotel's restaurant, Seasons, offers a menu with a focus on fresh, regional ingredients, while the Garden Terrace lounge is the capital's top spot for afternoon tea.

211 rooms. Pets accepted, some restrictions. Wireless Internet access. Restaurant, bar. Fitness center, spa. Indoor pool, whirlpool. Airport transportation available. $$$$

Washington, D.C.

THE HAY-ADAMS ★ ★ ★ ★

1800 16th St. N.W., Washington, D.C., 202-638-6600, 800-424-5054;
www.hayadams.com

Set on Lafayette Square across from the White House, this hotel has welcomed notables since the 1920s. The guest rooms are a happy marriage of historic preservation (carved plaster ceilings and ornamental fireplaces) and 21st-century conveniences (high-speed Internet access and CD players). Windows frame views of the White House, St. John's Church and Lafayette Square. All-day dining is available at Lafayette, while the Off the Record bar is a popular watering hole for politicians and hotel guests.

145 rooms. $$$$

MANDARIN ORIENTAL, WASHINGTON, D.C. ★ ★ ★ ★

1330 Maryland Ave. S.W., Washington, D.C., 202-554-8588, 888-888-1778;
www.mandarinoriental.com

Overlooking the Tidal Basin with views of the Jefferson Memorial, this Washington outpost of the Asian hotel brand delivers a scenic and central location on the Potomac River. Guest rooms mix an Eastern sensibility with East Coast style (think preppy plaids and toiles alongside clean-lined furniture and fresh-clipped orchids). Contemporary Asian-influenced cuisine is served in the two restaurants, while the Empress Lounge is a more casual alternative with cocktails and small plates like lobster salad BLT. A 10,000-square-foot spa, fitness center and indoor pool offer waterfront views, a full spa menu and on-call personal trainers.

400 rooms. Pets accepted, some restrictions; fee. Wireless Internet access. Two restaurants, two bars. Fitness center, spa. Indoor pool, whirlpool. Airport transportation available. $$$$

THE RITZ-CARLTON, GEORGETOWN ★ ★ ★ ★

3100 South St. N.W., Washington, D.C., 202-912-4100, 800-241-3333; www.ritzcarlton.com

Embassy delegations often stay at the Ritz-Carlton, Georgetown for its contemporary décor and historic setting. Many of the guest rooms offer views of the Potomac River, along with feather duvets, goose-down pillows, rich wood accents, contemporary furnishings and marble baths. Sip one of the fire-red martinis in the sleek Degrees Bar and Lounge, and then dine on American/Italian cuisine in Fahrenheit. Try a facial at the on-site spa, or slip in a workout at the fully-equipped fitness center.

86 rooms. Airport transportation available. $$$$

THE RITZ-CARLTON, WASHINGTON ★ ★ ★ ★

1150 22nd St. N.W., Washington, D.C., 202-835-0500, 800-241-3333; www.ritzcarlton.com

The Ritz-Carlton provides noteworthy attention to detail along with innovative amenities. On-call technology butlers assist with computer woes, while frequent visitors can have items stored for their next stay. Even the nightly turndown service is distinctive, leaving a freshly baked brownie on your pillow. Guest rooms are spacious and comfortable and provide pleasing vistas of the garden courtyard or various Washington landmarks. If you are staying in the Club Level rooms, you will be treated to five food and beverage presentations each day. All guests are granted access to the Sports Club/LA fitness complex next door.

300 rooms. Airport transportation available. $$$$

FOUR STAR RESTAURANTS

Washington, D.C.

CITYZEN ★ ★ ★ ★

1330 Maryland Ave. S.W., Washington, D.C., 202-787-6006; www.mandarinoriental.com

Under Chef Eric Ziebold, CityZen serves modern American-French cuisine. There's a new three-course prix-fixe menu every month which includes appetizers such as purèe of Savoy cabbage soup with a lobster custard, globe artichoke ravioli, sashimi of Japanese hamachi and broiled

Boston mackerel. Desserts include crispy brioche bread pudding, a CityZen peanut butter cup or a chocolate mint julep. Ziebold also offers a multi-course tasting menu, available as a vegetarian option. The restaurant and the lounge, designed by the acclaimed Tony Chi, feel intimate despite the large space and vaulted ceilings.

American, French menu. Dinner. Closed Sunday-Monday. Bar. Business casual attire. Reservations recommended. Valet parking. $$$$

MICHEL RICHARD CITRONELLE ★ ★ ★ ★

3000 M St. N.W., Washington, D.C., 202-625-2150; www.citronelledc.com
Chef Michel Richard won the James Beard award for outstanding chef in 2007 for his fresh and bright cuisine. The restaurant is equally uplifting with its colorful mood wall and glass-enclosed open kitchen that provides a bird's-eye view of the show. The chef manages to wow diners by highlighting the simple flavors of each dish's main component. A la carte entrées may include duck with persimmon and black cherry-anise sauce or squab with macaroni gratin and foie gras-syrah sauce.

French menu. Dinner. Bar. Business casual attire. Reservations recommended. Valet parking. Outdoor seating. $$$$

PALENA ★ ★ ★ ★

3529 Connecticut Ave. N.W., Washington, D.C., 202-537-9250;
www.palenarestaurnat.com
Starting with the fresh baked-on-the-premises whole-grain breads, chef/owner Frank Ruta's authentic Italian-influenced fare is rustic and exceptional. After working in the White House kitchen in the 1980s with retired pastry chef Ann Amernick, the two opened this small, stylish eatery and were greeted by instantaneous success. The seasonal tasting menu remains the best way to experience Ruta's culinary expertise, but à la carte dishes including sea scallops with chestnut puree or gnocchi with roasted endive, turnips, black truffle and shaved pecorino, are no less impressive.

Continental menu. Dinner. Closed Sunday-Monday. $$$

FOUR STAR SPAS

Washington, D.C.

THE SPA AT THE MANDARIN ORIENTAL, WASHINGTON, D.C. ★ ★ ★ ★

1330 Maryland Ave. S.W., Washington, D.C., 202-787-6100
The staff at the spa promote the time ritual concept, a customized two- or three-hour experience during which clients receive a one-on-one consultation with a therapist to determine which treatments are best-suited to their needs. All of the facials, massages and body therapies are

enhanced with Eastern philosophies and techniques. The spa's signature Cherry Blossom Scrub uses cherry tea leaves, sugar and nourishing oils to strengthen the immune system and remove dead skin cells.

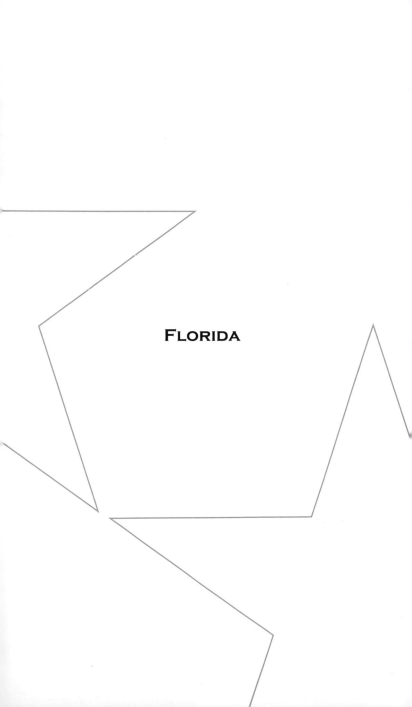

FLORIDA

FLORIDA

Naples

THE RITZ-CARLTON, NAPLES ★ ★ ★ ★ ★

280 Vanderbilt Beach Rd., Naples, 239-598-3300, 800-241-3333;
www.ritzcarlton.com

Three miles of white sand beaches attract visitors to this Mediterranean-inspired resort. While here, take part in water sports, sample the menu at the full-service spa or take the shuttle to the Ritz Carlton Golf Resort just down the road. Guest rooms reflect a European-style décor and the hotel's multi-million dollar art collection of 18th- and 19th-century British and American pieces is on prominent display throughout the property. Restaurants run the gamut from casual poolside cafés and beach pavilions to formal establishments that encourage guests to dress for dinner.

463 rooms. High-speed Internet access. Seven restaurants, six bars. Children's activity center. Fitness center, fitness classes available, spa. Beach. Two outdoor pools, children's pool, whirlpool. Golf, 36 holes. Tennis. Airport transportation available. Business center. $$$$

Palm Beach

FOUR SEASONS RESORT PALM BEACH ★ ★ ★ ★ ★

2800 S. Ocean Blvd., Palm Beach, 561-582-2800, 800-332-3442;
www.fourseasons.com

This resort unites the best of Palm Beach in one spot. The hotel is set on a secluded stretch of golden beach, just minutes from the alluring boutiques of Worth Avenue and the challenges of three championship golf courses. The guest rooms have a sophisticated tropical décor, with floral prints, pastel colors and casually elegant furnishings. Southeastern regional dishes are the specialty at the Restaurant, while the patio setting of the Atlantic Bar & Grill and the canopied terrace of the Ocean Bistro are perfect for casual meals and tropical drinks. A small spa and well-equipped fitness center round out the experience.

210 rooms. Pets accepted, some restrictions. High-speed Internet access. Four restaurants, four bars. Fitness center, Fitness classes available, spa. Outdoor pool, whirlpool. Children's activity center. Tennis. Airport transportation available. Business center. $$$$

THE RITZ-CARLTON, PALM BEACH ★ ★ ★ ★ ★

100 S. Ocean Blvd., Manalapan, 561-533-6000, 800-241-3333;
www.ritzcarlton.com

This luxury resort recently underwent a major renovation. Tucked away on seven oceanfront acres on the southern tip of Palm Beach Island, the property boasts two outdoor pools, exquisite on-site dining and a 3,000-square-foot oceanfront terrace complete with an evening fire pit. Guest rooms artfully blend Florida style with European elegance with their inviting golden hues, rich upholstered fabrics and modern amenities including flatscreen TVs, DVD players and wireless Internet access. Looking to unwind with a hot bath? Let a bath butler run you the perfect soak in one of the suites' oversized oceanview bathtubs. Try the Ocean Café and Bar for lunch or enjoy afternoon tea at the Lobby Lounge. The children's programs at this resort are especially imaginative. Whether you're looking for a romantic getaway weekend or a family vacation, you can't go wrong with this Palm Beach jewel.

270 rooms. Pets accepted, some restrictions; fee. High-speed Internet access. Three restaurants, three bars. Children's activity center. Fitness center, spa. Beach. Outdoor pool, whirlpool. Tennis. Business center. $$$$

FOUR STAR HOTELS

Amelia Island

THE RITZ-CARLTON, AMELIA ISLAND ★ ★ ★

4750 Amelia Island Pkwy., Amelia Island, 904-277-1100, 800-241-3333; www.ritzcarlton.com

Located on a barrier island off Florida's northeastern coast, this resort captures the essence of this magical place, where time seems to stand still. The guest rooms are decorated with floral prints and pastel colors and all offer coastal or ocean views. Spend the day by the beach or try tennis, golf, horseback riding or sailing. For young guests, there are Ritz Kids activity programs, a playground and a nanny service. Fernandina Beach, a quaint Victorian area with specialty boutiques, is just down the road. The resort's numerous restaurants and lounges serve up a variety of specialties with a focus on seafood.

444 rooms. Wireless Internet access. Three restaurants, four bars. Fitness center, spa. Beach. Indoor, outdoor pool, whirlpool. Tennis. Golf. Business center. $$$$

Aventura

FAIRMONT TURNBERRY ISLE RESORT & CLUB ★ ★ ★

19999 W. Country Club Dr., Aventura, 305-933-6937, 800-441-1414; www.fairmont.com

Located near Fort Lauderdale in Aventura, Turnberry Isle underwent a $100 million renovation in 2006. The hotel, set on the Atlantic Ocean, is reminiscent of a palatial private estate featuring terra-cotta tiles and pastel color schemes in its rooms. Four restaurants and five lounges serve delectable seafood and continental dishes. Two Robert Trent Jones, Sr. golf courses provide a challenge, while the famous Island Green 18th hole continues to be one of the more difficult holes. Turnberry's two tennis centers are often counted among the country's best.

392 rooms. Pets accepted, some restrictions; fee. Four restaurants, five bars. Fitness center, spa. Indoor pool. Golf. Tennis. Business center. $$$$

Fort Lauderdale

ST. REGIS RESORT ★ ★ ★ ★

1 N. Fort Lauderdale Beach Blvd., Fort Lauderdale, 954-465-2300;
www.stregis.com

Elegant, contemporary and utterly luxurious, this oceanfront resort is a stylish escape in busy Fort Lauderdale. Rooms, decorated in neutral tones with mahogany furniture, feature flat-screen TVs with DVD players, beds wrapped in Pratesi linens and balconies with views of the ocean. An 8,500-square foot spa offers a full menu of treatments while the sprawling fitness center has spinning classes and a Pilates studio. Cero, the on-site restaurant, serves fresh seafood in a sophisticated setting overlooking the water, and the wine room is a chic place to sample one of the many reserves and chat with the sommelier.

187 rooms. Wireless Internet access. Restaurant, bar. Fitness center. Spa. Pool. Beach. Business Center. $$$$

Key Biscayne

THE RITZ-CARLTON, KEY BISCAYNE ★ ★ ★ ★

455 Grand Bay Dr., Key Biscayne, 305-365-4500, 800-241-3333;
www.ritzcarlton.com

Located minutes from downtown Miami, this resort delivers the intimacy of a private island escape but with all the convenience of a city hotel. Situated on 12 acres of oceanfront property, the resort has a 20,000-square-foot spa and 11-court tennis center. The guest rooms feature British colonial furnishings and pastel colors. Cioppino, the resort's signature restaurant, has an Italian-influenced menu with an accent on local seafood.

490 rooms. Wireless Internet access. Two restaurants, two bars. Children's activity center. Fitness center, spa. Beach. Two outdoor pools, children's pool, whirlpool. Tennis. Airport transportation available. Business center. $$$$

Miami

FOUR SEASONS HOTEL MIAMI ★ ★ ★ ★

1435 Brickell Ave., Miami, 305-358-3535, 800-332-3442;
www.fourseasons.com

This contemporary hotel is located in downtown Miami's newly buzzing Brickell neighborhood. Guest rooms and suites are decorated with cool earth tones and distinctive artwork. The 50,000-square-foot Splash Spa at the on-site Sports Club/LA has 10 treatment rooms, including a Turkish steam room. The hotel features a fine-dining restaurant, Acqua, which serves up Latin-inspired fare, and two lounges, including the skytop, poolside Bahia where locals and travelers alike gather for cocktails.

305 rooms. Pets accepted, some restrictions. High-speed Internet access. Restaurant, two bars. Children's activity center. Fitness center, fitness classes available, spa. Outdoor pool, children's pool, whirlpool. Airport transportation available. Business center. $$$

MANDARIN ORIENTAL, MIAMI ★ ★ ★ ★

500 Brickell Key Dr., Miami, 305-913-8288, 866-888-6780;
www.mandarinoriental.com

With its waterfront location and contemporary interior design, this hotel is an island of calm in the middle of downtown Miami. Located on tiny Brickell Key opposite the city center, this outpost of the Asian hotel group is a favorite among Miamians for its skyline views, Azul restaurant, and its man-made white sand beach. Guests can sign up for the hotel's South Beach Experience, which includes transportation to South Beach, a private beach cabana and access to the pool and restaurant at the famed South Beach mansion-turned private club Casa Casuarina. Come back to one of the luxurious guest rooms decorated in a contemporary Asian-influenced style with bamboo hardwood floors, simple furnishings and white fabrics.

327 rooms. Pets accepted, some restrictions; fee. High-speed Internet access. Two restaurants, two bars. Fitness center, fitness classes available, spa. Beach. Outdoor pool, whirlpool. Airport transportation available. Business center.

THE RITZ-CARLTON COCONUT GROVE ★ ★ ★ ★

3300 S.W. 27th Ave., Miami, 305-644-4680, 800-241-3333;
www.ritzcarlton.com

This palatial hotel is recognized for its impeccable service—technology, travel, bath and even pet butlers cater to your every whim. Rooms are classically decorated and offer views of the city and Biscayne Bay. The spacious spa offers dozens of treatments, and a shimmering pool with views over Coconut Grove is a prime spot for sunbathers and people-watchers.

The lobby lounge serves cocktails and afternoon tea, while Bizcaya Grill offers steaks prepared to perfection.

115 rooms. High-speed Internet access. Restaurant, three bars. Fitness center, spa. Outdoor pool. Airport transportation available. Business center. $$

Miami Beach

LOEWS MIAMI BEACH HOTEL ★ ★ ★ ★

1601 Collins Ave., Miami Beach, 305-604-1601, 800-235-6397;
www.loewshotels.com

The architecture here blends an Art Deco landmark with new construction to form a thoroughly modern hotel. As one of the largest resorts on South Beach, occupying 900 feet of prime oceanfront, you can't miss its cone-shaped 18-story tower perched high above the rest of Collins Avenue. Guest rooms are decorated in the soothing hues of sun, sand and sea, and have modern amenities including flat-screen TVs, in-room iPods and Bloom toiletries. The enormous oceanfront pool is a landmark in itself with space to accommodate couples, families and conventioneers alike, while still exuding an aura of relaxation and luxury. Celeb chef Emeril Lagasse gives the seafood-heavy menu at his on-site restaurant, Emeril's South Beach, a Creole accent and tourists and locals flock to the 'see and be seen' atmosphere.

790 rooms. Pets accepted. High-speed Internet access. Three restaurants, three bars. Children's activity center. Fitness center, fitness classes available, spa. Beach. Outdoor pool, whirlpool. Airport transportation available. Business center. $$$

THE RITZ-CARLTON, SOUTH BEACH ★ ★ ★ ★

1 Lincoln Rd., Miami Beach, 786-276-4000, 800-241-3333;
www.ritzcarlton.com

This landmark property, originally designed by legendary Miami architect Morris Lapidus, boasts an ideal location—the foot of South Beach's Lincoln Road Mall on the Atlantic Ocean. Rooms feature nautical hues, views of the ocean and luxury touches like marble baths and feather-topped beds. The 16,000-square-foot La Maison de Beaute Carita spa is the centerpiece of the resort. Dining choices abound, including restaurants that feature Caribbean, New American, and Floridian cuisine served in a variety of elegant and informal settings.

376 rooms. Pets accepted, some restrictions; fee. High-speed Internet access. Four restaurants, four bars. Children's activity center. Fitness center, spa. Beach. Outdoor pool, whirlpool. Airport transportation available. Business center. $$$$

THE SETAI ★ ★ ★ ★

2001 Collins Ave., Miami Beach, 305-520-6000; www.setai.com

Set on the oceanfront, rooms at the Setai are sleek and simple with hardwood floors, neutral tones, crisp white linens and black granite bathrooms. Luxurious amenities include in-room tubs, Aqua di Parma bath products, waterfall showers and plasma televisions. The Spa at the Setai features private suites with ocean views and a fully-equipped gym with personal trainers. At the end of the day, satiate your appetite with a meal at the Restaurant, where a menu of French and Asian-inspired fare awaits.

75 rooms. High-speed Internet access. Restaurant, bar. Fitness center, Fitness center, spa. Outdoor pool.

Naples

THE RITZ-CARLTON GOLF RESORT, NAPLES ★ ★ ★ ★

2600 Tiburon Dr., Naples, 239-593-2000, 800-241-3333;
www.ritzcarlton.com

Greg Norman's award-winning Tiburon golf course is the focal point at the Ritz-Carlton Golf Resort, Naples. Just three miles down the road from its beachfront sister property, the course here is legendary for its beauty and athletic challenge, and the on-site Rick Smith Golf Academy is respected for its innovative instructional techniques. The resort's architecture presents a fresh take on a Mediterranean villa, with sunny, vibrant colors, a red-tiled roof and striped awnings. Guests may take advantage of the sister property's spa and other amenities, though many choose to stay put here and enjoy the fantastic dining options and splendid views.

295 rooms. Pets accepted, some restrictions; fee. High-speed Internet access. Restaurant, two bars. Children's activity center. Fitness center. Outdoor pool, whirlpool. Golf, 36 holes. Tennis. Airport transportation available. Business center. $$$

Orlando

THE PEABODY ORLANDO ★ ★ ★ ★

9801 International Dr., Orlando, 407-352-4000, 800-732-2639;
www.peabodyorlando.com

Famous for the flock of ducks that parade through the hotel's lobby twice daily, this hotel is located across from the Orange Convention Center and near Orlando's theme parks. The athletic club, pool and tennis courts lure guests away from their rooms, while top-rated golf is just a short drive away. The Peabody's restaurants have something for everyone, from a 1950s-style diner to a sophisticated steakhouse.

891 rooms. Wireless Internet access. Three restaurants, three bars. Fitness center (fee), spa. Outdoor pool, children's pool, whirlpool. Tennis. Business center. $$$

THE RITZ-CARLTON ORLANDO, GRANDE LAKES ★ ★ ★ ★

4012 Central Florida Pkwy., Orlando, 407-206-2400, 800-241-3333;
www.ritzcarlton.com

The Ritz-Carlton Orlando was inspired by the grand palazzos of Italy and is a stylish retreat for families visiting Disney World. In between visits to nearby attractions, drop the kids off at the Ritz Kids Club and rest up at the 40,000-square-foot spa, which features 40 treatment rooms. Golfers will love the Greg Norman-designed 18-hole golf course. The hotel also has 11 on-site restaurants, including the elegant Norman's. Guest rooms have private balconies, marble bathrooms and plush robes. There's complimentary transportation to SeaWorld and Universal Orlando.

584 rooms. High-speed Internet access. Six restaurants, bar. Children's activity center. Fitness center, fitness classes, spa. Outdoor pool, children's pool, whirlpool. Golf, 18 holes. Tennis. Business center. $$$

Palm Beach

THE BREAKERS, PALM BEACH ★ ★ ★ ★

1 S. County Rd., Palm Beach, 561-655-6611, 888-273-2537;
www.thebreakers.com

Dating to 1896, the Breakers earned its moniker from the crashing waves on this resort's stretch of beach. Travelers have come here for more than 100 years to admire the ocean views, as well as the Venetian chandeliers, hand-painted ceilings and priceless antiques inside. Guest rooms feature traditional furnishings and modern treats such as CD players and Playstations. The resort includes 10 tennis courts, 36 holes of championship golf, four oceanfront pools, fine shopping, a full-service fitness center and a luxury spa. Restaurants serve everything from beachside lobster clubs to foie gras.

560 rooms. Wireless Internet access. Eight restaurants, four bars. Children's activity center. Three fitness centers, spa. Five outdoor pools, children's pool. Beach. Golf, 36 holes. Tennis. Business center. $$$$

Sarasota

THE RITZ-CARLTON, SARASOTA ★ ★ ★ ★

1111 Ritz-Carlton Dr., Sarasota, 941-309-2000, 800-241-3333;
www.ritzcarlton.com

Located in the city's cultural district overlooking Sarasota Bay, the Ritz-Carlton is close to the boutiques and galleries of the city but maintains a resort feel. The hotel's lobby sets an elegant tone—think rich marble floors and crystal chandeliers—that carries throughout the property. Rooms feature rich colors, sumptuous fabrics and antiques. The hotel also offers an 18-hole Tom Fazio-designed golf course. From the technology butlers on call to assist with computer woes to the bath menu drawn by the bath butlers, the service is superlative.

266 rooms. Pets accepted, some restrictions; fee. High-speed Internet access. Four restaurants, two bar. Children's activity center. Fitness center, fitness classes, spa. Beach. Outdoor pool, whirlpool. Golf, 18 holes. Tennis. Airport transportation available. Business center. $$$

Sunny Isles Beach

TRUMP INTERNATIONAL SONESTA BEACH RESORT
★ ★ ★ ★

18001 Collins Ave., Sunny Isles Beach, 305-692-5600, 800-461-8501; www.trumpsonesta.com

Standing 32 stories above the white, sandy beaches of Sunny Isles, the Trump International Sonesta Beach Resort is a distinctive tower of luxury near Bal Harbour. Guests here have everything at their fingertips, including privileges at three nearby golf courses and access to jet skis, catamarans and kayaks. The comfortably sized, contemporary guest rooms are equipped with wet bars, microwaves, refrigerators, CD players, radios, and cable television. For complete rejuvenation, head to the 8,000-square-foot Aquanox Spa. The resort's signature restaurant, Neomi's, offers contemporary American cuisine with a tropical flair.

390 rooms. Pets accepted, some restrictions; fee. High-speed Internet access. Restaurant, two bars. Children's activity center. Fitness center, spa. Beach. Outdoor pool, whirlpool. Tennis. Airport transportation available. Business center. $$$$

FOUR STAR RESTAURANTS

Coral Gables

LA PALME D'OR ★ ★ ★ ★

1200 Anastasia Ave., Coral Gables, 305-445-8066; www.biltmorehotel.com

Located inside the Biltmore Hotel in Coral Gables, La Palme d'Or is a 1920s-era dining room decked out in flowers and tropical foliage, with mirrored columns, ornate light fixtures and a view of the hotel's beautiful, oversized swimming pool. In addition to the à la carte choices, the chef offers a six-course prix fixe experience and a nine-course tasting menu. Each menu can be paired with wine for an additional fee. The food here is varied in influence, with many contemporary French choices and several dishes inspired by Spain, Italy and Morocco.

French menu. Dinner. Bar. Business casual attire. Valet parking. Closed Sunday-Monday. $$$$

Lake Buena Vista

VICTORIA AND ALBERT'S ★ ★ ★ ★

4401 Floridian Way, Lake Buena Vista, 407-939-3463; www.disney.com

Victoria and Albert's is tailor-made for those craving sophistication. The setting is Victorian by design, with thick drapes, plush carpeting and elegant table settings. To match the regal ambience, the kitchen provides an equally impressive seven-course prix fixe menu. Dinner begins with an assortment of amuse bouche and ends with petit fours and a large selection of Madeiras, ports and cognacs. The wine list is diverse and extensive, and wine pairings are offered at an extra charge.

French, International menu. Dinner. Bar. Jacket required. Reservations recommended. Valet parking. $$$$

Miami

AZUL ★ ★ ★ ★

500 Brickell Key Dr., Miami, 305-913-8358; www.mandarinoriental.com

Mediterranean and Asian flavors marry at Azul at the Mandarin Oriental Miami, where chef Clay Conley crafts a menu made from the day's fresh catch and seasonal ingredients. Miso-marinated hamachi is accompanied by edamame rice, shrimp dumplings and sake butter sauce, while a grilled lamb chop might rest alongside a harissa-marinated lamb loin with smoked eggplant. Wash down these delicacies with an exclusive wine from a selection that boasts more than 700 bottles. Views through the huge windows (which overlook Biscayne Bay) make the restaurant's bar a prime spot for lingering with after-dinner drinks.

Lunch, dinner. Bar. Children's menu. Business casual attire. Reservations recommended. Valet parking. Outdoor seating. $$$$

Miami Beach

BLUE DOOR ★ ★ ★ ★

1685 Collins Ave., Miami Beach, 305-674-6400; www.delano-hotel.com

You don't have to take a test to eat at Blue Door, which is housed in the legendary Delano Hotel, but a certain level of cultural literacy is necessary to fully appreciate the experience. For example, you must know that the chef giving Blue Door's French cuisine a Pan-Asian and tropical twist (think: duck breast with nine-spice ginger sauce) is the acclaimed Claude Troisgras. And uber-architect Philippe Starck designed the all-white, tropical-cool décor. Dinner here is pure theater, and it always earns a rave review.

French, Brazilian menu. Breakfast, lunch, dinner, Sunday brunch. Bar. Children's menu. Business casual attire. Reservations recommended. Valet parking. Outdoor seating. $$$$

WISH ★ ★ ★ ★

801 Collins Ave., Miami Beach, 305-674-9474; www.wishrestaurant.com

Dining at Wish is a little slice of paradise. Avocado, watermelon, plantains, cilantro and ginger are used to perfectly accent everything on the menu, from ceviche to poultry and beef. The kitchen is careful to balance the familiar with the exotic so that the menu remains exciting. There's a house cocktail list in addition to an extensive international wine list. When the weather is at its best, dine in the outside courtyard which is surrounded by palm trees but still allows glimpses of the action on Collins Avenue.

American, pan-Asian menu. Breakfast, lunch, dinner. Tuesday-Sunday. Bar. Children's menu. Business casual attire. Reservations recommended. Valet parking. Outdoor seating. $$$

Naples

ARTISANS IN THE DINING ROOM ★ ★ ★ ★

280 Vanderbilt Beach Rd., Ritz-Carlton, Naples, 239-598-3300,
800-241-3333; www.ritzcarlton.com

Artisans is an intimate space that gives the feeling of dining in a private home. The space is elaborately decorated with dark wood china cabinets, tropical floral arrangements and 19th-century paintings. The capable kitchen staff prepares a menu degustation and a blind tasting menu, a selection of dishes prepared at the chef's whim. The gifted wine stewards will confidently assist in pairing wines with the meal. The Champagne brunch on Sundays comes with live jazz and enough food to keep you satiated for the rest of the week.

Seafood menu. Dinner, Sunday brunch. Closed Monday; also August-early September. Bar. Children's menu. Business casual attire. Reservations recommended. Valet parking. Outdoor seating. $$$$

Orlando

NORMAN'S ★ ★ ★ ★

4012 Central Florida Pkwy., Orlando, 407-393-4333, 800-241-3333;
www.normans.com

The Ritz-Carlton Grande Lakes Resort is home to the Orlando outpost of Norman's, owned by celebrity chef and fusion pioneer Norman Van Aken. Menu items change frequently to reflect whatever is fresh and in season. Appetizers include ahi tuna ceviche or green curry scented lobster ravioli. Classic main dishes include whole roasted chicken with savory bread pudding. Dinner would not be complete without sampling one of Van Aken's spice creams, such as Mexican chocolate and chipotle spice.

All menu items are available with signature wine pairings. Norman's also has a private dining room and an outdoor terrace with views of the golf course.

American, Caribbean menu. Dinner. Bar. Business casual attire. Reservations recommended. Valet parking. Outdoor seating. $$$

Palm Beach

CAFÉ BOULUD ★ ★ ★ ★

301 Australian Ave., Palm Beach, 561-655-6060; www.danielnyc.com
Southern France meets southern Florida at the Palm Beach branch of Café Boulud. Here, Lyon-born chef Daniel Boulud offers the same pitch-perfect French cuisine as that of his New York restaurants, with deftly prepared standards like potato-leek soup and red wine-braised short ribs. The dining room is formal, but not stuffy, thanks to a tropical palette of yellows and oranges, illuminated through ample windows and French doors. The restaurant also boasts a prime location in the historic Brazilian Court Hotel, just steps from the shops of Worth Avenue.

American, French menu. Breakfast, lunch, dinner. Bar. Business casual attire. Reservations recommended. Valet parking. Outdoor seating. $$$

L'ESCALIER AT THE FLORENTINE ★ ★ ★ ★

1 S. County Rd., Palm Beach, 561-659-8480; www.thebreakers.com
The wine list at L'Escalier, an old-world charmer inside the Breakers resort includes 1,400 bottles. The resort's collection contains 25,000 bottles, 7,800 of which are on display in the Wine Cellar adjacent to L'Escalier. In other words, if you love wine, this is the restaurant for you. The menu here is innovative yet rooted in French tradition. Seasonal ingredients are sourced from specialty purveyors, and the kitchen delicately adds layers of flavor to the plate, allowing the quality of the ingredients to shine.

French menu. Dinner. Closed Sunday-Monday. Bar. Reservations recommended. Valet parking. $$$$

THE RESTAURANT ★ ★ ★ ★

2800 S. Ocean Blvd., Palm Beach, 561-533-3750, 800-432-2335;
www.fourseasons.com
The Four Seasons Resort in Palm Beach reopened its signature restaurant in September 2006 after a massive renovation. The new contemporary and tropically-inspired dining room gives every seat an ocean view. The menu melds the flavors of the South, the Caribbean and Central and South America, and comes in prix fixe versions with three, four and five courses. Appetizers include such creations as jumbo lump crab with alligator pear, golden tomato coulis and crispy potato lace, while entrées can include black duck foie gras with wild rice, passion fruit and baby root vegetables. A few Palm Beach classics remain from the previous menu,

including the chateaubriand for two.

American menu. Dinner. Closed Monday. Bar. Children's menu. Jacket required. Reservations recommended. Valet parking. $$$

Sarasota

VERNONA RESTAURANT ★ ★ ★ ★

1111 Ritz-Carlton Dr., Sarasota, 941-309-2008, 800-241-3333;
www.ritzcarlton.com

The ambience at this restaurant inside the Ritz-Carlton, Sarasota resembles that of a Tuscan villa, complete with crystal chandeliers and elegantly arched windows. The menu, though, is contemporary American and features locally-sourced organic ingredients. Signature favorites include lobster macaroni and cheese, roasted ratatouille soup, sage-orange braised veal short ribs and olive oil-poached prime beef tenderloin. Be sure to save room for the Sarasota key lime pie.

American menu. Breakfast, lunch, dinner, Sunday brunch. Bar. Children's menu. Casual attire. $$$

FOUR STAR SPAS

Amelia Island

WILLOW STREAM, THE SPA AT THE FAIRMONT TURNBERRY ISLE RESORT & CLUB ★ ★ ★ ★

19999 W. Country Club Dr., Aventura, 305-933-6930, 800-327-7028;
www.fairmont.com

This spa has it all, from massages and facials to body therapies and exotic rituals. The spa features 16 treatment rooms where 13 different kinds of massages inspired by techniques from around the world, including lomi lomi, hot rock and reflexology, are offered. The facials range from classic European and deep-pore cleansing treatments to aromatherapy, rejuvenating, revitalizing and oxygenating options. Citrus chiffon and coco-mango scrubs are sweet ways to buff and polish skin. Experience Balinese cultural traditions like a royal Javanese lulur ritual, originally created for brides from regal families, or aboriginal Australian customs such as mala mayi and lowanna, both of which offer a blend of nourishing body treatments to restore your energy. Enjoy Thai relaxation techniques with a mud wrap or a Dead Sea water bath.

Boca Raton

SPA PALAZZO AT BOCA RATON RESORT & CLUB ★ ★ ★ ★

501 E. Camino Real, Boca Raton, 561-447-3240, 888-491-2622;
www.spapalazzo.com
Spa Palazzo reflects the beauty of the Mediterranean in its architecture and seductive design. Modeled after Spain's Alhambra Palace, this spa offers services in which nature is the inspiration. Body wraps use grapefruit, peppermint, moor mud and algae, while the facials incorporate botanical extracts, Florida citrus, and aromatherapy oils. Signature treatments include Thai massage, aromatherapy massage, Palazzo stone therapy, the double oxygen facial and the Florida citrus scrub and wrap.

Key Biscayne

THE RITZ-CARLTON SPA, KEY BISCAYNE ★ ★ ★ ★

455 Grand Bay Dr., Key Biscayne, 305-365-4500; www.ritzcarlton.com
You don't have to travel far to find a tropical paradise. This luxurious spa, located at the Ritz-Carlton on Key Biscayne just a few minutes from downtown Miami, has 21 treatment rooms, a wellness center and a full-service salon, all set on a secluded stretch of sand that seems miles away from the city. Try the signature 42 movement minerale massage, which combines slow and long strokes with Thai massage. The Seawater Therapy restores and balances the skin with a pure, freeze-dried seawater bath. Wellness services include personal training, body sculpting and kickboxing, as well as classes such as tai chi and yoga.

Kissimme

CANYON RANCH SPACLUB AT GAYLORD PALMS RESORT ★ ★ ★ ★

6000 W. Osceola Pkwy., Kissimmee, 407-586-2051, 800-742-9000;
www.canyonranch.com
An outpost of the award-winning Arizona-based spa chain, the Canyon Ranch SpaClub at Gaylord Palms reflects its sister properties' dedication to excellence. The euphoria treatment begins with a scalp massage followed by a botanical body mask, a gentle buffing and a warm water soak, and ends with a relaxing oil massage. Marine products from the coast of Brittany serve as the inspiration behind the aqua lift replenishing facial, while the Canyon stone massage uses oils and warm basalt stones to release tension. From deep-cleansing and antioxidant facials to shiatsù and head, neck, or shoulder massages, this spa has something to satisfy every need.

Little Torch Key

SPATERRE AT LITTLE PALM ISLAND ★ ★ ★ ★

28500 Overseas Hwy., Little Torch Key, 305-515-3028, 800-343-8567; www.littlepalmisland.com

Reconnecting with body and soul is the philosophy behind Little Palm Island's SpaTerre. The menu is filled with massages and body treatments, many inspired by Indonesian and Thai techniques and traditions. Spend an hour unwinding with a Swedish, sports or aromatherapy massage, or let heated volcanic river rocks do the work in a hot stone massage. If your skin needs a little TLC, try the detoxifying Caribbean seaweed body mask or the rehydrating cucumber and aloe wrap. $$

Miami

THE SPA MANDARIN ORIENTAL, MIAMI ★ ★ ★ ★

500 Brickell Key Dr., Miami, 305-913-8332; www.mandarinoriental.com

This three-story, 15,000-square-foot spa is a destination in itself. Miamians book massage appointments here months in advance to take full advantage of the views and the work of the expert technicians. The décor makes the most of earthy materials, from natural stone to bamboo floors. The six VIP suites occupy the top floor of the spa and include private relaxation rooms, some with personal multi-jet tubs. Those who can't pry themselves from the beach can opt for a massage in one of the beachfront cabanas. The spa also features a full fitness facility, salon services, and pilates, yoga and tai chi classes.

Miami Beach

THE RITZ-CARLTON, SOUTH BEACH SPA ★ ★ ★ ★

1 Lincoln Rd., Miami Beach, 786-276-4000, 800-241-3333; www.ritzcarlton.com

Sybarites book appointments at this Carita spa to experience therapies that beautify and detoxify. Carita is well known for its anti-aging treatments, which can be experienced in many of the facial and body treatments. Relaxation is paramount here, where massage therapists cover everything from Swedish, Shiatsu and deep tissue varieties to the more unique sand stone therapy, which uses heated and cooled stones. Services include pre-and post-party therapies. Those who overindulged at the beach can seek solace in the spa's nourishing after-sun treatments. There's also a powershower with 23 body sprays.

THE SPA AT THE SETAI ★★★★

2001 Collins Ave., Miami Beach, 305-520-6100; www.setai.com

Asian simplicity and elegance are the inspiration for this tranquil oceanfront retreat. Surrounded by lush gardens and with views of the Atlantic Ocean, the Spa at the Setai feels like a remote haven tucked away in a corner of Southeast Asia. Four treatment suites feature private steam rooms and showers for quiet relaxation before or after treatments. The Balinese massage is a deep-pressure technique that relieves muscular tension and stimulates the lymphatic system. Or try the Langkawi Bamboo Body Polish, during which tiny rejuvenating pearls of bamboo and ginseng are used to improve circulation and leave you feeling invigorated.

Naples

THE RITZ-CARLTON SPA, NAPLES ★★★★

280 Vanderbilt Beach Rd., Naples, 239-598-3300, 800-241-3333; www.ritzcarlton.com

This tranquil spa exudes luxury with its Mediterranean-style décor. The spa features 33 treatment rooms, hot and cold plunge pools, saunas and steam rooms. Try the Sea Holistic, an exfoliating relaxation experience utilizing marine salt crystals. For an exfoliating body treatment, there's the Golden Shimmer, which uses extracts of pure gold and artemisia. Massage treatments range from classic (Swedish) to cutting edge (watsu). The on-site fitness center offers personal training, group exercise classes from yoga to kickboxing and nutrition consultation. The Spa Café's chefs serve tasty, healthy cuisine and even offer cooking classes.

Orlando

THE SPA AT THE RITZ-CARLTON ORLANDO, GRANDE LAKES ★★★★

4012 Central Florida Pkwy., Orlando, 407-206-2400, 800-241-3333; www.ritz-carlton.com

From citrus body polishes to orange-inspired manicures and pedicures, Florida's famous fruit is the basis for many of the treatments at this 40,000-square-foot facility, which also has a lap pool, meditation room, fitness center and salon. Bindi, Thai and shiatsu massage are offered along with shirodhara and Javanese Lulur rituals. Kids and teens have their own menu, including treatments such as the Princess Fizzing pedicure (which uses aromatherapy fizzing balls) or kids massage. Fitness consultations and salon services are also available.

Palm Beach

THE SPA AT THE BREAKERS ★ ★ ★ ★

1 S. County Rd., Palm Beach, 561-653-6656, 888-273-2537;
www.thebreakers.com

This 20,000-square-foot facility overlooking the Atlantic Ocean features 17 treatment rooms, eight salon stations, an outdoor lap pool and an ocean terrace for outdoor massages. Even the state-of-the-art fitness center offers oceanfront vistas. Try the kiwi-coconut scrub, combining Bali sea salts and hydrating coconut to soften and rejuvenate your skin. Or splurge with an Orchidée Impériale facial which utilizes the anti-aging properties of the orchid flower and Guerlain's Impériale cream to reshape and brighten your skin. Regular yoga and tai chi classes are also available oceanside.

Sarasota

THE RITZ-CARLTON MEMBERS CLUB SPA, RITZ-CARLTON SARASOTA ★ ★ ★ ★

1111 Ritz-Carlton Dr., Sarasota, 941-309-2000, 800-241-3333;
www.ritz-carlton.com

This exclusive spa, for use only by guests of the resort and members of the Ritz-Carlton Members Club, combines state-of-the-art design with European technique. More than 100 treatments make up the comprehensive menu. Ten varieties of facials cater to clients with varying skin types. Hand and foot treatments go beyond the basic manicure or pedicure to include citrus anti-aging manicures and mineral powder pedicures. Salon services include hair care and styling, as well as makeup application and lessons.

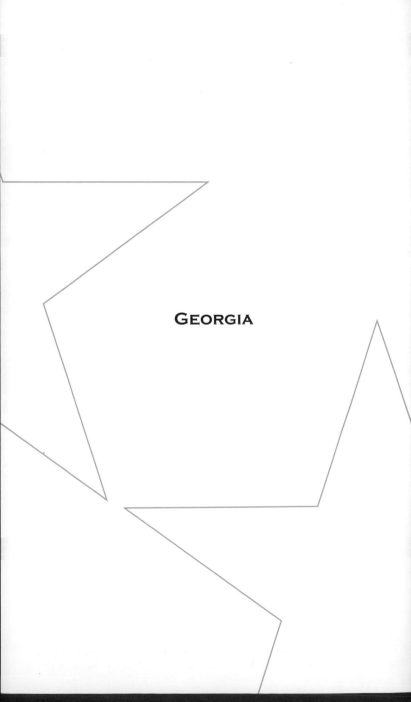

GEORGIA

GEORGIA

Atlanta

FOUR SEASONS HOTEL ATLANTA ★ ★ ★ ★ ★

75 14th St., Atlanta, 404-881-9898, 800-332-3442; www.fourseasons.com
This Neoclassical tower rises over Atlanta's Midtown, where world-class culture, flourishing businesses and enticing stores line the streets. Well-suited for both business and leisure travelers, this hotel offers its guests fine accommodations and flawless, intuitive service. Earth tones and polished woods set a relaxed elegance in the rooms and suites. The state-of-the-art fitness center is complete with an indoor pool and sun terrace. Park 75's fresh approach to American cuisine earns praise from locals and hotel guests alike. Service is top-notch, from the twice-daily turndown service to the affable staff at the door.

244 rooms. Pets accepted, some restrictions. High-speed Internet access. Restaurant, bar. Fitness center. Indoor pool, whirlpool. Business center. $$$$

St. Simons Island

THE LODGE AT SEA ISLAND GOLF CLUB ★ ★ ★ ★ ★

100 Retreat Ave., St. Simons Island, 912-638-3611, 888-732-4752; www.seaisland.com
Generations of privileged travelers have made Sea Island their vacation destination of choice. Created in the spirit of European sporting estates, this resort features first-rate tennis and equestrian facilities, three championship golf courses and tastefully decorated accommodations with private balconies. The spa includes Japanese baths and a special chair massage that uses sound and physical vibrations. There are also several good dining options, including an ice cream parlor.

40 rooms. Complimentary continental breakfast. Wireless Internet access. Three restaurants, two bars. Fitness center, spa. Beach. Whirlpool. Golf, 36 holes. Tennis. Business center. $$$$

Atlanta

INTERCONTINENTAL BUCKHEAD ★ ★ ★ ★

3315 Peachtree Rd. N.E., Atlanta, 404-946-9000, 800-972-2404; www.intercontinental.com
Recognized as one of the leading business hotels in the area, offering the largest meeting and event facilities in Buckhead, this luxe hotel is also

perfect for leisure travelers thanks to its location within walking distance of Lenox Square, the largest shopping mall in the Southeast, as well as the upscale Phipps Plaza. Guest rooms are replete with pillow top bedding, floor-to-ceiling windows and large marble bathrooms. It also boasts the only day spa in an Atlanta hotel. The lovely grounds add to the property's southern elegance. Early risers enjoy a complimentary breakfast from 5 to 7 a.m.

422 rooms. Wireless Internet access. Restaurant, bar. Spa. $$$

THE RITZ-CARLTON, BUCKHEAD ★ ★ ★

3434 Peachtree Rd. N.E., Atlanta, 404-237-2700, 800-241-3333;
www.ritzcarlton.com
This hotel in one of the city's most fashionable neighborhoods offers a warm and luxurious experience. A recent renovation made way for updated rooms with antique furnishings and amenities like pillow-top mattresses and flat-screen TVs. Bay windows in each room or suite showcase views of the downtown skyline. Afternoon tea in the Lobby Lounge is a Georgia tradition, especially after a day of perusing the area's shops, and the Café is a popular gathering place for casual fare. After an extensive kitchen overhaul, The Dining Room has reopened under acclaimed chef Arnaud Berthelier and serves award-winning French cuisine.

533 rooms. Pets accepted, some restrictions; fee. Wireless Internet access. Restaurant, bar. Fitness center. Indoor pool, whirlpool. Airport transportation available. Business center. $$$

Greensboro

THE RITZ-CARLTON LODGE, REYNOLDS PLANTATION ★ ★ ★

1 Lake Oconee Trail, Greensboro, 706-467-0600, 800-542-8680;
www.ritzcarlton.com
The Ritz-Carlton Lodge has one of the most enviable locations in the South. Located an hour from Atlanta, this resort on the 8,000-acre Reynolds Plantation overlooks Lake Oconee, Georgia's second-largest lake. Fill your days with fishing, boating or water-skiing. Golf is a major attraction, with 99 holes designed by legends like Jack Nicklaus, Rees Jones, Tom Fazio and Bob Cupp. The comfortable guest rooms are designed with a rich blend of American and European fabrics and furniture.

251 rooms. Pets accepted, some restrictions; fee. High-speed Internet access. Three restaurants, three bars. Children's activity center. Fitness center, fitness classes, spa. Beach. Indoor pool, outdoor pool, children's pool, whirlpool. Golf, 99 holes. Tennis. Airport transportation available. Business center. $$$

Sea Island

THE CLOISTER ★ ★ ★ ★

100 First St., Sea Island, 912-634-3964;www.cloister.com

This 80-year-old resort recently underwent an impressive $350 million renovation, which included the addition of a magnificent spa. Wood-beamed rooms are now decorated with rich, jewel-toned Turkish rugs and plush, pillow-topped beds and the spacious Turkish stone bathrooms boast deep-soaking tubs and heated towel bars. The many restaurants include a casual raw bar and grill, where after-beach oysters and cocktails are the specialty. Whether it's roaming along the five miles of private beach or taking a dip in one of the resorts three large pools, relaxation is inevitable.

212 rooms. Complimentary continental breakfast. Restaurants, bar. Children's activity center. Whirlpool. Golf, 54 holes. Airport transportation available. $$$$

FIVE STAR RESTAURANTS

Atlanta

THE DINING ROOM ★ ★ ★ ★ ★

3434 Peachtree Rd. N.E., Atlanta, 404-237-2700, 800-241-3333;
www.ritzcarlton.com

Prepare for an extraordinary experience when dining in the masterful hands of chef Arnaud Berthelier, who creates menus influenced by the lively flavors of France, Spain and Northern Africa at the Dining Room in the Ritz-Carlton, Buckhead. The restaurant closed in early 2008 for three months of kitchen renovations. During that time, the chef was dispatched to Spain and the sommelier to California to find new inspiration for the restaurant's menus. Dishes served in the classically elegant room (think deep, tufted banquettes cloaked in Victorian green silk) include sweetbread kebobs with tomato confit, lobster and citrus cocotte, or truffle-stuffed guinea hen. After dessert and a cheese course, sample the petit fours, which arrive in numbers.

French menu. Dinner. Closed Sunday-Monday. Jacket required. Reservations recommended. Valet parking. $$$$

Sea Island

THE GEORGIAN ROOM ★ ★ ★ ★ ★

100 First St., Sea Island, 800-732-4752; www.seaisland.com

When the Cloister opened its doors in 2006 following a complete renovation, the magnificent Georgian Room, an elegant fine-dining restaurant was tucked inside. The décor of the room is stunning, with bas-relief details, gilded chandeliers and a carved stone fireplace. Tables are set with crisp white linens, silver flatware and hand-painted china. What graces those plates is a work of art, with cuisine inspired by seasonal, fresh ingredients and the bounty of the sea. Dishes might include butter-poached sea bass with frog's leg confit and herb dumplings, or succulent Kobe beef filet with smoked morel mushrooms. Service is polished and perfect, with staff guiding diners through the meal seamlessly. There's also a vegetarian and wellness menu which features lighter dishes. A gorgeous private dining room for up to 10 guests makes special events even more memorable.

Continental cuisine. Dinner. Jacket and tie required. Reservations required. $$$$

FOUR STAR RESTAURANTS

Atlanta

BACCHANALIA ★ ★ ★

1198 Howell Mill Rd., Atlanta, 404-365-0410; www.starprovisions.com
Set in a renovated factory complex, this urban dining room has a sleek, industrial feel. The dramatic vaulted ceiling and exposed brick-trimmed factory windows are the perfect foil to the long, low-lit, sexy bar. Chefs Anne Quatrano and Clifford Harrison create vibrant, seasonal American menus that change daily based on whatever organic and small-farm produce is available. Plates are presented with little fuss but lots of flavor. The wine list includes a thoughtful collection of food-friendly choices by the bottle or the glass.

American menu. Dinner. Bar. Business casual attire. Reservations recommended. Outdoor seating. $$$

PARK 75 AT THE FOUR SEASONS ATLANTA ★ ★ ★

75 14th St. N.E., Atlanta, 404-253-3840, 800-332-3442;
www.fourseasons.com
Located in the Four Seasons Hotel, Park 75 is a classic choice for tranquil and comfortable fine dining. The serene, pale-yellow dining room is warmed by iron candelabras, custom lighting and oversized watercolor murals. The cross-cultural menu takes its cue from the season, offering the finest local vegetables, meats and fish. The signature Park 75 surf and turf combines butter-braised Maine lobster with milk-fed veal filet and foie gras. The wine list is mostly American, with some boutique and international selections. For a special treat, reserve the chef's table and enjoy an eight-course menu with wines to match.

American menu. Breakfast, lunch, dinner, Sunday brunch. Bar. Children's menu. Business casual attire. Reservations recommended. Valet parking. $$$

QUINONES AT BACCHANALIA ★ ★ ★ ★

1190 Howell Mill Rd., Atlanta, 404-365-0410; www.starprovisions.com
Quinones at Bacchanalia has a cozy dining area—there are only 11 tables—
and an intimate atmosphere with pressed Irish linens and oil lamps on
the tabletops. A 10-course prix-fixe contemporary American menu
features new creations daily. Sample Southern-influenced dishes such
as squab with turnips, turnip greens and butter beans, or flounder with
local pecans, apples and butternut squash. Desserts are elegant takes on
Southern classics, like the pecan tart with vanilla bean ice cream.

Contemporary American menu. Dinner. Closed Sunday-Tuesday.
Business casual attire. Reservations recommended. $$$$

FOUR STAR SPAS

Greensboro

THE RITZ-CARLTON LODGE SPA, REYNOLDS PLANTATION ★ ★ ★ ★

1 Lake Oconee Trail, Greensboro, 706-467-0600, 800-241-3333;
www.ritzcarlton.com
This 26,000-square-foot spa facility features an array of massages, body
treatments, facials and other therapies designed to soothe and rejuvenate.
The deep forest muscle repair uses a linen wrap infused with pine,
rosemary, peppermint and fir to calm aching muscles. Massage techniques
include Swedish, deep tissue and refloxology. The resort's wellness center
features advanced cardiovascular equipment, an indoor lap pool, health
screenings and consultations with counselors who will design an individual
exercise program.

Sea Island

THE CLOISTER SPA ★ ★ ★ ★

100 First St., Sea Island, 912-638-3611, 888-732-4752; www.seaisland.com
After a major renovation, the Cloister Spa defines the complete spa
experience. The focus is on customization, with 26 treatment rooms
dedicated and an extensive menu of offerings. Each guest is paired with a
spa guide to design an experience that includes anything from nutritional
consultations to body work, baths, wraps and energy treatments. Try one
of the Turkish or Japanese baths. The latter involves a ginger grass polish
and wild cherry blossom rice bluff, followed by a hinoki mint soak, wild
lime silk oil massage and more. A special KidSpa program for spa-goers
ages eight to 15 promotes healthy skin care and includes kid-friendly
massages, sports and nature hikes.

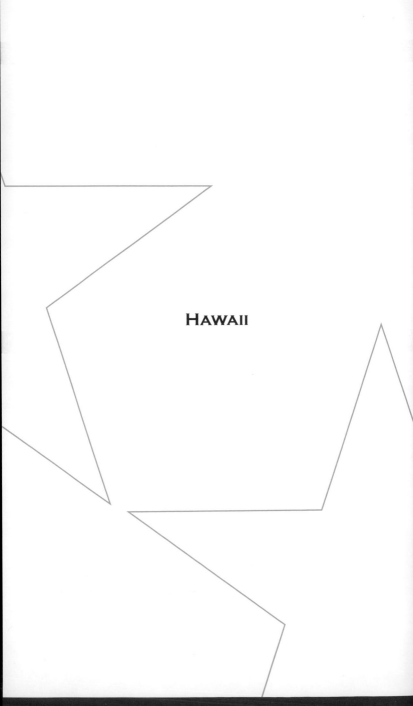

HAWAII

HAWAII

Wailea

FOUR SEASONS RESORT MAUI AT WAILEA ★ ★ ★ ★

3900 Wailea Alanui, Wailea, 808-874-8000, 800-268-6282;
www.fourseasons.com/maui

Blessed with abundant sunshine and perfect white-sand beaches, Wailea is one of Maui's best destinations, and this resort is the most exclusive. Guest rooms are studies in laid-back sophistication, with pastel colors, tropical patterns, rattan furnishings and oversized marble bathrooms. You'll never be bored, either, thanks to the lighted tennis courts, water sports, indoor and outdoor exercise facilities, off-site golf and shimmering pools.

380 rooms. Pets accepted, some restrictions. High-speed Internet access. Three restaurants, three bars. Children's activity center. Fitness center, fitness classes, spa. Beach. Three outdoor pools, children's pool, whirlpool. Tennis. Airport transportation available. Business center. $$$$

Honolulu

HALEKULANI ★ ★ ★ ★

2199 Kalia Rd., Honolulu, 808-739-8888, 800-367-2525;
www.halekulani.com

Located on the western side of Waikiki Beach, Halekulani's understated tropical elegance and exceptional service make it unforgettable. Guest rooms have deep soaking tubs and large lanais. Handmade chocolates left in the rooms nightly by the staff are a reminder of the resort's attention to detail. Try surfing and snorkeling lessons on the beach, or take a bike ride around nearby Diamond Head. Besides occupying a prime spot on one of Hawaii's most popular beaches, the resort boasts the superb SpaHalekulani, which celebrates the cultures of Hawaii, Asia and the South Pacific.

455 rooms. Wireless Internet access. Three restaurants, three bars. Children's activity center. Fitness center, spa. Beach. Outdoor pool. Airport transportation available. Business center. $$$$

KAHALA HOTEL AND RESORT ★ ★ ★ ★

5000 Kahala Ave., Honolulu, 808-739-8888, 800-367-2525;
www.kahalaresort.com

Besides powdery beaches and beautiful views, this hotel offers a 26,000-square-foot lagoon occupied by Atlantic bottlenose dolphins. The Dolphin Quest program is a highlight, offering face-to-face encounters with the adorable mammals. Complimentary surfing and scuba classes are available, while the Spa Suites provide plenty of pampering. Rooms have plantation-style décor with canopied beds, luxury linens and deep soaking tubs. The resort's restaurants serve up superb variations on seafood, from Japanese recipes at Tokyo Tokyo to fresh catches at Plumeria Beach House.

364 rooms. Pets accepted, some restrictions. Wireless Internet access. Five restaurants, four bars. Children's activity center. Fitness center, fitness classes, spa. Beach. Outdoor pool, children's pool, whirlpool. Airport transportation available. Business center. $$$$

Kapalua

THE RITZ-CARLTON, KAPALUA ★ ★ ★ ★

1 Ritz-Carlton Dr., Kapalua, 808-669-6200, 800-262-8440;
www.ritzcarlton.com

Fresh from a complete makeover, this resort has views of the Pacific stretching all the way to Molokai. Rooms have been updated with flatscreen TVs, marble bathrooms and Hawaiian artwork. Part of a 23,000-acre working pineapple plantation, the resort also has two championship golf courses, a three-tiered swimming pool and beaches that are about 10 minutes away by foot (a complimentary shuttle transports guests around the property). A new 14,000-square-foot spa has 15 private treatment rooms, including several new couples cabanas. A sushi restaurant has been added to the hotel's collection of eateries.

548 rooms. Pets accepted. High-speed Internet access. Five restaurants, four bars. Children's activity center. Fitness center, fitness classes, spa. Beach. Outdoor pool, two whirlpools. Golf. Tennis. Airport transportation available. Business center. $$$$

Ka'upulehu

FOUR SEASONS RESORT HUALALAI AT HISTORIC KA'UPULEHU ★ ★ ★ ★

100 Ka'upulehu Dr., Ka'upulehu, 808-325-8000, 800-332-3442;
www.fourseasons.com

Located at the southern end of the Kahala Coast, this property is 15 minutes from the Kona airport. The luxurious rooms, which reflect the island setting with their rattan chaises and batik fabrics, all have ocean views with a private lanai. Regional cuisine takes center stage at both Pahu i'a and the Hualalai Grille by Alan Wong. Laid-back island sophistication is the idea behind both restaurants, which serve creative dishes crafted from fresh fish and local ingredients. The Beach Tree Grill & Bar has a well-rounded menu and also offers Italian and beach barbecue buffet nights each week.

243 rooms. Pets accepted. Wireless Internet access. Three restaurants, two bars. Children's activity center. Fitness center, Fitness classes available, spa. Beach. Five outdoor pools, children's pool, whirlpool. Golf, 18 holes. Tennis. Business center. $$$$

Lana'i City

FOUR SEASONS RESORT LANAI AT MANELE BAY ★ ★ ★ ★

1 Manele Bay Rd., Lana'i City, 808-565-2000, 800-819-5053; www.fourseasons.com

This Mediterranean-style resort set on red lava cliffs is near Hulopoe, which is considered the island's best beach. The guest rooms have private lanais and countless other amenities including CD and DVD players, duvet-topped bed and luxurious marble bathrooms. Local musicians playing Hawaiian tunes accompany cocktail hour at the Hale Ahe Ahe Lounge. Golfers will appreciate the Challenge, a gorgeous course designed by great Jack Nicklaus.

249 rooms. High speed Internet access. Restaurant, bar. Children's activity center. Fitness center, spa. Beach. Outdoor pool, whirlpool. Golf, 18 holes. Tennis. Airport transportation available. Business center. $$$$

FOUR SEASONS RESORT THE LODGE AT KOELE ★ ★ ★ ★

1 Keomoku Hwy., Lanai City, 808-565-2000, 800-819-5053; www.fourseasons.com

Located upcountry at the center of Lanai, this Victorian-style lodge has extensive and perfectly manicured grounds and a more sophisticated feel than its sister resort, the beachfront Four Seasons Manele Bay. The resort boasts one of the best championship golf courses in the world, designed by PGA legend Greg Norman. Other amenities include children's programs, babysitting services, a health club, yoga classes, tennis, swimming pools and live evening music in the Great Hall.

102 rooms. High-speed Internet access. Restaurant, bar. Fitness center. Outdoor pool, two whirlpools. Golf, 18 holes. Tennis. $$$$

Honolulu

CHEF MAVRO ★ ★ ★ ★

1969 S. King St., Honolulu, 808-944-4714; www.chefmavro.com

This restaurant is the creation of award-winning French chef George Mavrothalassitis, who moved to Honolulu in 1988 and has focused his talents on perfecting a cuisine that couples French technique with fresh Hawaiian ingredients. The restaurant has no wine list—instead, each dish is served with a glass of wine that complements its ingredients. For special occasions, the six-course meal, priced at $220 with wine pairings, is an indulgence you won't forget.

Hawaiian menu. Dinner. Closed Monday. Business casual attire. Reservations recommended. Valet parking. $$$

LA MER ★ ★ ★ ★

2199 Kalia Rd., Honolulu, 808-923-2311; www.halekulani.com

Pocketed along the coast on Waikiki's west side, La Mer makes good use of its enviable location inside the Halekulani hotel. Pocket doors open up to welcome in the tradewind breezes and the sound of the ocean. A private dining room accommodates up to 16 guests, ideal for celebrating a special occasion. A popular dish at this French restaurant is the medallions of milk-fed veal with golden brown Roquefort on a ragout of flageolet beans. For dessert, it's hard to pass on La Mer's Dreams of Chocolate, a decadent blend of cherry brandy chocolate mousse, white-and-dark chocolate tear drops and gianduja ice cream, all served in a chocolate cup.

French menu. Dinner. Bar. Children's menu. Reservations recommended. Valet parking. $$$$

Lahaina

GERARD'S ★ ★ ★ ★

174 Lahainaluna Rd., Lahaina, 808-661-8939, 877-661-8939;
www.gerardsmaui.com

Chef Gerard Reversade is an internationally recognized master of French cuisine, but that doesn't mean his namesake restaurant doesn't also celebrate its Hawaiian location. He uses ahi tuna in his Basque-inspired fisherman's stew, and a poha berry compote accompanies a seared duck foie gras appetizer. The flourless chocolate gâteau is created with macadamia nuts and Kona coffee liqueur, while the apple tarte tatin includes tropical fruit. Gerard's décor blends perfectly with the Victorian charm of its host hotel, the Plantation Inn. Request a table on the veranda or the garden patio.

French, Hawaiian menu. Dinner. Children's menu. Business casual attire. Reservations recommended. Outdoor seating. $$$$

Lana'i City

THE DINING ROOM AT THE FOUR SEASONS RESORT THE LODGE AT KOELE ★ ★ ★ ★

1 Keomoku Hwy., Lanai City, 808-565-7300, 800-819-5053;
www.fourseasons.com.
This fine-dining room is somewhat of an anachronism in laid-back Hawaii. The room is elegant and formal with white-linen topped tables, but there are distinct island influences as well. The food features American classics with a focus on local produce and seafood, showcased in dishes such as butter-poached lobster with salsify, fennel and caviar.

American menu. Breakfast, lunch, dinner. Bar. Children's menu. Jacket required. Reservations recommended. Valet parking. $$$$

Wailea

SPAGO ★ ★ ★ ★

3900 Wailea Alanui, Wailea, 808-879-2999; www.wolfgangpuck.com
Wolfgang Puck shows that, despite recent culinary forays into fast food and canned soups, he remains a master of the fine-dining experience. Puck catapulted to international fame back in 1982 with the first Spago on Sunset Boulevard, and he currently operates three Spago outposts on the mainland: two in California and one in Las Vegas. Each Spago maintains its own identity, and that's good news for anyone visiting here. The menu incorporates the best of the islands, fusing traditional Hawaiian tastes and locally sourced ingredients with Asian influences and Puck's signature California style.

Hawaiian, Pacific-Rim/Pan-Asian menu. Dinner. Bar. Children's menu. Business casual attire. Reservations recommended. Valet parking. Outdoor seating. $$$

FOUR STAR SPAS

Honolulu

SPA SUITES AT KAHALA HOTEL & RESORT ★ ★ ★ ★

5000 Kahala Ave., Honolulu, 808-739-8938, 800-367-2525;
www.kahalaresort.com
Named for different Hawaiian flowers, each of the five 550-square-foot spa suites at this spa is decorated in an authentic island style. All but one of the spa treatments begins with an ESPA welcoming foot ritual that uses Hawaiian sea salts and aromatic water. The spa's signature treatments

include the pi'ha kino therapy, which uses a spearmint-aloe blend for a full-body exfoliation before a massage with aromatherapy oils. The kua lani back, face and scalp massage begins with a deep cleansing and exfoliation and continues with a massage, an energizing facial and a Hawaiian scalp massage with volcanic clay, apricot and watercress.

SPA HALEKULANI ★ ★ ★ ★

2199 Kalia Rd., Honolulu, 808-931-5322, 800-367-2343;
www.halekulani.com

The healing traditions of the Pacific Islands, including Samoa, Tonga and Tahiti, inspire this spa's authentic treatments, which use only fresh island ingredients, such as coconut, orchid, hibiscus, seaweed and papaya. All of the spa's massages, body treatments and facials begin with a ritual foot pounding, an exotic way to treat neglected feet. In addition to traditional Swedish and shiatsu massages, Samoan-inspired nonu, Japanese amma and Hawaiian lomi lomi, hapai and pohaku massages are offered. Therapists will even customize a massage based on your needs and preferences. Facials are individually crafted for specific skin types, and the body scrubs and wraps come complete with a steam shower and a mini massage.

Ka'upulehu

HUALALAI SPORTS CLUB AND SPA, FOUR SEASONS RESORT HUALALAI ★ ★ ★ ★

100 Ka'upulehu Dr., Ka'upulehu-Kona, 808-325-8440, 800-983-3880;
www.fourseasons.com

Featuring an open-air gym, a grass yoga and meditation courtyard, an Olympic-style lap pool, a sand volleyball court and eight tennis courts, the Hualalai Sports Club and Spa at the Four Seasons Resort has dozens of ways to stay fit. Try climbing the 24-foot climbing wall, join fitness hikes or take a kickboxing, tai chi or water aerobics class. After working up a sweat at the fitness center, unwind in the sensational spa. The facility offers a variety of massages, such as lomi lomi, Swedish and sports. Signature body treatments include the Hualalai herbal wrap, which uses hibiscus (the state flower) to stimulate the release of toxins, while Hawaiian red clay, mineral-rich salts and essential oils make up the deep-cleansing Hualalai salt glow.

Manele Bay

THE SPA AT MANELE BAY ★ ★ ★ ★

1 Manele Bay Rd., Manele Bay, 808-565-2000, 800-819-5053,
www.fourseasons.com

This spa is a sanctuary of pampering and rejuvenation with 11 state-of-the-art treatment rooms, red cedar dry heat saunas, eucalyptus steam rooms, rainforest showers, and signature treatments that incorporate centuries-old native skin and beauty rituals. Revitalize your skin with a full-body tropical fruit and sea salt scrub, or soothe tired feet with the hehi lani treatment, which uses hot eucalyptus towels, exfoliation and massage. Traditional or Hawaiian lomi lomi massages take place in the spa, the privacy of a guest room or poolside. For ultimate privacy, opt for the "spa after hours" experience, allowing groups up to eight to use the facilities and enjoy treatments after the spa closes.

Wailea

SPA GRANDE AT GRAND WAILEA RESORT ★ ★ ★ ★
3850 Wailea Alanui Dr., Wailea, 808-875-1234, 800-888-6100;
www.grandwailea.com
The Grand Wailea's 50,000-square-foot spa has elegant interiors, a comprehensive fitness center and extensive spa menu. Most treatments include a one-hour Wailea hydrotherapy session, in which you can choose to lounge in five aromatic baths, a bubbling Japanese Furo bath or a massaging waterfall. Afterward, take in the cold plunge pool, eucalyptus steam room and Roman jacuzzi, or Swiss jet shower. Spa Grande's sizable menu includes a blend of classic treatments, Hawaiian favorites and eastern therapies. Experience pure bliss with a deep shiatsu barefoot massage, or try the anti-aging facial using seashells.

THE SPA AT FOUR SEASONS RESORT MAUI AT WAILEA ★ ★ ★ ★
3900 Wailea Alanui Dr., Wailea, 808-874-8000, 800-334-6284;
www.fourseasons.com
While the signature massages at this spa introduce guests to Hawaiian traditions, the body treatments expose them to the bounty of the islands. Using native and natural ingredients, these unique treatments rejuvenate skin, and smell and feel heavenly while doing so. The mango salt glow uses mango sorbet to exfoliate skin while the Hawaiian nut-sugar scrub employs a blend of macadamia, coconut and kukui nut to smooth skin. The papaya-pineapple body scrub combines those fruits with finely crushed grape seeds. The ultimate foot treatment delivers what it promises with its orchid and sea salt bath, mango salt exfoliation, refreshing moisturizing treatment and divine reflexology massage.

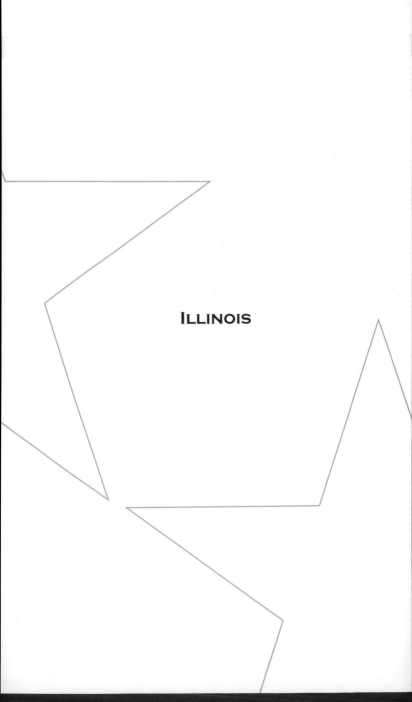

Illinois

ILLINOIS

Chicago

FOUR SEASONS HOTEL CHICAGO ★ ★ ★ ★ ★

120 E. Delaware Place, Chicago, 312-280-8800; www.fourseasons.com/chicago

Located in a 66-story building on Michigan Avenue, the Four Seasons Hotel Chicago is a shopper's paradise. More than 100 stores, including Gucci and Bloomingdales, are located downstairs from the hotel. The recently renovated rooms, decorated with contemporary furniture and soothing, neutral fabrics, are stylish and comfortable. With amenities like DVD players and flat-screen TVs, it may be hard to leave the luxury of your room. If you do, there's a Roman-columned indoor pool, well-stocked fitness center and full-service spa. Edible indulgences include American and French dishes at Seasons restaurant and continental favorites at the Café. The Seasons Lounge, with its working fireplace and live piano, is a favorite gathering spot for cocktails or tea.

343 rooms. Pets accepted, some restrictions. Wireless Internet access. Two restaurants, bar. Fitness center, spa. Indoor pool, children's pool, whirlpool. Airport transportation available. Business center. $$$$

THE PENINSULA CHICAGO ★ ★ ★ ★ ★

108 E. Superior St., Chicago, 312-337-2888, 866-288-8889; www.peninsula.com

The unparalleled level of service and meticulous attention to detail make this hotel a standout. Rooms, with classic and elegant décor, are outfitted with bedside electronic control panels and plush, comfy beds. The sprawling spa and fitness center (and beautiful sky-high indoor pool) feature the most up-to-date equipment and cutting edge treatments. Pets at the Peninsula are pampered as much as their masters with special beds, their own room service menus and doggie massages. The hotel's restaurants, including the fine-dining room Avenues and more casual Shanghai Terrace, are some of the city's most acclaimed.

339 rooms. Pets accepted, some restrictions. Wireless Internet access. Four restaurants, bar. Fitness center, fitness classes available, spa. Indoor pool, whirlpool. Airport transportation available. Business center. $$$$

THE RITZ-CARLTON, A FOUR SEASONS HOTEL ★ ★ ★ ★ ★

160 E. Pearson St., Chicago, 312-266-1000, 800-621-6906;
www.fourseasons.com

Situated on the upper levels of Water Tower Place on the city's Magnificent Mile, this hotel boasts a prized location only minutes from world-class shopping, acclaimed restaurants and the shores of Lake Michigan. The lobby is open and airy, and carries a sense of sophisticated grandeur with a sculptured fountain and opulent floral bouquets. Guest rooms have extra large picture windows showcasing breathtaking views of Lake Michigan or the city, and a décor of rich fabrics and lavish detailing. Suites are outfitted with Bulgari toiletries, personalized stationary and fresh-cut flowers. Book an in-room massage, or visit the hotel's full-service spa. Pets can feast on filet mignon and salmon from room service.

435 rooms. Pets accepted, some restrictions. High-speed Internet access. Two restaurants, two bars. Fitness center, fitness classes available, spa. Indoor pool, whirlpool. Airport transportation available. Business center. $$$$

FIVE STAR RESTAURANTS

Chicago

ALINEA ★ ★ ★ ★ ★

1723 N. Halsted St., Chicago, 312-867-0110; www.alinearestaurant.com

A dimly lit corridor provides the dramatic entrance to chef/owner Grant Achatz's stunning restaurant. Once inside, you can catch a glimpse of the spotless open kitchen and watch a team of chefs cook with scientific precision. The four intimate dining rooms, appointed with dark mahogany tables, provide the perfect setting for the adventurous cuisine. The restaurant offers two types of menus: a 12- or 24-course degustation feast. Steaming eucalyptus leaves, smoking cinnamon sticks or lavender air-filled pillows are just some of the unusual elements that may be incorporated in the presentation of some dishes. The knowledgeable and affable waitstaff are passionate about every guest's experience and deflate any sense of pretension.

American menu. Dinner. Closed Monday-Tuesday; July 4. Business casual attire. Reservations recommended. Valet parking. $$$$

CHARLIE TROTTER'S ★ ★ ★ ★ ★

816 W. Armitage Ave., Chicago, 773-248-6228; www.charlietrotters.com

Set inside an unassuming brick brownstone, this Lincoln Park legend is an intimate, peaceful place. Upon entry, you are greeted by a well-stocked two-story bar and a profusion of aromatic floral bouquets. Each of the four dining rooms is light and elegant, and remains earnestly unpretentious. The menu features French and Italian influences and seasonal ingredients.

Trotter prefers saucing with vegetable juice-based vinaigrettes, light emulsified stocks and purees, as well as delicate broths and herb-infused meat and fish essences. The result is flavors that are remarkably intense, yet light. Staying true to its accommodating reputation, the staff will adjust, adapt and substitute to match personal preferences.

American menu. Dinner. Closed Sunday-Monday. Bar. Jacket required. Reservations recommended. Valet parking. $$$$

FOUR STAR RESTAURANTS

Chicago

AVENUES ★ ★ ★ ★

108 E. Superior St., Chicago, 312-573-6754; www.peninsula.com
Cutting edge, contemporary cuisine awaits diners at Avenues, located within Chicago's Peninsula Hotel. Foodies will jump at the chance to order the multi-course tasting menu that showcases chef Graham Elliot Bowles' considerable talent at preparing straightforward, clean interpretations of fresh ingredients. Plan ahead if you'd like to be seated at the Chef's Bar, which overlooks the exhibition kitchen. The service there and in the main dining room is confident and welcoming.

American menu. Dinner. Closed Sunday-Monday. Bar. Business casual attire. Reservations recommended. Valet parking. $$$$

EVEREST ★ ★ ★ ★

440 S. LaSalle St., Chicago, 312-663-8920; www.leye.com
Perched high atop the city on the 40th floor of the Chicago Stock Exchange building, Everest affords spectacular views and equally fabulous contemporary French cuisine. Chef and owner Jean Joho blends European influences with local, seasonal American ingredients and he's not afraid to pair noble ingredients like caviar with potatoes or turnips. Everest's dining room is luxuriously decorated with vaulted draped ceilings, mirrored walls, reflective paintings by Adam Seigel and floor-to-ceiling windows.

French menu. Dinner. Bar. Business casual attire. Reservations recommended. Valet parking. $$$$

LES NOMADES ★ ★ ★ ★

222 E. Ontario St., Chicago, 312-649-9010; www.lesnomades.net
Les Nomades is a serene spot tucked away off Michigan Avenue in an elegant turn-of-the-century townhouse. Romantic and intimate with a fireplace, hardwood floors, deep, cozy banquettes and gorgeous flowers, Les Nomades was originally opened as a private club. Chef Chris Nugent has crafted a traditional French menu that features dishes such as white asparagus soup with wild mushrooms and truffle froth.

French menu. Dinner. Closed Sunday-Monday. Bar. Jacket required. Reservations recommended. Valet parking. $$$$

SEASONS ★ ★ ★ ★

120 E. Delaware Place, Chicago, 312-280-8800; www.fourseasons.com/chicagofs
Seasons restaurant has a diverse menu that changes depending upon the availability of fresh ingredients. You might find something like surf and turf tartare, which features American Kobe beef with violet mustard, or ahi tuna with wasabi sorbet and tamarind-soy gelee. Groups of six or more can request the Chef's Table and receive a personally guided eight-course meal with wine pairings. The traditional, hushed dining room features tables set with vintage china. Service is affable and attentive, and every meal ends with freshly made petit fours.

American menu. Breakfast, lunch, dinner, Sunday brunch. Bar. Children's menu. Business casual attire. Reservations recommended. Valet parking. $$$

TRU ★ ★ ★ ★

676 N. St. Clair St., Chicago, 312-202-0001; www.trurestaurant.com
Tru's modern, airy dining room is a stunning stage for chef and co-owner Rick Tramonto's progressive French creations and co-owner pastry chef Gale Gand's incredible, one-of-a-kind sweet and savory endings. Tramonto offers plates filled with ingredients that are treated to his unmatched creativity and artistic flair. The wine list, with more than 1,800 selections, is overseen by sommelier Scott Tyree. Museum quality artwork is on display, including pieces by Andy Warhol, Maya Lin and Gerhard Richter. A lounge area offers a somewhat less formal but no less memorable dining experience.

French menu. Dinner. Closed Sunday. Bar. Jacket required. Reservations recommended. Valet parking. $$$$

FOUR STAR SPAS

Chicago

THE PENINSULA SPA, CHICAGO ★ ★ ★ ★

108 E. Superior St., Chicago, 312-573-6860, 866-288-8889;
www.peninsula.com
This downtown spa combines Asian-inspired techniques with a full menu of traditional massages, body envelopments, skin care and salon services. Some massages incorporate reflexology to increase energy flow, while facials target shiatsu pressure points to counter stress. In the ESPA body envelopment treatment, the skin is brushed, exfoliated and oiled, then the whole body is encased in algae, marine mud or Oshadi clay, depending upon the goal—detoxificiation, de-stressing or an immune system boost. The crowning touch is an acupressure head massage.

THE SPA AT FOUR SEASONS CHICAGO ★ ★ ★ ★

120 E. Delaware Place, Chicago, 312-280-8800, 800-819-5053;
www.fourseasons.com

This spa, located off Chicago's Michigan Avenue, features five sound-proofed treatment rooms, ideal for escaping the noise of the city. The décor of the space is as sophisticated as the Four Seasons' urban location, with creamy, white-washed walls and neutral-tones throughout. Unwind with a Swedish, hot stone, sports conditioning or scalp rejuvenating massage. The elixir paraffin wrap combines olive stones, lavender, juniper berries and grapefruit to produce baby-soft skin. To sooth parched winter skin, try the Magnificent Mile facial, which rehydrates and leaves faces glowing. The facility also features a fitness center and indoor swimming pool.

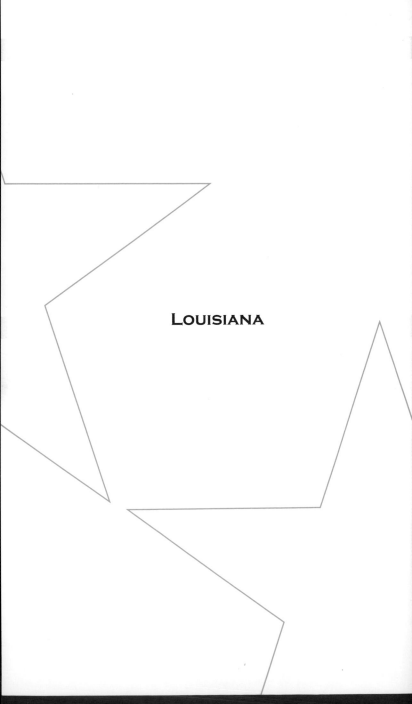

Louisiana

Louisiana

New Orleans

WINDSOR COURT HOTEL ★ ★ ★ ★

300 Gravier St., New Orleans, 504-523-6000, 888-596-0955,
www.windsorcourthotel.com
Located in the city's business district and a short walk to the historic French
Quarter, the Windsor Court brings a bit of the English countryside to
New Orleans. Guest rooms feature traditional English furnishings
and artwork, Italian marble bathrooms and elegant touches such as
complimentary imported chocolates or pralines at turndown. Balconies
or bay windows provide scenic views of the city and the Mississippi River
from every room. This full-service hotel also includes a pool, sundeck,
business and fitness centers and terrific restaurants.

324 rooms. Pets accepted, some restrictions; fee. High-speed Internet
access. Restaurant, bar. Fitness center. Outdoor pool. Business center.
$$

New Orleans

BAYONA ★ ★ ★ ★

430 Dauphine St., New Orleans, 504-525-4455; www.bayona.com
A little slice of the romantic Mediterranean awaits you at Bayona, a jewel
of a restaurant tucked into a 200-year-old Creole cottage in the heart
of the French Quarter. The cozy room is often set with fresh flowers
and is warmed by sunny lighting and bright colors. Chef Susan Spicer
serves up her own interpretation of New Orleans cuisine, blending the
ingredients of the Mediterranean with the flavors of Alsace, Asia, India
and the Southwest. You'll find an outstanding waitstaff eager to guide you
and answer questions about the menu. The restaurant has a great selection
of beers, including several local brews, plus an extensive wine list.

International menu. Lunch, dinner. Closed Sunday-Monday, Mardi
Gras. Business casual attire. Reservations recommended. Outdoor
seating. $$$

THE NEW ORLEANS GRILL ★ ★ ★ ★

300 Gravier St., New Orleans, 504-522-1994, 888-596-0955;
www.windsorcourthotel.com

Dining at The New Orleans Grill (located inside the Windsor Court Hotel) may be one of the most luxurious ways to spend an evening in New Orleans. With a menu that changes monthly and features locally grown and organic foods whenever possible, the restaurant is known for its fabulous contemporary American cuisine. Gumbo is taken to a new level here with locally-raised organic chicken and native-grown rice. Enjoy live music on Friday nights in the lounge.

French-influenced menu. Breakfast, lunch, dinner. Bar. Children's menu. Jacket required. Reservations recommended. Valet parking. $$$

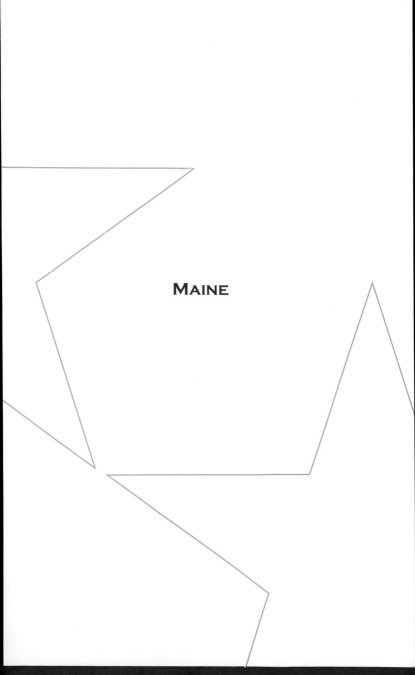

MAINE

MAINE

Kennebunkport

THE WHITE BARN INN ★ ★ ★ ★

37 Beach Ave., Kennebunkport, 207-967-2321; www.whitebarninn.com

This cluster of cottages, restored barns, and a circa-1860s house make up the White Barn Inn, a quaint spot that delivers quiet luxury on the coast of Maine. The charming rooms and suites are decorated with antiques and feature wood-burning fireplaces, whirlpool tubs and flat screen TVs with DVDs and CD players. Simple pleasures here include relaxing by the stone swimming pool, riding a bike along the coast, experiencing a spa treatment, and having afternoon tea by the fire in the comfortable sitting room. The inn has one of the region's most acclaimed restaurants, which serves New England cuisine in a rustic, candlelit setting.

25 rooms. Complimentary full breakfast. Wireless Internet access. Restaurant. Bar. Spa. Outdoor pool. Business center. $$$$

THE WHITE BARN INN RESTAURANT ★ ★ ★ ★ ★

37 Beach Ave., Kennebunkport, 207-967-2321; www.whitebarninn.com

A New England classic, this charming candlelit space inside the White Barn Inn is filled with fresh flowers and white linen-topped tables. Chef Jonathan Cartwright creates delicious regional dishes expertly accented with a European flair. The four-course prix fixe menu changes weekly, highlighting seafood from Maine's waters as well as native game and poultry. The vast wine selection perfectly complements the cuisine, and a rolling cheese cart offers some of the best local artisans' products.

American menu. Bar. Jacket required. Reservations recommended. Valet parking. Dinner. Closed three weeks in January. $$$$

SPA AT WHITE BARN INN ★ ★ ★ ★

37 Beach Ave., Kennebunkport, 207-967-2321; www.whitebarninn.com

Though located in a traditional New England country inn, the décor at the Spa at White Barn Inn has a hint of minimalism without compromising on luxury. Guests can request a light-of-the-moon plunge, which is a fizz of marine pebbles infused with mandarin orange and lemon essential oils, or an aroma sea bath. The nearby Kennebunk River provides the materials used in the spa's signature stone massage, while natural marine algae and Maine sea salts are incorporated into the body wraps.

MARYLAND

MARYLAND

Baltimore

CHARLESTON ★ ★ ★

1000 Lancaster St., Baltimore, 410-332-7373; www.charlestonrestaurant.com
Chef/owner Cindy Wolf's regional American/French restaurant serves up dishes such as sauteed heads-on Gulf shrimp with andouille sausage and Tasso ham with creamy stone-milled grits. The restaurant also has an impressive wine program that includes several dozen sparkling wines and a selection of about 600 well-chosen whites and reds from the New World (Australia, South Africa, New Zealand and Chile) and the Old (France, Italy and Spain). Charleston also offers more than a dozen microbrews and imported beers.

American, French menu. Dinner. Closed Sunday. Bar. Business casual attire. Reservations recommended. Valet parking. Outdoor seating. $$$

Easton

THE INN AT EASTON ★ ★ ★

28 S. Harrison St. Easton, 410-822-4910
Housed in a Federal-style mansion, the dining room at the Inn at Easton delivers the unexpected. The room is fresh and contemporary, not stuffy, and the food is modern Australian, not classic American. Chef Andrew Evans puts his knowledge of clean, unfussy, fresh Down Under cuisine (he spent a year cooking in Brisbane and married an Aussie) to work in recipes like barramundi en papillote with red Thai curry and jasmine rice, or coffee-crusted rack of lamb with potato purée and wilted spinach. The wine list draws heavily from Australian produces, whose bold shirazes and chardonnays pair well with Andrews' inventive food.

Australian menu. Dinner. Closed Monday-Tuesday. Business casual attire. Reservations recommended. Outdoor seating. $$

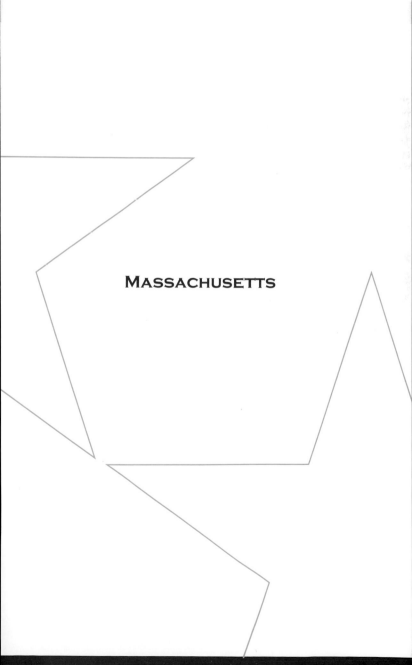

MASSACHUSETTS

MASSACHUSETTS

Boston

FOUR SEASONS HOTEL BOSTON ★ ★ ★ ★ ★

200 Boylston St., Boston, 617-338-4400, 800-330-3442;
www.fourseasons.com

The Four Seasons offers its guests a prime location overlooking the Public Garden and Boston Common. The recently renovated contemporary lobby, complete with a dramatic yellow marble and black granite floor, gleams. Antiques, fine art, sumptuous fabrics, period furniture and sleek technology such as flat screen televisions and wireless Internet access bring the guest rooms and suites up to date, while impeccable and attentive service heightens the experience. Canines are pampered with everything from dog bones to a convenient dog-walking service. The Bristol Lounge is where Boston's power players come to celebrate their success.

273 rooms. High-speed Internet access. Two restaurants, two bars. Airport transportation available. $$$$

BOSTON HARBOR HOTEL ★ ★ ★ ★ ★

70 Rowes Wharf, Boston, 617-439-7000, 800-752-7077; www.bhh.com

Occupying an idyllic waterfront location, this quietly luxurious, subtly sophisticated hotel is situated across from Boston's financial district and along a stretch of land that was once dominated by an elevated highway, but now is poised to become the new Rose Kennedy Greenway. The staff at this full-service property takes care of every possible need. Rooms and suites are beautifully appointed in rich colors—it's worth paying extra for a room with a view. In the summer, live music, dancing and an outdoor movie night take place on the outdoor patio. The hotel's Meritage restaurant is the domain of chef Daniel Bruce, who dreams up seasonal dishes based on the freshest local ingredients and pairs them with imaginative wines by the glass or bottle from around the world. The Rowes Wharf water taxi whisks guests straight to the airport, avoiding Boston's notorious traffic.

230 rooms. High-speed Internet access. Three restaurants, two bars. Airport transportation available. $$$$

Lenox

BLANTYRE ★ ★ ★ ★ ★

16 Blantyre Rd., Lenox, 413-637-3556; www.blantyre.com

Gilded Age charm abounds at this Tudor-style mansion in the Berkshire Mountains. Blantyre's rooms maintain a decidedly British country style, with floral fabrics and overstuffed furniture. Fireplaces are available in many rooms. Country pursuits such as croquet, tennis and swimming fill summer afternoons, while cultural events at nearby Tanglewood and Jacob's Pillow offer after-dark diversions. Dining at Blantyre is a special occasion, whether you're lingering over breakfast in the conservatory or enjoying a candlelit dinner. The chef even packs gourmet picnics for afternoons spent lounging on the grounds.

25 rooms. Children over 12 years only. Complimentary continental breakfast. High-speed Internet access. Spa. Restaurant. Bar. $$$$

FOUR STAR HOTELS

Boston

XV BEACON ★ ★ ★ ★

15 Beacon St., Boston, 617-670-1500, 877-982-2226; www.xvbeacon.com
This turn-of-the-century Beaux Arts building on Beacon Hill belies the sleek décor found within. Original artwork commissioned specifically for the hotel by well-known artists fill the walls. The eclectic guest rooms and suites are decorated in a palette of rich chocolate browns, blacks and creams. Rooms feature canopy beds with luxurious Italian linens and gas fireplaces covered in cool stainless steel. Completed in crisp white with simple fixtures, the bathrooms are a modernist's dream. A new modern steakhouse called Mooo occupies the hotel's ground floor.

63 rooms. High-speed Internet access. Restaurant. Bar. Airport transportation available. Pet. Fitness center. $$$$

TAJ BOSTON ★ ★ ★ ★

15 Arlington St., Boston, 617-536-5700, 877-482-5267; www.tajhotels.com
Boston's hotel scene changed forever when the Taj hotel chain bought out the old Ritz-Carlton on Arlington Street. Many were optimistic that the new owners would do this restored 1920s landmark justice—and they have. In the lobby, the property looks much the same—"wedding cake" ceiling details, elaborate moldings, lavish carpets and graceful marble staircases. The guest rooms are still heavenly, with feather beds, soft robes, Molton Brown amenities and luxe marble bathrooms (suites include wood-burning fireplaces with butler service). Even the hotel's oldest tradition of proper afternoon tea is still going strong.

273 rooms. High-speed Internet access. Restaurant, two bars. $$$$

THE RITZ-CARLTON, BOSTON COMMON ★ ★ ★ ★

10 Avery St., Boston, 617-574-7100, 800-241-3333; www.ritzcarlton.com
In a town known for its historic buildings, this contemporary hotel is a fresh and stylish alternative. Located near the city's theater district and overlooking the country's oldest public space, the Ritz-Carlton, Boston Common is convenient for business and leisure travelers alike. The guest rooms and suites have a distinctly serene feel with muted tones and

polished woods. After a night of indulgence, guests often head to the massive Sports Club/LA, the city's most exclusive health club. Dogs are welcomed in style with the Pampered Pet Package, which includes bowls, biscuits and a personalized dog tag.

193 rooms. High-speed Internet access. Restaurant. Bar. $$$$

Edgartown

THE CHARLOTTE INN ★★★★

27 S. Summer St., Edgartown, Massachusetts 02539, 508-627-4151,
fax 508-627-4652, www.relaischateaux.com

The Charlotte Inn offers guests a quintessential Martha's Vineyard experience. This inn has a central location among Edgartown's quaint streets and stately sea captains' homes. Artwork, antiques and other decorative objects lend a hand in creating a historical feel in the bedrooms. Individually designed, some rooms feature canopy beds. Light French cuisine enhanced by American and French wine is served in the restaurant, where candlelit dinners in the garden are particularly unforgettable.

23 rooms. Children over 14 years only. Restaurant. $$$

Nantucket

THE WAUWINET ★★★★

120 Wauwinet Rd., Nantucket, 508-228-0145, 800-426-8718;
www.wauwinet.com

Secluded on a quiet section of the island, the Wauwinet is a welcome retreat from the throngs of summer travelers who flock to the island every year. Built in 1876 by ship captains, this is a grand resort, with sophisticated rooms and suites decorated in fresh, pretty chintzes. Service is friendly and seemingly laidback (but this crew is on top of their game, day and night). Private beaches front the harbor and Atlantic Ocean and the resort's stable of bikes make exploring the area easy. Toppers restaurant has a 20,000-bottle wine cellar and offers fresh-from-the-ocean seafood in an elegant setting.

36 rooms. Children over 18 only. Complimentary full breakfast. Restaurant. Tennis. Closed late October-early May. $$$$

FOUR STAR RESTAURANTS

Boston

AUJOURD'HUI ★★★★

200 Boylston St., Boston, 617-338-4400, 617-423-0154; www.fourseasons.com

With floor-to-ceiling windows overlooking Boston's Public Garden, Aujourd'hui is a beautiful spot for a business lunch or an intimate dinner.

Tables are set with Italian damask linens and decorated with antique plates and fresh flowers. The kitchen aims to please with an innovative selection of seasonal modern French fare prepared with regional ingredients. The predominantly American wine list complements the delicious food. A lighter menu of more nutritional choice is also available.

French menu. Dinner, Sunday brunch. Bar. Children's menu. Business casual attire. Reservations recommended. Valet parking. $$$

CLIO ★ ★ ★ ★

370 Commonwealth Ave., Boston, 617-536-7200; www.cliorestaurant.com

Chef/owner Ken Oringer treats ingredients like notes in a melody—each one complements the next, and the result is a culinary symphony. Fresh fish plays a big role on the menu, and for those who prefer their seafood raw, Clio has a separate sashimi bar, Uni, that features a pricey selection of rare fish from around the world. Each meal begins with Oringer's signature tomato water martini, a palate-awakening concoction that takes the flavor of the fruit to its most honest essence. Where you go from there depends on what's in season, but might include Toro Tartare, St. Pierre in Crisped Bread or Spiced Pear 'Biscuit Coulant'. The rooms are perpetually packed with Boston's media and financial elite.

French, Pan-Asian menu. Breakfast, dinner. Bar. Business casual attire. Reservations recommended. Valet parking. Closed Monday. $$$

L'ESPALIER ★ ★ ★ ★

30 Gloucester St., Boston, 617-262-3023; www.lespalier.com

Housed in a charming 19th-century townhouse, L'Espalier feels like a Merchant-Ivory film come to life. The place captures the elegance of another era, while the French-influenced New England recipes are completely modern. Chef Frank McClelland prepares prix fixe and tasting menus, as well as a caviar special for those feeling indulgent. A monster of a wine list offers an amazing variety of vintages, with many great choices under $50. The afternoon teas are a favorite with the local ladies who lunch.

French menu. Dinner, Saturday tea. Bar. Children's menu. Business casual attire. Reservations recommended. Valet parking. No Disabled Facilities. Closed Sunday-Monday in January-April and July-October. $$$$

MERITAGE ★ ★ ★ ★

70 Rowes Wharf, Boston, 617-439-3995, 800-752-7077; www.bhh.com

Fulfilling chef Daniel Bruce's quest to pair great wine with food, Meritage is an oenophile's playground where more than 900 varities of wine are on hand to enhance the flavors of the seasonal menu. Bruce matches his eclectic dishes with wine flavors rather than varietals, progressing from light to heavy and usually offering tastes of each grape by the glass. Fennel-cured smoked salmon is matched with sparkling wines, while herb-and-mustard-marinated filet comes with a pairing of robust reds. All menu items are available as large or small plates.

International menu. Dinner, Sunday brunch. Bar. Business casual attire. Reservations recommended. Valet parking. Closed Monday. $$$

No. 9 PARK ★ ★ ★ ★

9 Park St., Boston, 617-742-9991; www.no9park.com

In the shadow of the State House on historic Beacon Hill sits chef/owner Barbara Lynch's No. 9 Park. Her effort to support top-of-the-line local producers is evident on the seasonal menu where many ingredients are identified by farm. Perfectly prepared with a healthy dose of flavor and style, Lynch's sophisticated, tempting modern European fare includes beef, fish, venison and pheasant. Lynch is particulary known for her masterful hand at preparing fresh gnocchi, which usually appears on the menu with seared foie gras and Vin Santo glaze. Wine director Cat Silirie selects a thoughtful and unique list, and trains the friendly wait staff to be as knowledgeable as she is.

French, Mediterranean menu. Lunch, dinner. Bar. Business casual attire. Reservations recommended. Valet parking. Closed Sunday. $$$

Chatham

TWENTY-EIGHT ATLANTIC ★ ★ ★ ★

Pleasant Bay Rd., Chatham, 508-432-5400, 800-225-7125;
www.wequassett.com

Black truffle risotto, salmon tartare and a petite clambake are among the enticing entrees offered at this waterfront restaurant located in the Wequassett Resort. The Shaker-style décor, Limoges china and hand-blown glass chandeliers create a subdued, eclectic elegance, while enormous windows offer panoramic views of Pleasant Bay. Chef Bill Brodsky's menu utilizes Cape Cod's local ingredients to create inventive combinations such as Chatham "day boat" scallops and peekytoe crab or coffee and brown sugar cured beef tenderloin. Don't skip the brulee-covered banana rum compote. It's heavenly.

American menu. Breakfast, lunch, dinner. Bar. Children's menu. Business casual attire. Reservations recommended. Outdoor seating. Closed December-March. $$$

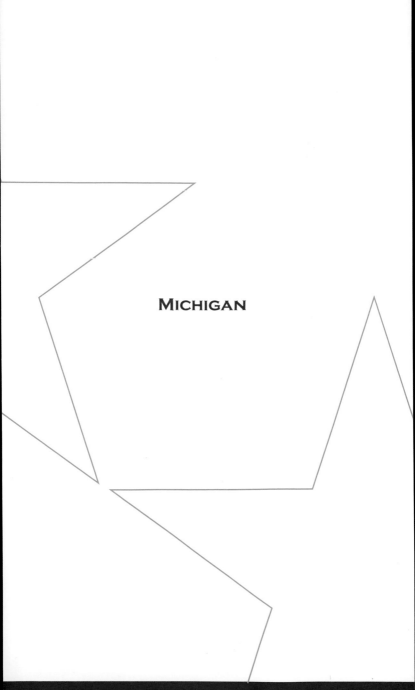

MICHIGAN

MICHIGAN

Birmingham

THE TOWNSEND HOTEL ★ ★ ★ ★

100 Townsend St., Birmingham, 248-642-7900, 800-548-4172;
www.townsendhotel.com
Located in the quiet, upscale community of Birmingham, where tree-lined streets brim with boutiques and cafés, this hotel is conveniently located less than an hour from Detroit. The guest rooms are handsomely furnished with jewel tones, four-poster beds and full kitchens in the suites and penthouses. The cherrywood paneling and the warm glow of the fireplace make the Rugby Grille an inviting space. The dark and sleek interior of the Corner Bar is a perfect match for its Asian-inspired appetizers and creative cocktails.

152 rooms. Pets accepted, some restrictions; fee. High-speed Internet access. Restaurant, bar. Fitness center. Airport transportation available. Business center. $$$$

Bloomfield

THE LARK ★ ★ ★ ★

6430 Farmington Rd., West Bloomfield, 248-661-4466; www.thelark.com
Dining at the Lark is like escaping to a quiet European hideaway. The room—a beautiful space with Portuguese-style tile murals and a trellised terrace—is warm and welcoming. The ambitious menu features classics like bouillabaisse and lobster Thermidor, as well as heartier dishes like rack of lamb Genghis and Chinese oven-roasted duck with figs, dates, almonds and brandy. The world-class wine list perfectly compliments the French-influenced menu. The Lark is also known for its dessert trolley, loaded with every kind of cake, tart, cookie and pastry imaginable.

French menu. Dinner. Closed Sunday-Monday. Bar. Jacket required. Reservations recommended. Outdoor seating. $$$

Ellsworth

TAPAWINGO ★ ★ ★ ★

9502 Lake St., Ellsworth, 231-588-7971, 866-588-7881; www.tapawingo.net
To find this magnificent restaurant, you'll have to travel about seven miles on a winding country road until you hit a place surrounded by gardens. The dining room is charming, with a stone fireplace, lots of windows, a

stunning wine room (the wine list is a find as well), and an elegant private room with its own veranda. But the best part of Tapawingo (the Indian name for the land on which it sits) is the food, which is simply divine—a pleasure to look at and to eat. You'll find seasonal and earthy flavors in dishes such as seared dayboat diver scallops with chorizo ragu and white bean purée, Aspen Hill Farm rabbit with baby leeks, English peas and pearl onions, and spiced filet mignon with Yukon Gold potato purée, Chanterelle mushrooms, baby bok choy, sweet corn and a gorgonzola fondue.

Contemporary American menu. Lunch, dinner. Closed Sunday-Wednesday in winter. Business casual attire. Reservations recommended. Outdoor seating. $$$

Grand Rapids

1913 ROOM ★★★★

187 Monroe N.W., Grand Rapids, 616-774-2000; www.amwaygrand.com
Housed in the historic Amway Grand Plaza, this fine-dining restaurant is ideal for special occasions. The Louis XVI-style room is filled with white-linen topped tables and is overseen by a polished, confident staff. The menu, which features classic dishes with French influences, includes standouts like grilled beef filet and lobster terrine, or seared Atlantic salmon with horseradish crust. A chef's tasting menu with accompanying wines is available.

Continental menu. Lunch, dinner. Reservations recommended. $$$

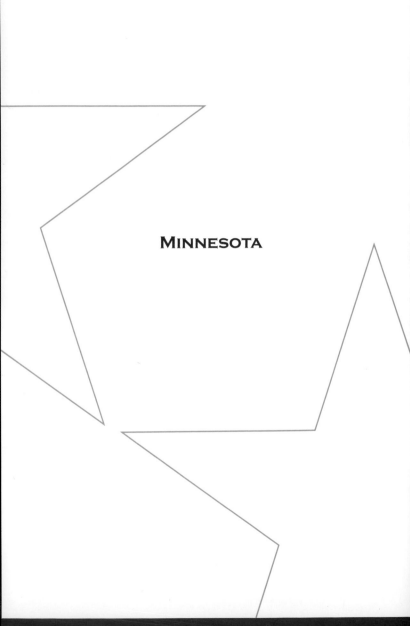

MINNESOTA

Minneapolis

LA BELLE VIE ★ ★ ★ ★

510 Groveland Ave., Minneapolis, 612-874-6440; www.labellevie.us

Located in downtown Minneapolis near the Walker Arts Center, La Belle Vie brings new meaning to pre-theater dining. This restaurant is not just the first act, but it is the entire show with its talented team of chefs who deliver applause-worthy performances. The staff is equally well-trained and the atmosphere is sophisticated and refined—appropriate for its location within the elegant 510 Groveland residence building. There's a five-course prix-fixe menu and flights of wine can be selected to round out the experience. Or order from the à la carte menu, with selections such as succulent pork tenderloin and flavorful sea bass with a saffron-orange emulsion.

Continental menu. Dinner. **$$**

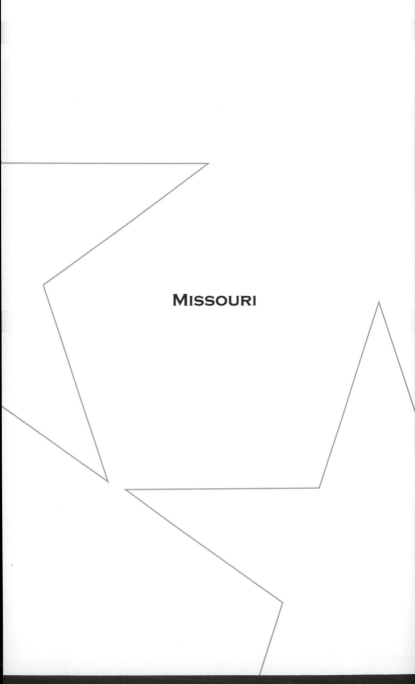

Missouri

MISSOURI

Clayton

THE RITZ-CARLTON, ST. LOUIS ★ ★ ★ ★

100 Carondelet Plaza, Clayton, 314-863-6300, 800-241-3333;
www.ritzcarlton.com

Nestled in the upscale Clayton neighborhood, this sophisticated hotel is conveniently located near the city's business district as well as bustling restaurants and cultural landmarks. The rooms are spacious and polished with plush furnishings, large marble bathrooms and private balconies offering views of the city skyline. A comprehensive fitness center includes lap and hydrotherapy pools, a steam room and sauna. For a cocktail, head to the Lobby Lounge or try the Wine Room, a unique spot for sampling one of the hotel's more than 7,000 bottles of wine. The Restaurant offers a fine dining experience.

301 rooms. Pets accepted; fee. Wireless Internet access. Two restaurants, bar. Fitness center. Indoor pool, whirlpool. Airport transportation available. Business center. $$$$

Kansas City

AMERICAN ★ ★ ★ ★

200 E. 25th St., Kansas City, 816-545-8000; www.theamericankc.com

The flagship restaurant of the Crown Center, the American has attracted Kansas City diners for 40 years. With a concept designed by the legendary James Beard, the father of American cooking, and Joe Baum, the restaurateur of the former Windows on the World in New York City, the place is as elegant as ever, with downtown views, polished service, and one of the city's best wine lists. The kitchen staff, led by chef Celina Tio, prepares American fare using local seasonal produce.

American menu. Lunch, dinner. Closed Sunday. Bar. Children's menu. Business casual attire. Reservations recommended. Valet parking. $$$

St. Louis

TONY'S ★★★★

410 Market St., St.Louis, 314-231-7007; www.tonysstlouis.com

Italian food may bring to mind images of pasta with red sauce, but at Tony's you'll find a menu of authentic Italian fare prepared with a measured and sophisticated hand. Expect appetizers like smoked salmon with mascarpone cheese and asparagus and Belgian endive, and entrées such as tenderloin of beef with foie gras in a port wine demi-glaze. The room has an urban, postmodern style, with sleek low lighting, linen-topped tables, and glossy, wood-paneled walls. The chef's tasting menu is a nice choice for gourmands with healthy appetites.

Italian menu. Dinner. Closed Sunday; also first week of January and first week of July. Bar. Jacket required. Reservations recommended. Valet parking. $$$

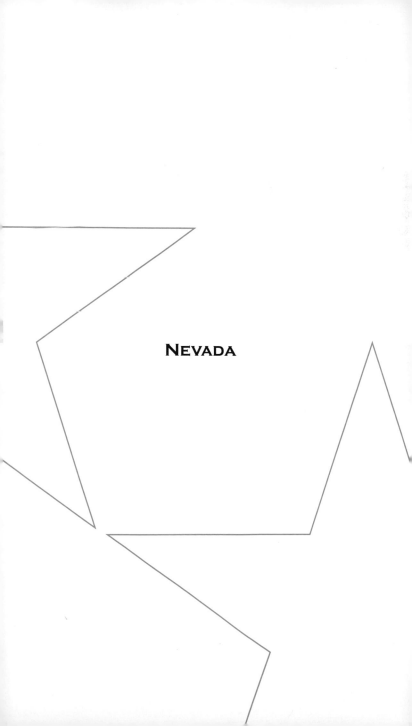

Nevada

NEVADA

Las Vegas

THE TOWER SUITES AT WYNN LAS VEGAS ★ ★ ★ ★ ★

3131 Las Vegas Blvd. S., Las Vegas, 702-770-7100, 877-321-9966;
www.wynnlasvegas.com

As if the regular guest rooms at the ultra-posh Wynn resort weren't luxurious enough, the 50-story Wynn features apartment-like suites located in their own tower that raise the bar for luxury. Upon arrival, guests are whisked up in private elevators to the suites, which overlook either the city lights or the Wynn Country Club—the only golf course on the Strip. Guests get priority access to high-stakes tables and slots in the 111,000-square foot casino, and entry to an exclusive pool where servers will even clean your sunglasses for you. Ranging in size from 640 to nearly 2,000 square feet, the rooms are filled with replicas of artwork from Steve Wynn's impressive collection and have floor-to-ceiling windows covered by sleek, electronic draperies. Marble baths feature bubble-jet tubs, enclosed showers, two sinks and LCD televisions. A restful night's sleep is guaranteed on the signature Wynn bed, with fluffy pillow-top mattresses and ultra-soft European linens. Tableau, the restaurant in the Tower Suites, turns out impeccable American cuisine. Dinner is served to all hotel guests but breakfast and lunch are reserved for suites-only customers.

653 rooms. High-speed Internet access. Restaurant, bar. Spa. Casino. Golf. Pool. $$$$

Las Vegas

BELLAGIO ★ ★ ★ ★

3600 Las Vegas Blvd. S., Las Vegas, 702-693-7111, 888-987-6667;
www.bellagiolasvegas.com

A fantastic casino is only the beginning at this all-encompassing hotel, with a beautifully landscaped pool, arcade of fine shopping and celebrity-chef restaurants. Visitors will gaze with awe at the exotic botanical gardens and magnificent hand-blown glass flowers by renowned artist Dale Chihuly in the lobby. Of course, the star of the show is the eight-acre man-made lake, where the popular fountain and light show takes place every half-hour. The Bellagio is also home to Cirque du Soleil's *O*, a mesmerizing aquatic performance. The rooms have luxurious fabrics and Italian marble. The only downside here is that you have to go through the casino to get everywhere. But then again, that's the point.

3,933 rooms. Wireless Internet access. Twelve restaurants, Five bars. Spa. Casino. $$

Four Seasons Hotel Las Vegas ★ ★ ★ ★

3960 Las Vegas Blvd. S., Las Vegas, 702-632-5000, 877-632-5000; www.fourseasons.com

The Four Seasons Hotel is a palatial refuge in glittering Las Vegas. Located on the southern tip of the Strip on the top floors of the Mandalay Bay Resort tower, it's close to the action but also provides a welcome respite when you need it. The sumptuous rooms at this non-gaming hotel have floor-to-ceiling windows overlooking the city. The glorious pool is a lush oasis with its swaying palm trees and attentive poolside service and the sublime spa offers innovative treatments. Steak lovers will enjoy Charlie Palmer Steak, while the sun-filled Verandah offers a casual dining alternative.

424 rooms. High-speed Internet access. Two restaurants, bar. Spa. Business Center. $$$

The Ritz-Carlton Lake Las Vegas ★ ★ ★ ★

1610 Lake Las Vegas Pkwy., Henderson, 702-567-4700; www.ritzcarlton.com

Exchange the over-the-top glitz of the Las Vegas strip for the serenity of the Mediterranean-inspired Ritz-Carlton on Lake Las Vegas. A 35-minute ride from the Strip, the resort is nestled in a valley surrounded by low-lying desert mountains. A replica of Florence's Ponte Vecchio extends across the 320-acre lake, and singing gondoliers take guests on a romantic trip under the bridge. After playing the tables at the nearby MonteLago Village Resort, wind down with a massage at the spa or with a round of golf on one of two championship golf courses. Guests can dine at the Medici Café and Terrace, which overlooks the resort's Florentine gardens or have a cocktail in the Firenze Lobby Lounge.

349 rooms. Wireless Internet access. Restaurant, bar. Spa. Pets accepted. Golf. Tennis. Business Center. $$

The Venetian Resort Hotel Casino ★ ★ ★ ★

3355 Las Vegas Blvd. S., Las Vegas, 702-414-1000, 877-883-6423; www.venetian.com

From the masterfully re-created Venetian landmark buildings to the frescoed ceilings and gilded details, the Venetian faithfully re-creates the splendor that is Venice in the heart of the Las Vegas Strip. Guests walk down winding alleys and glide past ornate architecture in gondolas. From the moment you enter through the Doge's Palace and walk through the lobby to the casino with its frescoes, you'll be impressed. The suites are large and luxurious, with sunken living rooms and walk-in closets. Some of the biggest names in American cuisine operate award-winning restaurants here, including Lutece. The Venetian's Guggenheim showcases rotating exhibits while the Canyon Ranch Spa offers the same pampering treatments as the famed spa based in Arizona. The Grand Canal Shoppes is a who's who of designers, from Chanel to Jimmy Choo.

4,027 rooms, all suites. Nineteen restaurants, six bars. Spa. Casino. Pool. $$

WYNN LAS VEGAS ★ ★ ★ ★

3131 Las Vegas Blvd. S., Las Vegas, 702-770-7100, 888-320-9966;
www.wynnlasvegas.com

You won't find any world wonders or replicas here. This is the haute version of Las Vegas. The rooms, with deep orange walls, impressive art work and richly appointed couches, are decorated to make you feel like you're staying in someone's apartment in London or Manhattan. Open the drapes with the push of a button and soak in the tub while watching the flat screen LCD in the bathroom. On the main level there are two spacious pools, a European-style bathing pool and the Cabana Bar, where you can play poolside blackjack in season. (Guests of the suites enjoy two quieter pools.) Then there's the championship golf course and the boutiques. Shops include Manolo Blahnik, Dior, Louis Vuitton and Oscar de la Renta. There's even a Ferrari dealership, and some of the most revered chefs, including Daniel Boulud, have opened restaurants here.

2,716 rooms. 18 restaurants, bars. Spa. Casino. Pool. $$$$

FIVE STAR RESTAURANTS

Las Vegas

ALEX ★ ★ ★ ★ ★

3131 Las Vegas Blvd. S., Las Vegas, 702-248-3463, 888-352-3463;
www.wynnlasvegas.com

Famed chef Alessandro Stratta has brought his sumptuous French cuisine to this stunning restaurant at the Wynn, which has a grand hour-glass-shaped staircase, chandeliers and mahogany furniture. The artfully presented dishes might include Robiola cheese agnolotti with black truffles and aged Parmigiano or the Dover Sole with a potato crust, artichokes and tomato confit. Desserts by pastry chef Jenifer Witte are just as imaginative and special. Request one of two private seating areas overlooking a private courtyard, or reserve the popular chef's table.

French menu. Dinner. Closed Monday. Bar. Reservations recommended. Valet parking. Outdoor seating. $$$$

JOËL ROBUCHON AT THE MANSION ★ ★ ★ ★ ★

3799 Las Vegas Blvd. S., Las Vegas, 702-891-7925; www.mgmgrand.com

Foodies everywhere salivated when they heard of Joël Robuchon's arrival in Sin City. His first of three restaurants in North America, Joël Robuchon at the Mansion, located in the MGM Grand, is a super-luxe temple of haute cuisine, showcasing the signature cooking style that earned Robuchon his reputation as one of the world's greatest chefs. The menu, which reflects simplicity and a respect for fine ingredients, includes signatures dishes like crispy amadai snapper with pistachio oil, truffled langoustine ravioli with diced cabbage and scallops in a ginger bouillon with baby leeks. Additional highlights include the bread cart (which showcases nearly two dozen different kinds of breads baked fresh daily) and a petit four cart with fanciful confections. The intimate Art Deco space has 17-foot ceilings and features cream-colored walls, black lacquered furniture and a black and white tiled entrance lit by a stunning crystal chandelier. The knowledgeable and graceful staff almost seems invisible. No doubt you'll remember a meal here for years to come.

French menu. Dinner. Bar. Children's menu. Jacket required. Reservations recommended. Valet parking. Outdoor seating. $$$$

FOUR STAR RESTAURANTS

Las Vegas

AUREOLE ★ ★ ★ ★

3950 Las Vegas Blvd. S., Las Vegas, 702-632-7401; www.aureolerestaurant.com
A branch of chef Charlie Palmer's New York original, Aureole wows patrons with its centerpiece four-story wine tower. Be sure to order a bottle just to see the catsuit-clad climber, suspended by ropes, locate your vintage. The extensive wine list complements Palmer's seasonal contemporary American cuisine typified by dishes such as Peking duck with foie gras ravioli and roast pheasant with sweet potato gnocchi. The modern but romantic room with encircling booths sets the stage for event dining at Mandalay Bay.

American menu. Dinner. Bar. Reservations recommended. Valet parking. $$$

BRADLEY OGDEN ★ ★ ★ ★

3570 Las Vegas Blvd. S., Las Vegas, 877-346-4642; www.caesarspalace.com
Bradley Ogden's eponymous restaurant at Caesars Palace—his first outside of California—is a sure bet. The décor is sleek and contemporary with exposed wood beams lining the high ceilings and a glossy cement floor. For a more romantic ambiance, head to the back of the restaurant where a large stone fireplace warms diners tableside. Although this modern Las Vegas location is a world away from the farms and ranches Ogden depends on when preparing his innovative take on American cuisine, no expense is spared in bringing it all in. Dishes include oak-grilled lamb rack with fava bean and cumin spaetzel, and hot and cold foie gras with kumquats.

American menu. Dinner. Bar. Business casual attire. Reservations recommended. Valet parking. $$$$

MICHAEL MINA ★★★★

3600 Las Vegas Blvd. S., Las Vegas, 877-234-6358; www.bellagiolasvegas.com
This luxurious, contemporary dining room bathed in creamy neutral tones and golden light is just past the botanical gardens at the Bellagio. The menu here is in the care of a talented group of chefs trained and transported from San Francisco, who create innovate seafood dishes with California ingredients. The menu is extensive and offers à la carte selections in addition to a pair of five-course tasting menus, one vegetarian and one seasonal. Classic dishes include savory black mussel soufflé with saffron and Chardonnay cream and Maine lobster pot pie. The wine list focuses on American producers and contains some gems from small vineyards.

Seafood menu. Dinner, late-night. Bar. Reservations recommended. Valet parking. $$$

MIX RESTAURANT ★★★★

3950 Las Vegas Blvd., Las Vegas, 702-632-9500; www.mandalaybay.com
It was only a matter of time before culinary mastermind Alain Ducasse took his place on the Strip. And in classic Ducasse style, the result is nothing less than grand. Located on the 64th floor of the hotel at Mandalay Bay, Mix is something of a futuristic fantasy. The light and airy, Patrick Jouin-designed interior features a 24-foot, $500,000 Champagne-bubble chandelier consisting of more than 15,000 glass spheres, massive floor-to-ceiling windows that offer spectacular 360-degree views of Las Vegas, and tables with white faux leather-covered chairs. The staff inside the $2-million open kitchen turns out Ducasse's classic French cuisine, but with a contemporary twist. Dishes include duck foie gras with date-apricot chutney, and beef tenderloin Rossini with potato galette and black truffle sauce. The extensive wine collection, consisting of approximately 7,000 bottles, lines an entire wall at the dining room's entrance.

French, American menu. Dinner. Bar. Business casual attire. Reservations recommended. Valet parking. $$$

PICASSO ★★★★

3600 Las Vegas Blvd. S., Las Vegas, 877-234-6358; www.bellagiolasvegas.com
Considered by many to be the most popular of Las Vegas restaurants, Picasso impresses with its ambience and food. Gold and red surround the dining room like holiday wrapping paper, drawing attention to authentic oil paintings and ceramics of the master artist. Chef Julian Serrano's French-Mediterranean cuisine more than competes for similar accolades. The prix-fixe menu changes daily, but certain favorites may be available, including poached oysters, roasted ruby red shrimp or sautéed center cut filet of swordfish, all of which are artfully presented.

French, Spanish menu. Dinner, late-night. Closed Tuesday. Bar. Jacket recommended. Reservations recommended. Valet parking. Outdoor seating. $$$$

RESTAURANT GUY SAVOY ★ ★ ★ ★

3570 Las Vegas Blvd. S., Las Vegas, 877-346-4642; www.caesarspalace.com
Perfect for a romantic dinner or a night out with friends, Restaurant Guy Savoy offers a fine-dining experience in a chic atmosphere with dark wood lattice, dramatic high ceilings and contemporary art. The creative French cuisine includes specialties such as artichoke black truffle soup, crispy sea bass with delicate spices and butter-roasted veal sweetbreads. Restaurant Guy Savoy is located in Caesar's Palace on the second floor of the Augustus Tower.

French menu. Dinner. Closed Monday-Tuesday. Bar. Business casual attire. Reservations recommended. Valet parking. $$$$

FOUR STAR SPAS

Las Vegas

CANYON RANCH SPACLUB AT THE VENETIAN ★ ★ ★ ★

3355 Las Vegas Blvd. S., Las Vegas, 702-414-3606, 877-220-2688; www.canyonranch.com
For years, Canyon Ranch has been the gold standard in the spa industry, known for its innovative approach to healthy living. The focus here is on fitness, nutrition and stress management. This 65,000-square-foot facility has the largest fitness center on the Las Vegas Strip and includes cutting-edge classes, state-of-the-art equipment and a 40-foot rock-climbing wall. After a vigorous workout, reward yourself with one of the spa's massages (from neuromuscular therapy to Thai) or body treatments. There's also a full-service salon.

SPA BELLAGIO AT BELLAGIO ★ ★ ★ ★

3600 Las Vegas Blvd. S., Las Vegas, 702-693-7472, 888-987-3456; www.bellagio.com
This Roman-style spa is the height of luxury, even in over-the-top Las Vegas. The facility includes a redwood sauna, eucalyptus steam room and cold plunge pools. The staff attends to your every whim. You'll feel pampered as you sip a latte served in Bernadaud china that fits perfectly into the armrest of a pedicure chair. Try a lemon-ginger stone or deluxe scalp massage. Hot toe-voodoo can be added to any massage and is a wonderfully relaxing treatment in which warm stones are placed between your toes to re-energize tired feet. The lemon-ginger scrub is another fantastic treatment for rough skin. Facials target common problems, such as sun damage, dehydration and wrinkles, and eye and lip treatments can

be added to these services. Hydrotherapy services include thalasso seaweed baths, revitalizing mineral baths and aromatic Moor mud baths.

THE RITZ-CARLTON SPA, LAKE LAS VEGAS ★ ★ ★ ★

1610 Lake Las Vegas Pkwy., Henderson, 702-567-4700, 800-241-3333;
www.ritzcarlton.com

This Mediterranean-influenced, 30,000-square-foot facility is a sanctuary from the hot desert sun. Treatment rooms are luxurious and spacious—several have outdoor terraces that overlook the lake, and some are designed exclusively for couples. The La Culla treatment includes an array of body and facial treatments, accompanied by music and other sounds and aromatherapy. The signature facial uses an exclusive marine concentrate. The spa facilities include a complete fitness center, movement studio for yoga and pilates, full service salon and a boutique. Nutritional and wellness counseling, physician-directed cosmetic dermatology and extensive recreations programs and activities are available.

THE SPA AT FOUR SEASONS HOTEL LAS VEGAS ★ ★ ★ ★

3960 Las Vegas Blvd. S., Las Vegas, 702-632-5000, 800-819-5053;
www.fourseasons.com

A Buddhist goddess greets visitors at this Asian-inspired spa. The 16 treatment rooms offer elegant details and the Zen lounge is a true sanctuary of relaxation with soothing music and aromas. Try the 80-minute JAMU massage, which blends Hindu, Chinese and European styles and techniques (including acupressure and skin rolling) with essential oils to work out every last kink. Other treatments include Balinese foot washes, aromatherapy scalp massage and reflexology. There are also a variety of herbal wraps, salt glows and European facials such as the Golden Veil, which utilizes the anti-aging properties of gold to revitalize and rejuvenate your skin.

THE SPA AT THE WYNN LAS VEGAS ★ ★ ★ ★

3131 Las Vegas Blvd. S., Las Vegas, 702-770-3900, 877-321-9966;
www.wynnlasvegas.com

A soothing atmosphere with shades of cream and gold, decadent treatments and luxurious, well-appointed amenities will make this spa your new reason for return trips to Las Vegas. Available exclusively to guests of the resort, the spa focuses on providing individualized treatments. Whether you opt for a facial, massage or hydrotherapy, the staff will make you feel as if this tranquil sanctuary were created exclusively for you. Slip into a velvety robe and slippers and relax in the lounge area until you're swept away to one of the 45 garden-themed treatment rooms. The signature Good Luck Ritual includes a customized massage along with a lemon verbena and peppermint foot treatment, moisturizing hand therapy and stimulating scalp treatment. The radiance facial brightens skin and improves circulation, while the brown sugar body treatment uses a light, warming massage with sugar-infused formulas to nourish skin.

New Mexico

New Mexico

Santa Fe

Inn of the Anasazi ★ ★ ★ ★

113 Washington Ave., Santa Fe, 505-988-3030; www.innoftheanasazi.com
Located just off the historic Plaza, the inn was designed to resemble the traditional dwellings of the local Anasazi. Enormous handcrafted doors open to a world of authentic artwork, carvings and textiles synonymous with the Southwest. The lobby sets the scene for arriving guests with its rough-hewn tables, leather furnishings, unique objects and huge cactus plants in terra-cotta pots. The region's integrity is maintained in the guest rooms, which have fireplaces and four-poster beds and bathrooms stocked with toiletries made locally with native cedar extract. The restaurant earns praise for honoring the area's culinary heritage.

57 rooms. Restaurant, bar. Pets accepted. Fitness center. $$$

Santa Fe

Geronimo ★ ★ ★ ★

724 Canyon Rd., Santa Fe, 505-982-1500; www.geronimorestaurant.com
Housed in a restored 250-year-old landmark adobe building, Geronimo (the name of the restaurant is an ode to the hacienda's original owner, Geronimo Lopez) offers robust southwestern-spiked global fusion fare in a stunning and cozy space. Owners Cliff Skoglund and Chris Harvey treat each guest like family. The interior is like a Georgia O'Keeffe painting come to life, with its wood-burning cove-style fireplace, tall chocolate-and-garnet-leather seating and local Native American-style artwork decorating the walls. The food is remarkable, fusing the distinct culinary influences of Asia, the Southwest and the Mediterranean. Vibrant flavors, bright colors and top-notch seasonal and regional ingredients come together in such dishes as Maryland soft-shell tempura crabs with soba noodle and asian pear salad, or mesquite-grilled New York strip steak with French onion tart and polenta fries with green pepper corn and mustard sauce. When it's warm outside, sit on the patio for prime Canyon Road people watching.

International menu. Lunch, dinner, Sunday brunch. Bar. Casual attire. Reservations recommended. Valet parking. Outdoor seating. $$$

NEW YORK

NEW YORK

New York

FOUR SEASONS HOTEL NEW YORK ★ ★ ★ ★ ★

57 E. 57th St., New York, 10022, 212-758-5700, 800-545-4000;
www.fourseasons.com
Designed by legendary architect I.M. Pei, the Four Seasons is the tallest
hotel in New York. An opulent tone is immediately set with an entry foyer
boasting 33-foot ceilings and massive marble columns. The rooms and
suites have a chic style with neutral tones, English sycamore furnishings
and state-of-the-art technology. Floor-to-ceiling windows showcase the
dazzling city skyline or the verdant swath of Central Park. Some rooms
offer furnished terraces so that guests can further admire the views. Frette
linens and blackout blinds guarantee a restful night's sleep. But it's the
service that defines the Four Seasons experience: the staff is wonderfully
helpful and courteous.
370 rooms. Wireless Internet access. Restaurant, bar. Airport
transportation available. Fitness center. Spa. Business center. Pets
accepted. $$$$

MANDARIN ORIENTAL, NEW YORK ★ ★ ★ ★ ★

80 Columbus Circle, New York, 212-805-8800, 866-801-8880;
www.mandarinoriental.com/newyork
This luxury hotel occupies 54 floors high atop the Time Warner Center,
offering spectacular views of Central Park, the Hudson River and the
city skyline. Guest rooms are serene and relaxing, and there's much to
indulge outside your room. Take a swim in the 36th-floor pool or have
a Balinese body massage at the spa. The hotel's Asian theme carries over
into Asiate, which serves French and Japanese fusion cuisine, and MObar,
which features drinks like the East Meets West, a combination of pear and
cinnamon-infused brandy, chilled Champagne and a sugar cube. Want to
be dazzled by one of the world's best chefs? Make reservations at one of
the much talked-about restaurants in the Time Warner Center, including
Thomas Keller's Per Se and Masa Takayama's Masa.
248 rooms. Wireless Internet access. Two restaurants, bar. Fitness center.
Spa. Pool. Business Center. $$$$

THE RITZ-CARLTON NEW YORK, CENTRAL PARK ★ ★ ★ ★ ★

50 Central Park S., New York, 212-308-9100, 800-542-8680;
www.ritzcarlton.com
Rising above Central Park and flanked by prestigious Fifth Avenue and

fashionable Central Park West, this hotel has one of the most coveted locations in town. This genteel property is exquisite down to every last detail, from the priceless antiques and artwork in the glamorous lobby to the floral displays. The rooms and suites have sumptuous fabrics and plush furnishings. No detail is overlooked; rooms facing the park include telescopes for closer viewing. The white-glove service makes this a top choice of well-heeled travelers. The hotel includes an outpost of the renowned European La Prairie Spa and star chef Laurent Tourondel's BLT Market.

261 rooms. Wireless Internet access. Restaurant, bar. Fitness Center, spa. Airport transportation available. Business Center. $$$$

THE ST. REGIS ★ ★ ★ ★ ★

2 E. 55th St., New York, 10022, 212-753-4500; 888-625-4988;
www.stregis.com/newyork
Located just off Fifth Avenue, the St. Regis reigns as New York's grande dame. Opened in 1904, this Beaux Arts landmark defines elegance with its gleaming marble, glittering gold leafing and sparkling chandeliers. The guest rooms are elegantly decorated in soft pastel colors with Louis XVI-style furnishings. The Astor Court is the perfect place to enjoy traditional afternoon tea. Renowned for its famous Red Snapper cocktail and bewitching Maxfield Parrish mural, the King Cole Bar is a favorite of hotel guests and locals alike. Be sure to ask the bartender why crafty Old King Cole is smirking.

229 rooms. Wireless Internet access. Restaurant, bar. Fitness Center, spa. Airport transportation available. Business Center. $$$$

Saranac Lake

THE POINT ★ ★ ★ ★ ★

Hwy. 30, Saranac Lake, 518-891-5674, 800-255-3530;
www.thepointresort.com
This former great camp of William Avery Rockefeller revives the spirit of the early 19th century Adirondacks, when the wealthy came to this sylvan paradise. No signs direct visitors to this intimate camp, and a decidedly residential ambience is maintained. The resort has a splendid location on a 10-acre peninsula on Upper Saranac Lake. Rooms feature Adirondack twig furnishings, stone fireplaces, elegant bathrooms and exquisite antiques. Outdoor activities include snowshoeing and cross-country skiing to water sports, trail hikes and croquet. Champagne and truffled popcorn at 4 a.m.? No problem. Gourmet dining figures largely in the experience, and with a nod to the patrician past, guests don black-tie attire twice weekly at the communal dining table in the resort's great room.

11 rooms. No children allowed. Restaurant, bar. Beach. Tennis. $$$$

New York

THE CARLYLE, A ROSEWOOD HOTEL ★ ★ ★ ★

35 E. 76th St., New York, 212-744-1600, 888-767-3966; www.thecarlyle.com

Discreetly tucked away on Manhattan's Upper East Side, the Carlyle has maintained the allure of being one of New York's best-kept secrets for more than 70 years. A favorite of movie stars, presidents and royals, the Carlyle feels like an exclusive private club. Its art collection is extraordinary, from Audubon prints and Piranesi architectural drawings to English country scenes by Kips. Frequented by power brokers and socialites, the Carlyle Restaurant defines elegance. Bemelmans Bar proudly shows off its murals by *Madeline* creator Ludwig Bemelmans, while Café Carlyle is one of the city's most beloved piano bars.

179 rooms. Pets accepted; fee. Wireless Internet access. Two restaurants, bar. Fitness center, fitness classes available, spa. Airport transportation available. Business center. $$$$

THE LOWELL ★ ★ ★ ★

28 E. 63rd St., New York, 212-838-1400, 800-221-4444;
www.lowellhotel.com

Located in a landmark 1920s building on the Upper East Side, the Lowell captures the essence of an elegant country house with a delightful blend of English prints, floral fabrics and Chinese porcelains. Many suites boast wood-burning fireplaces. All rooms are individually decorated, and the Lowell's specialty suites are a unique treat. The glamour of the 1930s silver screen is recalled in the Hollywood Suite, while the English influences extend to the Pembroke Room, where a proper tea is served, as are breakfast and brunch. The clubby Post House, a well-respected New York steakhouse, serves terrific chops.

70 rooms. Complimentary continental breakfast. Wireless Internet access. Two restaurants, bar. Airport transportation available. $$$$

THE NEW YORK PALACE ★ ★ ★ ★

455 Madison Ave., New York, 212-888-7000, 800-804-7035;
www.newyorkpalace.com

Return to the Gilded Age at the New York Palace. Marrying the historic 1882 Villard Houses with a 55-story contemporary tower, this hotel brings the two worlds together under one roof. The glorious public rooms are masterfully restored and recall their former incarnations as fin-de-siecle ballrooms and sitting areas. The Palace's rooms and suites are a blend of contemporary flair and period décor. The hotel's restaurant, Gilt, serves exceptional food in a dramatic, modern-yet-classic setting.

897 rooms. Wireless Internet access. Restaurant, bar. Spa. Airport transportation available. $$$$

THE PENINSULA NEW YORK ★ ★ ★ ★

700 Fifth Ave., New York, 212-956-2888, 800-262-9467; www.peninsula.com
The lobby of this turn-of-the-century Beaux Arts landmark hotel is magnificent with a sweeping staircase and elegant bar. Bellhops in crisp white uniforms escort guests to rooms and suites where lush fabrics and warm tones create a soothing ambience. A few rooms overlook the famed St. Patrick's Cathedral. Though the décor exudes old-world charm, modern amenities abound including flat screen plasma TVs, wireless Internet access and silent in-room fax machines. The glass enclosed fitness center, overlooking the city, is a favorite among those in the know. With its views above the city, the Pen-Top Terrace and Bar is a prime spot for a drink.

239 rooms. Wireless Internet access. Two restaurants, three bars. Fitness Center, spa. Airport transportation available. Business Center. $$$$

THE PIERRE NEW YORK, A TAJ HOTEL ★ ★ ★ ★

2 E. 61st. St., New York, 212-838-8000, 866-969-1825;
www.tajhotels.com/pierre
Regal and luxurious, this is the definition of a grand old hotel. Although guest rooms are undergoing a massive renovation, slated for completion in early 2009, banquet and meeting rooms are still available. The Pierre has been a city landmark since its construction in 1930. Rooms and suites have a traditional bent thanks to floral prints and antique reproductions. The Rotunda, where breakfast, lunch and afternoon tea are served, has a ceiling of trompe l'oeil murals.

201 rooms. Wireless Internet access. Two restaurants, bar. $$$$

THE RITZ-CARLTON NEW YORK, BATTERY PARK ★ ★ ★ ★

2 West St., New York, 212-344-0800, 800-542-8680;
www.ritzcarlton.com
Watch the world from the Ritz-Carlton New York, Battery Park. While only a 5-minute walk from Wall Street and the Financial District, the Ritz-Carlton seems removed from the fray thanks to its staggering views of the Hudson River, the Statue of Liberty and Ellis Island from its location on the southern tip of Manhattan. The 38-story glass and brick tower is a departure from the traditional Ritz-Carlton European style, with its contemporary artwork to the modern furnishings. The service however is distinctly Ritz-Carlton, with exceptional concierge service and amenities like Bath Butlers who create special concoctions for bath time. The view takes center stage throughout the hotel, whether you're gazing through a telescope in a harbor view room, enjoying a cocktail at Rise (the 14th-floor bar with outdoor space) or savoring a meal at 2 West.

298 rooms. Wireless Internet access. Restaurant, two bars. Fitness center, spa. Pets accepted. Business Center. $$$$

TRUMP INTERNATIONAL HOTEL & TOWER ★ ★ ★ ★

1 Central Park W., New York, 212-299-1000, 888-448-7867; www.trumpintl.com

Occupying an enviable site across from Central Park and the Time Warner Center on Manhattan's Upper West Side, the 52-story Trump International Hotel and Tower delivers glitz and glam. The guest rooms and suites reflect a contemporary European flavor, while the floor-to-ceiling windows focus attention on the views of Central Park and Columbus Circle. All suites and most rooms feature kitchens, and in-room chefs are available to craft memorable meals. Room service comes courtesy of top chef Jean-Georges Vongerichten, whose restaurant, Jean Georges, sits just off the lobby. The personal attaché service provides an apt pair of hands to take care of life's little details.

176 rooms. Wireless Internet access. Restaurant, bar. Spa. Airport transportation available. $$$$

Skaneateles

MIRBEAU INN & SPA ★ ★ ★ ★

851 W. Genesee St., Skaneateles, 315-685-5006, 877-647-2328; www.mirbeau.com

This 12-acre Finger Lakes country estate, filled with ponds, gardens and woodlands, seems to have leapt off the canvases of Claude Monet. Delightful Provençal fabrics and French country furnishings make the rooms cozy and comfortable, and fireplaces and soaking tubs add romance. The friendly staff is available when you need them and unobtrusive when you don't. The restaurant will make your stay even more pleasant, thanks to its winsome views of the lily pond and the fresh-from-the-garden taste of the food. The European-style spa is both modern and charming.

34 rooms. High-speed Internet access. Restaurant, two bars. Fitness center. Spa. Whirlpool. $$$

FIVE STAR RESTUARANTS

New York

JEAN GEORGES ★ ★ ★ ★ ★

1 Central Park W., New York, 212-299-3900; www.jean-georges.com

Perfection is a word that comes to mind when speaking of meals at Jean-Georges. Located in the Trump International Hotel and Tower, Jean-Georges is a shrine to haute cuisine. Drawing influences from around the world, the menu is conceived and impeccably executed by celebrity chef/owner Jean-Georges Vongerichten. Prix Fixe dishes include young garlic soup with thyme and sautéed frog legs, and mouth-watering Arctic char with miso-potato puree in a Granny Smith apple-jalapeno juice. If you can't secure a table at the restaurant, try your luck at Nougatine, the popular on-site café. It has a simple bar menu but will give you a taste of Vongerichten's cuisine. The bar is also a lovely place to meet for an aperitif or a cocktail before dinner or a walk through the park.

Continental, French menu. Breakfast, lunch, dinner, brunch. Bar. Business casual attire. Reservations recommended. Valet parking. Outdoor seating. $$$$

LE BERNARDIN ★ ★ ★ ★ ★

155 W. 51st St., New York, 212-554-1515; www.le-bernardin.com
This fabled restaurant has impressed foodies and newbies alike since it moved from Paris to Manhattan in 1986. Le Bernardin is very civilized and sophisticated, and it's certainly not the place for a quick bite. With service that is both precise and impeccably understated, diners are able to turn their full attention to their tastebuds. Chef Eric Ripert's food is light, aromatic and perfectly balanced and the presentations are museum-worthy. Seafood is the star, and the menu features such knockout dishes as poached halibut with marinated grapes and cherry tomatoes and organic Chilean turbot in a lemon-miso broth. The wine list is equally exquisite.
French, Seafood menu. Lunch, dinner. Closed Sunday. Bar. Jacket required. Reservations recommended. $$$$

MASA ★ ★ ★ ★ ★

10 Columbus Circle, New York, 212-823-9808; www.masanyc.com
You need deep pockets to indulge at Masa. This is the high roller's table for gourmands, given that you've already committed to spending $400 just by walking through the 2,500-year-old Japanese cedar door—before you've had a drink, tacked on tax or paid the gratuity. Chef/owner Masa Takayama creates a different dining experience each day based on market offerings. A mere shiitake mushroom, for example, is raised to shrine-worthy status. Every detail at Masa is aesthetically exquisite, from the amazing cuisine to the top-flight service.

Japanese, sushi menu. Lunch, dinner. Closed Sunday. Bar. Business casual attire. Reservations recommended. $$$$

PER SE ★ ★ ★ ★ ★

10 Columbus Circle, New York, 212-823-9335; www.perseny.com
Thomas Keller, the chef at the fabled French Laundry, calls his restaurant in the Time Warner Center "per se" because it's not exactly The French Laundry, per se. Both restaurants embrace rich copper floors, a harmonious mix of wood, marble and granite and a signature blue door. What's missing is the bucolic setting of the Napa Valley, but in its place are eye-popping views and equally incredible cooking. The best way to enjoy per se is to order the ever-changing nine-course tasting menu and settle

in for three hours of culinary surprises exemplified by small dishes such as truffles and custard in an eggshell and foie gras accompanied by various salts. Custom-made china and pristine table settings speak to the equally outstanding service details.

American, French menu. Lunch, dinner. Closed two weeks in late July-early August. Business casual attire. Reservations recommended. Valet parking. $$$$

FOUR STAR RESTUARANTS

New York

ASIATE ★ ★ ★ ★

80 Columbus Circle, New York, 212-805-8800; www.mandarinoriental.com
Asiate offers a spectacular view of Central Park and a modern Franco-Asian menu on the 35th floor of the Mandarin Oriental Hotel. World-renowned restaurant designer Tony Chi was the creative force behind this stunning space, which features a jeweled tree branch sculpture that hangs from the cathedral-styled ceiling. Like the ambience, Chef Noriyuki Sugies' inspired menu impresses even the most sophisticated traveler, borrowing from both Old Europe and New Asia. Highlights include the seafood yuzu ceviche, surf clam salad and pickled vegetables; grilled Maine lobster with cuttlefish noodles and goji berries; and chocolate fondant cake with raspberry compote.

Asian, French menu. Breakfast, lunch, dinner, brunch. Business casual attire. Reservations recommended. Valet parking. $$$$

AUREOLE ★ ★ ★ ★

34 E. 61st St., New York, 212-319-1660; www.charliepalmer.com/aureole_ny
Hidden inside an elegant brownstone on Manhattan's Upper East Side, Aureole is a luxurious space bathed in cream tones and warm lighting and furnished with overstuffed wine-colored banquettes. (An enclosed courtyard garden opens for warm-weather dining.) The restaurant is friendly and cozy and suited for just about any occasion, from couples looking for romance to colleagues seeking to have a luxe business dinner. Owner and celebrity chef Charlie Palmer offers his guests a wonderfully prepared menu of what he calls "progressive American" fare. There are always two tasting menus—one vegetarian and another inspired from the market—in addition to a parade of terrific à la carte selections. The extensive and celebrated wine program includes bold wines from California, Spain and Italy.

American menu. Lunch, dinner. Closed Sunday. Bar. Jacket required. Reservations recommended. $$$$

BOULEY ★ ★ ★ ★

120 W. Broadway, New York, 212-964-2525; www.bouleyrestaurants.com

Acclaimed chef David Bouley mans the stoves at this temple of haute French gastronomy. Housed in the renovated and impeccably decorated space that was once his more casual bistro, Bouley appeals to an epicurean-minded crowd. The elegant space is packed with well-heeled foodies, fashionistas, political pundits and celebs who understand that a night in Bouley's care is nothing short of perfection. The service is charming, the seasonal ingredients shine, the French technique is impeccable and the food is nothing short of brilliant. Indulge in the chef's canapé tasting menu or opt for succulent à la carte dishes including seared foie gras with Pruneaux d'Agen and apple-rosemary puree, and tea-smoked organic duckling with vanilla glazed baby turnips and porcini mushrooms.

French menu. Lunch, dinner. Jacket required. Reservations recommended. $$$$

COUNTRY ★ ★ ★ ★

90 Madison Ave., New York, 212-889-7100; www.countryinnewyork.com

Housed in a Beaux Arts building that includes the Carlton Hotel, this creation of chef Geoffrey Zakarian (with design by David Rockwell) combines classic Manhattan elegance with contemporary flair in both décor and cuisine. The seasonal, French-influenced menu comes in three-course pre-theater, four-course or six-course chef's tasting versions. Entrées change daily, and might include everything from Berkshire pork with apple jam, chestnut and polenta to snapper with clams and lemon. The space also includes a more casual café, which serves breakfast, lunch and dinner, as well as a Champagne lounge.

French, American menu. Breakfast, lunch, dinner. $$$

DANIEL ★ ★ ★ ★

60 E. 65th St., New York, 212-288-0033; www.danielnyc.com

Daniel is a dining experience that begins when you enter the palatial front room and continues as you sip an old-fashioned cocktail in the romantic, low-lit lounge. From there, it's on to the formal dining room where superstar chef Daniel Boulud serves sublime cooking in the most gracious of settings overflowing with flowers. Potato-crusted sea bass is a signature dish: a crisp, golden coat, fashioned from whisper-thin slices of potatoes, wraps the fish while it cooks and seals in the flavor. After dessert, there are petit fours and then the pièce de résistance: warm madeleines.

French menu. Dinner. Closed Sunday. Bar. Children's menu. Jacket required. Reservations recommended. $$$$

DANUBE ★ ★ ★ ★

30 Hudson St., New York, 212-791-3771; www.thedanube.net

Danube is the creation of David Bouley, the inspired and famed chef who has created many notable New York establishments. A stunning place to spend an evening, Danube has the feel of an old Austrian castle, with dark wood, plush banquettes and soft, warm lighting. Austrian-inspired dishes are interspersed with seasonal New American ones. Bouley's food is spectacular, though not for those who fear taking risks at dinner. The staff offers refined service, and the wine list is eclectic and extensive. As you would expect, it includes some gems from Austria.

Continental menu. Dinner. Closed Sunday. Bar. Business casual attire. Reservations recommended. $$$$

DEL POSTO ★ ★ ★ ★

85 Tenth Ave., New York, 212-497-8090; www.delposto.com
A dream team of star chefs—Joe Bastianich, Lidia Bastianich and Mario Batali—is behind this Italian restaurant, which has a menu that spans the many regions of the country and features dishes that range from classic to contemporary. The garganelli is topped with a ragú Bolognese any nonna would be proud of, while the rare tuna with bresaola is a more modern offering. The grand tasting menu (the whole table must participate in order to try it) offers seven courses and is a great way to sample the varied dishes the kitchen prepares. Service is polished and polite, and the presentation is pleasing. The enoteca serves reasonably-priced portions of the menu's more simple dishes like spaghetti and housemade gelati. Be sure to reserve a table well in advance—Del Posto requests a one-month notice.

Italian menu. Lunch, dinner. Bar. Business casual attire. Reservations recommended. $$$$

ELEVEN MADISON PARK ★ ★ ★ ★

11 Madison Ave., New York, 212-889-0905; www.elevenmadisonpark.com
Located across from the leafy, historic Madison Square Park, Danny Meyer's grand New American restaurant is a wonderful, soothing spot. The magnificent dining room boasts old-world charm with vaulted ceilings, clubby banquettes, giant floor-to-ceiling windows and warm, golden lighting. The crowd is equally stunning: a savvy blend of sexy, suited power types and chic, fashion-forward New Yorkers. The contemporary seasonal menu, created by Chef Daniel Humm, features updated American classics as well as a smart selection of dishes that borrow accents from Spain, France and Asia.

American menu. Lunch, dinner, brunch. Bar. Business casual attire. Reservations recommended. $$$

GILT ★ ★ ★ ★

455 Madison Ave., New York, 212-891-8100; www.giltnewyork.com
When the staff at New York's celebrated Le Cirque 2000 packed up their knives in 2004, foodies everywhere wondered what would take the

restaurant's place in the New York Palace Hotel's historic Villard Mansion. The answer: the opulent Gilt, whose name pays homage to the late 19th-century's Gilded Age, when the mansion was created. The 55-seat space, with carved-wood and gilded walls, cathedral ceilings and marble fireplaces, features contemporary elements that give the dining room a modern twist while retaining its historic beauty. Chef Christopher Lee's menu features New American options like crispy sea bass with chorizo, red bliss potatoes, garlic aioli, and saffron mussel broth. Wine is a large part of the experience, and Gilt offers an expansive (and expensive) selection to complement each dish on the Modern American menu.

Continental menu. Dinner. Closed Sunday-Monday. Bar. Jacket required. Reservations recommended. Valet parking. $$$$

GORDON RAMSAY AT THE LONDON ★ ★ ★ ★
151 W. 54th St., New York, 212-468-8888;
www.thelondonnyc.com/gordon_ramsay
The culinary world's mad genius now has a stateside playground in which to romp at the recently opened London NYC hotel. The menu is French influenced and sophisticated, and the room, designed by David Collins, matches that aesthetic. Chef de cuisine Josh Emmett interprets Ramsay's recipes when the star chef is away and dishes include everything from filet of beef with braised oxtail, baby onions and creamed mushrooms to pan-fried John Dory with eggplant, tomato and zucchini. Service is crisp and polished, and the wine list complements the cuisine perfectly.

French, continental. Lunch, dinner. Reservations recommended. $$$$

GOTHAM BAR & GRILL ★ ★ ★ ★
12 E. 12th St., New York, 212-620-4020; www.gothambarandgrill.com
Alfred Portale, the chef and owner of Gotham Bar and Grill, is an icon in New York's culinary circles. The leader of the "tall-food" movement and a passionate advocate of greenmarket seasonal ingredients, he has been a gastronomic force from behind the stove at his swanky, vaulted-ceilinged Gotham Bar and Grill for more than a decade. The room is loud, energetic and packed with a very stylish crowd at both lunch and dinner. The menu offers something for everyone—salad, fish, pasta, poultry, beef and game—and each dish is prepared with a bold dose of sophistication and plenty of architectural plating for extra drama.

American menu. Lunch, dinner. Bar. Casual attire. Reservations recommended. $$$

GRAMERCY TAVERN ★ ★ ★ ★
42 E. 20th St., New York, 212-477-0777; www.gramercytavern.com
Owner Danny Meyer's perpetually bustling New York eatery is warm and charming without a smidge of pretension. In the glorious, rustic main room, you can choose from a pair of seasonal tasting menus or a wide array

of equally tempting à la carte selections. The duck terrine smothered with onion and pistachio marmalade is an effusion of sweet and savory, and the smoked lobster on a bed of saffron-fennel strozzapreti and pancetta is not to be missed. If you don't have a reservation, stroll in, put your name on the list and you'll have the chance to sample some spectacular food at the bar. There's a terrific house cocktail list, too.

American menu. Lunch, dinner. Bar. Business casual attire. Reservations recommended. $$$

KAI ★ ★ ★ ★

822 Madison Ave., New York, 212-988-7277; www.itoen.com

Retreat to this restaurant and teahouse on the second floor of renowned tea merchant Ito En. Pop in for the afternoon tea featuring many of Ito En's premium teas and sweets like black sesame and green tea layered cake. It's also a good choice for lunch, for soups and dishes made with noodles, tea-scented rice, vegetables, seafood or beef. Bento boxes or sashimi are also popular choices. At dinner, order à la carte or a tasting menu such as the nine-course Iron Goddess, which features dishes like chilled puree of lily bulb soup and "live" unagi with seasonal vegetables and spicy miso.

Japanese menu. Lunch, dinner. Closed Sunday. Business casual attire. Reservations recommended. $$$

L'ATELIER DE JOËL ROBUCHON ★ ★ ★ ★

57 E. 57th St., New York, 212-758-5700; www.fourseasons.com/newyork

Housed in the Four Seasons Hotel, this offering from star French chef Joël Robuchon—his first in New York—delivers an intimate, sophisticated and unique dining experience. The name means "artist's workshop" and this concept, with outposts in Las Vegas, Paris and Tokyo, is a space for Robuchon and his well-trained staff to churn out small plates of perfectly executed culinary art. Diners sit at a 20-seat bar or at one of the 26 seats arranged around the dining room's tables and sample creations like truffled mashed potatoes or sea urchin in lobster gelée with califlower cream. Service is precise and professional, which allows the food in all its glory to take center stage.

French. Lunch, dinner. Reservations recommended. Upscale attire. $$$$

LA GRENOUILLE ★ ★ ★ ★

3 E. 52nd St., New York, 212-752-1495; www.la-grenouille.com

Housed in a former carriage house in Midtown, La Grenouille is an elegant New York classic overflowing with gorgeous flowers that mixes attentive service and beautifully prepared French fare. The floral aromas are bounteous and the deep red banquettes and gold-leaf sconces create an air of gilded fantasy. Sample the signature frog legs served sautéed Provençal style or the spectacular foie gras with sweet-sharp fig vinegar.

Those feeling less adventurous will be wowed by more standard fare including lobster and tarragon stuffed ravioli and grilled Dover sole with a mustard sauce

French menu. Lunch, dinner. Closed Sunday; also three weeks in August. Bar. Jacket required. Reservations recommended. $$$$

PICHOLINE ★ ★ ★

35 W. 64th St., New York, 212-724-8585; www.picholinenyc.com
Located on Manhattan's Upper West Side, Picholine is an obvious choice for dinner if you are attending an opera, ballet or play at Lincoln Center. But chef/owner Terrance Brennan's lovely, serene restaurant is also wonderful for any special occasion. Redesigned in 2006 to reflect the contemporary sensibilities of its tantalizing Mediterranean fare, the interior boasts hues of rich violet and boysenberry, impressive 10-foot velvet curtains and custom-made mirrors. The menu changes with the seasons, and the chef uses organic and local ingredients to create such dishes as the olive-oil poached halibut and morel and rabbit risotto.

French, Mediterranean menu. Lunch, dinner. Bar. Jacket required. Reservations recommended. $$$

SUGIYAMA ★ ★ ★

251 W. 55th St., New York, 212-956-0670; www.sugiyama-nyc.com
Zen-like, spare Sugiyama is well known for its prix fixe kaiseki-style meals (multi-course offerings that were originally part of elaborate, traditional Japanese tea ceremonies). At Sugiyama, the kaiseki dishes have evolved into a procession of beautifully presented little plates, holding small portions. Meals are tailored to suit your appetite and preferences and start with akizuke (an amuse bouche) followed by a seasonal special (zensai), soup, sashimi, sushi, salad, and beef or seafood cooked over a hot stone (ishiyaki), among other sumptuous Japanese delicacies.

Japanese menu. Dinner. Closed Sunday-Monday. Casual attire. Reservations recommended. $$$

Pocantico Hills

BLUE HILLS AT STONE BARNS ★ ★ ★

630 Bedford Rd., Pocantico Hills, 914-366-9600; www.bluehillstonebarns.com
An extension of Blue Hill restaurant in Manhattan and set in the Pocantico Hills, Blue Hill at Stone Barns is not only a restaurant, but a working farm and educational center dedicated to sustainable food production. The dining room is the former Rockefeller dairy barn, which has been converted to a lofty, modern space with vaulted ceilings, dark wood accents and earthy tones. Diners can choose three, four, or five courses from a variety of dishes such as pancetta wrapped trout or lamb with local rapini, chickpeas, and chorizo. Desserts are freshly made and hard to resist, like

the chocolate torte with salted peanuts, caramel and coffee ice cream. American menu. Dinner, Sunday lunch. Closed Monday-Tuesday. Bar. Business casual attire. Reservations recommended. $$$

Skaneateles

GIVERNY ★ ★ ★ ★

851 W. Genesee St., Skaneateles, 315-685-1927; www.mirbeau.com
Named after painter Claude Monet's French country home, this elegant dining room, under the confident direction of executive chef Edward Moro, delivers the best of Provençal cooking in a cozy, romantic setting. Try the four- or five-course tasting menu, or dine à la carte on dishes such as butter braised Maine lobster with squash risotto or sautéed foie gras with caramelized pear. The wine list includes selections from around the world, and around the corner, with local Finger Lakes wineries highlighted.

American, French menu. Breakfast, lunch, dinner. Bar. Business casual attire. Reservations recommended. Outdoor seating. $$$

FIVE STAR SPAS

New York

SPA AT MANDARIN ORIENTAL NEW YORK ★ ★ ★ ★ ★

80 Columbus Circle, New York, 212-805-8880;
www.mandarinoriental.com/newyork
This sleek hotel marries Asian sensibilities with New York panache, and its 14,500-square-foot spa is its showcase. Bamboo and natural stone are used throughout, while Chinese, Ayurvedic, Balinese and Thai healing therapies are the highlight of a visit to this facility. Signature therapies include lomi lomi massage, Chakra balancing and Thai yoga. This spa includes an Oriental tea room and a state-of-the-art fitness center, complete with a magnificent pool where swimmers can lap up the city skyline views.

FOUR STAR SPAS

New York

THE EMERSON SPA ★ ★ ★ ★

5340 Route 28, Mt. Tremper, 877-688-2828; www.emersonresort.com
This Asian-influenced upstate spa features 10 treatment rooms perfect for sampling a variety of Eastern-inspired treatments. Indian head massage, dosha balancing massage and abhyanga massage, involving two therapists in unison, are some of the bodywork offerings. Shirodhara (which

involves a stream of warm oil over the forehead) and a Bindi herbal body treatments round out the Ayurvedic menu. From aromatherapy facials and sea salt body scrubs to warm mud wraps, many of the treatments use natural ingredients for cleansing, detoxifying and healing the skin.

THE SPA AT FOUR SEASONS HOTEL NEW YORK ★ ★ ★ ★

57 E. 57th St., New York, 212-758-5700; www.fourseasons.com
Elegant, yet far from fussy, the spa at the Four Seasons mirrors the hotel's contemporary style. Try the signature Four Seasons in One treatment, which celebrates the seasons with a cooling scrub symbolizing winter, a floral body wrap for spring, a medley of massages for summer and a soothing scalp treatment for fall. In addition to shiatsu, aromatherapy and reflexology, this spa offers a full range of unique massage therapies. Facials harness the power of modern technology with microcurrent lifting, oxygen cellular renewal, and DNA molecular regeneration.

THE PENINSULA SPA, NEW YORK ★ ★ ★ ★

700 Fifth Ave., New York, 212-903-3910, 800-262-9467;
www.peninsulaspa.com
The Peninsula Spa is the embodiment of an urban oasis. The facial menu includes deep-cleansing, aromatherapy and sensitive skin treatments, while the specialty facials use June Jacobs or Valmont products. Microdermabrasion targets dull skin, while the body treatments include a papaya hydrating body mask or chai soy mud mask. Stressed-out executives head straight for the massage table to enjoy a Swedish, shiatsu, sports, deep-tissue or aromatherapy massage. Couples and pregnancy massages are also offered.

Skaneateles

SPA MIRBEAU ★ ★ ★ ★

851 W. Genesee St., Skaneateles, 315-685-5000; www.mirbeau.com
Fourteen-thousand square-feet of tranquility await at the Spa Mirbeau, where beautiful natural surroundings serve as the inspiration for everything from the herbal-infused steam rooms to body wraps and facials. After some pre-treatment relaxation in the resting area—complete with heated foot pools—you're ready to head to one of 18 treatment rooms. The Monet's Favorite Fragrance massage blends essential oils of herbs and flowers from the Finger Lakes region to create an aromatherapy treatment that stimulates the senses. The expansive fitness center offers everything from meditation to Pilates.

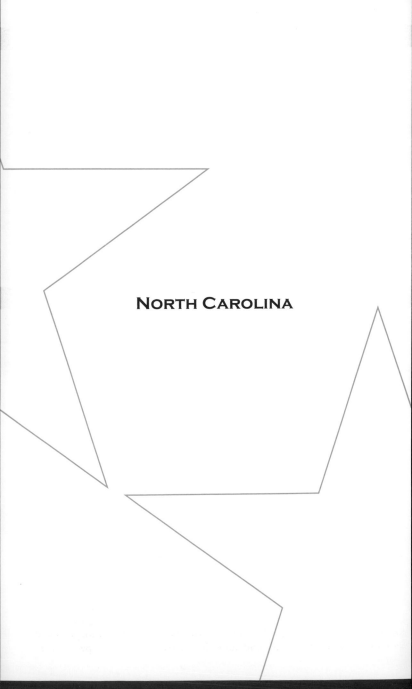

NORTH CAROLINA

North Carolina

Pittsboro

THE FEARRINGTON HOUSE COUNTRY INN ★ ★ ★ ★ ★

2000 Fearrington Village Center, Pittsboro, 919-542-2121; www.fearrington.com
The Fearrington House offers just the right mix of country style and
worldly sophistication. Part of a charming village of shops, this country
house hotel is located on Colonial-era farmland. The inn's former
incarnation as a dairy barn is evident today in the striped Galloway cows
that graze the grounds. The rooms and suites feature a country theme with
authentic details like salvaged church doors used as headboards. Canopied
beds and original art create a stylish look. Mornings start with hearty
breakfasts, while English afternoon tea curbs midday hunger pangs.

33 rooms. Children over 6 years only. Complimentary full breakfast.
High-speed Internet access. Restaurant, bar. Fitness center. Indoor pool,
outdoor pool, whirlpool. Tennis. Business center. $$$$

Asheville

INN ON BILTMORE ESTATE ★ ★ ★ ★

1 Antler Hill Rd., Asheville, 828-225-1660, 866-336-1240; www.biltmore.com
This hotel is located on the grounds of the historic Vanderbilt Biltmore
Estate, offering guests the chance to explore the same grounds that business
titan George Vanderbilt once roamed. The hotel's distinguished character
extends to its dining establishments—Bistro, Deerpark, the Dining Room
and Stable Café. Afternoon tea is a daily tradition and is served in the
library—piano music and views through the room's long windows set a
relaxing mood. The Lobby Lounge is ideal for informal meals. Carriage
rides, horseback riding and river float trips are just a few of the unique
recreational activities.

213 rooms. Wireless Internet access. Restaurant, bar. Spa. Airport
transportation available. $$$

RICHMOND HILL INN ★ ★ ★ ★

87 Richmond Hill Dr., Asheville, 828-252-7313, 800-549-9238;
www.richmondhillinn.com
Once the private home of an influential politician, the Queen Anne-style
mansion, croquet cottages and garden pavilion are set among nine acres
of formal, manicured gardens replete with waterfalls, floral displays and
a mountain brook. Rooms and suites have antiques and canopy or four-

poster beds and remarkable handcrafted woodwork. Many rooms also offer fireplaces and skylights. Enjoy delicious full country breakfasts at Ambassador's Grille before heading out to explore Asheville, the Biltmore Estate or the Blue Ridge Parkway. The restaurant, Gabrielle's, is heralded across the South for its continental menu.

37 rooms. Complimentary full breakfast. Wireless Internet access. Two restaurants, two bars. $$$

Cary

THE UMSTEAD RESORT & SPA ★ ★ ★ ★

100 Woodland Pond, Cary, 919-447-4000, 866-877-4141;
www.theumstead.com
Located in wooded suburban Cary, just outside Raleigh in the Research Triangle area, this contemporary, elegant hotel offers a full-service stylish stay. Rooms are decorated in muted neutrals and feature luxury linens, fully-stocked bars and plenty of room to spread out. The full-service Umstead Spa offers a quiet retreat after a day by the outdoor pool, or a workout in the state-of-the-art fitness center. Herons restaurant is a local favorite for its creative New American cuisine. The staff at the Umstead anticipate and meet every whim, from arranging a round of golf to suggesting the best local jogging trails.

150 rooms. Wireless Internet access. Restaurant, bar. Fitness center, spa. Pets accepted; fee. Pool. $$$

Charlotte

THE BALLANTYNE RESORT, A LUXURY COLLECTION HOTEL ★ ★ ★ ★

10000 Ballantyne Commons Pkwy., Charlotte, 704-248-4000, 866-248-4824; www.ballantyneresort.com
This elegant resort within Charlotte's city limits is a paradise for golf enthusiasts. It has one of the state's best 18-hole courses and is home to the renowned Dana Rader Golf School. Rooms are crisply and classically decorated, with lavish finishes, such as marble entrances and bathrooms. The Gallery Restaurant offers creative selections using seasonal ingredients, while the bar serves a tapas menu and lengthy selection of cocktails, whiskeys and after-dinner drinks.

249 rooms. Wireless Internet access. Restaurant, two bars. Fitness center, spa. Airport transportation available. $$

Pinehurst

THE CAROLINA HOTEL ★ ★ ★ ★

Carolina Vista Dr., Pinehurst, 910-295-6811, 800-487-4653;
www.pinehurst.com

The Carolina hotel, a National Historic Landmark, is the finest of the five different lodging venues available at Pinehurst. A dream destination for golfers with eight 18-hole courses designed by the sport's leading names, including Fazio, Jones, Maples and Ross. The 31 miles of golf at this property contain 780 bunkers and the largest number of golf holes in the world at a single resort. The Victorian-era Carolina hotel provides guests with handsomely furnished accommodations and first-class service. Two of the resort's nine restaurants and a luxurious spa are located here.

220 rooms. High-speed Internet access. Two restaurants, bar. Children's activity center. Fitness center, spa. Beach. Golf, 144 holes. Tennis. Airport transportation available. $$$

FOUR STAR RESTAURANTS

Cary

HERONS RESTAURANT AT THE UMSTEAD HOTEL ★ ★ ★ ★

100 Woodland Pond, Cary, 919-447-4200; www.theumstead.com/dining

Tucked inside a large hotel in Cary, a suburb of Raleigh/Durham, Herons puts a Southern spin on American cuisine in a fashionable setting complete with a 2500-bottle wine cellar. Cozy banquettes, original artwork and an open kitchen lend to a sense of casual sophistication. The food is seriously good, but not stuffy. Order the homemade cinnamon bun French toast with brown sugar streusel at breakfast and save room for the luscious brownie sundae baked Alaska after dinner. There's also a wellness menu designed for those participating in the hotel's spa program.

Southern/American menu. Breakfast, lunch, dinner. Bar. $$$

Chapel Hill

CAROLINA CROSSROADS ★ ★ ★ ★

211 Pittsboro St., Chapel Hill, 919-933-9277, 800-962-8519;
www.carolinainn.com

Set in the historic Carolina Inn, this restaurant is a picture-perfect example of Southern hospitality and charm. The dining room is elegant and classic, and the menu strikes delicious notes, with regional dishes incorporating local, seasonal ingredients prepared in a progressive American style. You'll find everything from a North Carolina pulled pork sandwich to dishes like salmon with grilled acorn squash in white-wine butter sauce, part of the chef's nightly six-course tasting menu.

Southern menu. Breakfast, lunch, dinner, brunch. Bar. Children's menu. Business casual attire. Reservations recommended. Valet parking. Outdoor seating. $$$

Charlotte

GALLERY RESTAURANT & BAR ★ ★ ★ ★

10000 Ballantyne Commons Pkwy., Charlotte, 704-248-4000,
866-248-4824; www.gallery-restaurant.com

The setting is relaxing and welcoming at Gallery Restaurant & Bar, located on the ground level of the Ballantyne Resort. Artfully presented dishes like cedar plank-roasted sea bass with blue crab, shallots and English pea risotto, or rosemary and citrus-roasted free-range chicken dazzle the palate, while the service makes dining here a delight. The wine list includes bottles from around the world, and the restaurant's bar is a comfortable spot for after-dinner drinks.

American menu. Breakfast, lunch, dinner. Bar. Business casual attire. Reservations recommended. Valet parking. Outdoor seating. $$$

Pittsboro

THE FEARRINGTON HOUSE RESTAURANT ★ ★ ★ ★

2000 Fearrington Village Center, Pittsboro, 919-542-2121; www.fearrington.com

This charming Victorian-style country restaurant is located on several rolling acres near Chapel Hill. The restaurant is accented with elegant antique furnishings and the food lives up to the lovely surroundings. The upscale menu is American, with techniques borrowed from France and robust flavors taken from the surrounding region. The thoughtful, seasonal menu is complemented by a deep international wine list that features close to 500 selections with a focus on California varietals.

American, French menu. Dinner. Bar. Jacket required. Reservations recommended. Valet parking. Outdoor seating. $$$

FOUR STAR SPAS

Cary

THE UMSTEAD SPA ★ ★ ★ ★

100 Woodland Pond, Cary, 919-447-4170; www.theumsteadspa.com

A tranquil, Asian-inspired space, this spa at the Umstead Hotel offers 14,000 square feet devoted to pampering treatments that run the gamut from hot stone massage to milk hydrotherapy baths. The treatment rooms epitomize understated luxury with rich creamy hues, silk draperies and soft lightening. Private spa suites, which accommodate four to six people, are perfect for parties and include access to a massage room, a color therapy tub and more. Guests receive fruit, Evian water and a bottle of Champagne. The spa also has a fitness center and salon services, and offers lunches prepared by the chefs of the renowned Herons restaurant.

Charlotte

THE SPA AT BALLANTYNE RESORT ★ ★ ★ ★

1000 Ballantyne Commons Pkwy., Charlotte, 708-241-4141;
www.ballantyneresort.com

Tucked inside Charlotte's luxurious Ballantyne Resort, this spa offers a classic pampering experience delivered by a friendly, well-trained staff. Treatments incorporate regional products made from natural and organic local ingredients, such as facials using apples and walnuts from North Carolina, or sand from thermal spring lakes. Complimentary wine and mimosas are offered with salon services, and fresh fruit-infused water is always on hand. Try the pumpkin pie or sweet wine body scrubs, which utilize pumpkin, yam, grains and muscaline grapes. The spa also offers a full range of nail and salon services.

Pinehurst

THE SPA AT PINEHURST ★ ★ ★ ★

1 Carolina Vista Dr., Pinehurst, 910-235-8320, 800-487-4653;
www.pinehurst.com

Pinehurst Resort is the setting for the refined Spa at Pinehurst. Featuring more than 40 different treatments, this spa is influenced by its southern location. Pine-inspired treatments dominate the menu, from the pine salt body rub to the exfoliating pine cream of the deluxe body treatment. The spa offers eight different massage therapies, including a special massage designed for golfers. The facials and skin care treatments target dryness, fine lines and wrinkles using botanical extracts and modern medicine.

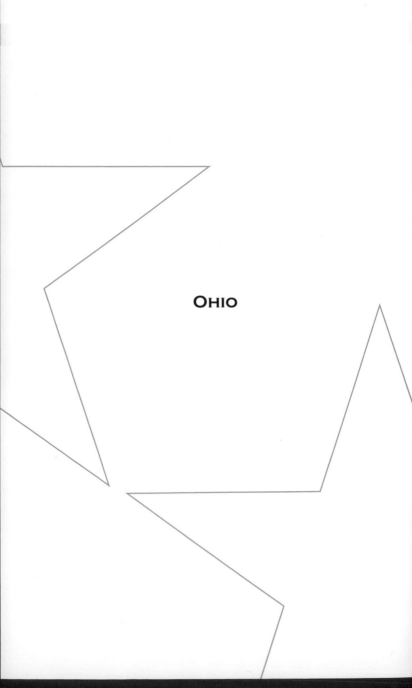

OHIO

OHIO

Cleveland

THE RITZ-CARLTON, CLEVELAND ★ ★ ★ ★

1515 W. Third St., Cleveland, 216-623-1300, 866-372-7868;
www.ritzcarlton.com

Adjacent to Cleveland's Tower City Center and close to the Cleveland
Indians' Jacobs Field, this elegant hotel offers downtown visitors a
place to stay in style. The guest rooms, with city and water views, are
luxuriously appointed, from the marble-clad bathrooms to the plush
terry robes. Even pets are pampered here, with cookies upon check-in,
a personalized water bowl and pet room-service menu (walking service is
available for a fee). All-day dining at Muse features a seafood-heavy menu
dotted with updated comfort-food like truffled macaroni and cheese.
By day, the Lobby Lounge serves afternoon tea, while in the evening live
entertainment attracts hotel guests and locals alike.

208 rooms. Pets accepted; fee. High-speed Internet access. Restaurant, two
bars. Fitness center, spa. Indoor pool, whirlpool. Airport transportation
available. Business center. $$

Cincinnati

CINCINNATIAN HOTEL ★ ★ ★ ★

601 Vine St., Cincinnati, 513-381-3000, 800-942-9000;
www.cincinnatianhotel.com

Open since 1882, the Cincinnatian hotel was one of the first hotels in
the world to have elevators and incandescent lighting and is now listed
on the National Register of Historic Places. The accommodations are
lovingly maintained and incorporate modern technology, like high-
speed Internet access and multi-line telephones. Furnishings lean toward
the contemporary, while some rooms feature balconies and fireplaces.
The eight-story atrium of the Cricket Lounge serves afternoon tea and
evening cocktails. The fine dining and impeccable service at the Palace
Restaurant make it one of the top tables in town.

146 rooms. Pets accepted. Wireless Internet access. Restaurant, bar.
Fitness center. $$

Cincinnati

JEAN-ROBERT AT PIGALL'S ★ ★ ★ ★

127 W. Fourth St., Cincinnati, 513-721-1345; www.pigalls.com

Jean-Robert at Pigall's serves the sort of inventive, high-quality food that has fans, who pay $75 for three courses, feel as though they've had a bargain. Chef Jean-Robert de Cavel reinvigorated the hoary Pigall's in 2002 with fresh, sophisticated décor and a lively new menu. The menu changes to reflect the season, but you might find things like cauliflower vichyssoise with truffles, crab and melon salad with caviar, and bacon-wrapped guinea fowl. The chef frequently comes up with surprise plates on the house.

French menu. Lunch, dinner. Closed Sunday-Monday. Bar. Business casual attire. Reservations recommended. Valet parking. $$$$

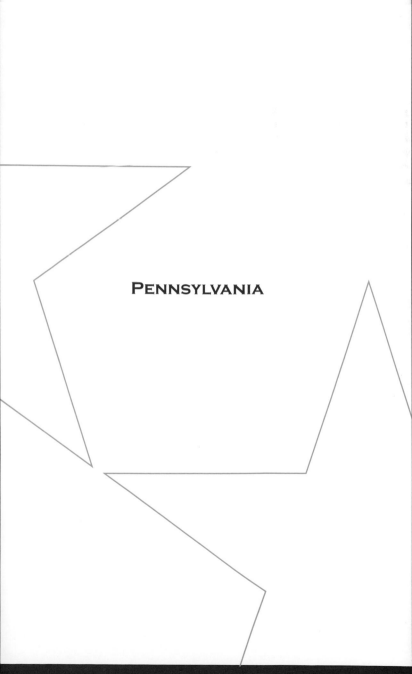

Pennsylvania

PENNSYLVANIA

Hershey

THE HOTEL HERSHEY ★ ★ ★

1 Hotel Rd., Hershey, 717-533-2171, 800-437-7439;
www.hersheys.com
Perched atop a hill overlooking town, the Hotel Hershey sits on 300 acres of formal gardens, fountains and reflecting pools. Instead of mints, you'll find chocolate kisses on your pillow at evening turndown. Recreational activities include 72 holes of golf, six miles of nature trails, basketball, volleyball, tennis courts and pools. Rest your sweet tooth with a meal at the Fountain Café, or grab snacks and light meals at the coffeehouse or fireside lounge. The Spa at Hotel Hershey is a wonderfully sinful place, with whipped cocoa baths and chocolate fondue wraps.
234 rooms. Children's activity center. Ski in/ski out. Airport transportation available. $$$

Farmington

NEMACOLIN WOODLANDS RESORT & SPA ★ ★ ★

1001 Lafayette Dr., Farmington, 724-329-8555, 866-344-6957;
www.nemacolin.com
Tucked away in Pennsylvania's scenic Laurel Highlands, this comprehensive resort offers a multitude of recreational opportunities, from the Hummer driving club, equestrian center and shooting academy, to the adventure and activities centers, culinary classes and art museums. Golfers come for the renowned golf academy and two courses. The guest accommodations at Chateau LaFayette have a European style, while the Lodge maintains a rustic charm. Families enjoy the spacious accommodations in the townhouses, while the luxury homes are perfect for group travel.
220 rooms. Children's activity center. Spa. Golf. $$$

Philadelphia

FOUR SEASONS HOTEL PHILADELPHIA ★ ★ ★

1 Logan Square, Philadelphia, 215-963-1500, 866-516-1100;
www.fourseasons.com/philadelphia
The eight-story Four Seasons located on historic Logan Square is a Philadelphia institution in itself, from its dramatic Swann Fountain to its highly rated Fountain Restaurant, considered one of the better dining establishments in town. The rooms and suites are a celebration of Federalist décor, and some accommodations incorporate deep soaking

tubs. Some rooms have city views of the Academy of Natural Science, Logan Square and the tree-lined Ben Franklin Parkway, while others offer tranquil views over the inner courtyard and gardens. The spa focuses on nourishing treatments, while the indoor pool resembles a tropical oasis with breezy palm trees and large skylights.

364 rooms. Restaurant. Fitness Center, spa. Airport transportation available. Business Center. $$$

FIVE STAR RESTAURANTS

Philadelphia

LE BEC-FIN ★ ★ ★ ★ ★

1523 Walnut St., Philadelphia, 215-567-1000; www.lebecfin.com
Still sparkling from its 2002 renovation, Georges Perrier's Le Bec-Fin, which opened in 1970, remains a shining star for haute French cuisine. The room is filled with fresh flowers, glass chandeliers, amber lighting and finely dressed tabletops. Perrier's signature crab cake with haricot verts is divine and joins an exciting menu divided between *les entrees* (appetizers); an impressive and unusual selection of *les poissons* (fish), depending on availability; and an equally terrific assortment of *les viandes* (meats), also listed according to season and availability.

French menu. Lunch, dinner. Closed Sunday. Bar. Jacket required. Reservations recommended. Valet parking. $$$$

FOUR STAR RESTAURANTS

Philadelphia

FOUNTAIN RESTAURANT ★ ★ ★ ★

1 Logan Square, Philadelphia, 215-963-1500; www.fourseasons.com/philadelphia
The Fountain is the stunning flagship restaurant of the Four Seasons Hotel Philadelphia. The wine list, which covers all of France as well as Germany, Italy, the United States, Australia, New Zealand and South America, is just one of the highlights of dining here. The kitchen often uses ingredients from local producers and includes the farms' names on the menu. As you'll see here, the best ingredients really do make a difference. Vegetarian items are available on request, and the kitchen offers several selections that are marked as healthy fare.

American, French menu. Breakfast, lunch, dinner, Sunday brunch. Bar. Children's menu. Jacket required. Reservations recommended. Valet parking. $$$

LACROIX AT THE RITTENHOUSE ★★★★

210 W. Rittenhouse Square, Philadelphia, 215-790-2533; www.rittenhousehotel.com
Set in the stately Rittenhouse Hotel, Lacroix is a restaurant of understated elegance. The kitchen plays up fresh local ingredients with a delicate French hand, while guests dine in posh, sophisticated luxury and enjoy views of the charming Rittenhouse Square. While acclaimed chef Jean-Marie Lacroix has retired, the kitchen is still in able hands under the direction of chef Matthew Levin. The flexible tasting menu is the best option here, where diners can choose three, four or five courses, and desserts are a gift from the chef. The Sunday brunch (where the buffet is set up in the kitchen) is a Philadelphia favorite.

French menu. Breakfast, lunch, dinner, Sunday brunch. Bar. Children's menu. Jacket required. Reservations recommended. Valet parking. $$$

STRIPED BASS ★★★★

1500 Walnut St., Philadelphia, 215-732-4444; www.stripedbassrestaurant.com
Set in a former brokerage house, Striped Bass boasts towering 28-foot ceilings, red marble columns and an open kitchen. The menu showcases virtually every fish in the sea, and magnificent raw bar tempts diners with briny oysters, sweet clams and plump, juicy shrimp. Be sure to go for the raw fish selection: a shimmering array of tartars, ceviches and carpaccios deliciously tinged with Asian, Latin American and Italian flavors.

Seafood menu. Dinner. Bar. Business casual attire. Reservations recommended. Valet parking. $$$

FOUR STAR SPAS

Farmington

WOODLANDS SPA AT NEMACOLIN RESORT ★★★★

1001 LaFayette Dr., Farmington, 724-329-8555, 800-422-2736;
www.nemacolin.com
Famed interior designer Clodagh created the look of this spa using natural materials and the guiding properties of feng shui. Achieving inner tranquility is the mission here, and the treatments embrace this guiding principle. An extensive massage menu includes favorites such as Swedish, sports, aromatherapy, shiatsu and deep tissue as well as Eastern methods such as reflexology and reiki. The body scrubs include everything from Japanese citrus and Balinese hibiscus to German chamomile and Greek mint. The on-site spa restaurant offers tasty healthy treats.

RHODE ISLAND

Rhode Island

Providence

MILL'S TAVERN ★ ★ ★ ★

101 N. Main St., Providence, 401-272-3331

The chefs at Mills Tavern have a knack for improving on the classics. From its smart design and energetic vibe to its appealing menu, this winning restaurant housed in a former mill turns tradition on its head. The menu echoes the classic-contemporary sentiment with a wide variety of creatively prepared American seasonal dishes, many utilizing the kitchen's wood-burning oven, wood grill and rotisserie. The warm, knowledgeable staff provides professional and thorough service without being stuffy or intrusive.

Contemporary American menu. Dinner. Bar. Business casual attire. Reservations recommended. Valet parking. $$$

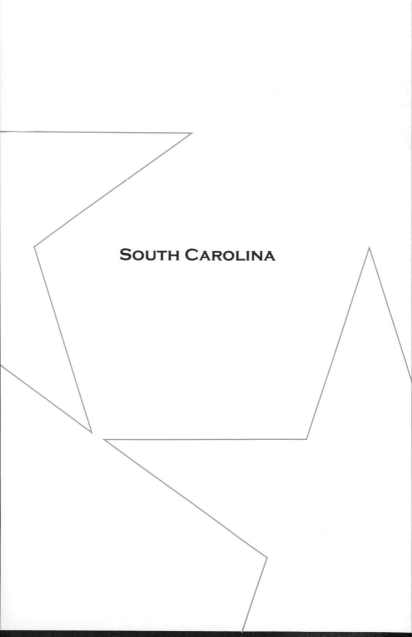

SOUTH CAROLINA

SOUTH CAROLINA

Summerville

THE SANCTUARY HOTEL AT KIAWAH ISLAND ★ ★ ★ ★ ★

1 Sanctuary Beach Dr., Kiawah Island, 843-768-6000, 877-683-1234;
www.thesanctuary.com

With five championship courses just outside the door, the Sanctuary Hotel at Kiawah Island is a natural choice for golfers. But this elegant seaside mansion resort appeals to a wide range of travelers with its fine dinning, first-class spa and beautiful setting. Separate outdoor adult and family pools attract couples looking for a romantic getaway as well as family vacationers. The rooms blend traditional early-American furnishings including handcrafted armoires and custom-made beds, with a crisp coastal ambience, and showcase ocean views from spacious balconies. Start the day with a workout at the state-of-the-art fitness center which offers personal training, hydro-toning classes and weight equipment. The service is impeccable and a friendly, gracious staff attends to your every need.

255 rooms. Wireless Internet access. Three restaurants, three bars. Children's activity center. Fitness center, spa. Beach. Indoor pool, children's pool, whirlpool. Airport transportation available. $$$$

WOODLANDS RESORT & INN ★ ★ ★ ★ ★

125 Parsons Rd., Summerville, 843-875-2600, 800-774-9999;
www.woodlandsinn.com

This country estate is a lovely retreat just down the road from some of the Low Country's most famous plantations and only minutes from historic Charleston. The 1906 Greek Revival Main House has casual, refined and lavishly appointed guest rooms designed by interior designer David Eskell-Briggs. Many rooms flaunt opulent sitting areas and romantic fireplaces, heated towel bars and rejuvenating whirlpool baths. Guests can take a dip in the pool, volley on the two clay tennis courts, play croquet matches on the lawn and ride bikes to the nearby town of Summerville. Sandalwoods Day Spa features Aveda products in all of its treatments. The Dining Room turns out delicious dishes in a cozy space.

19 rooms. Pets accepted. Restaurant, bar. Children's activity center. Outdoor pool. Tennis. Airport transportation available. Business center. $$$

Charleston

CHARLESTON PLACE ★ ★ ★ ★

205 Meeting St., Charleston, 843-722-4900, 800-611-5545;
www.charlestonplace.com

Located in Charleston's historic district, this hotel puts antebellum mansions, luscious gardens and colonial markets within an easy stroll. Guest rooms are a perfect blend of Southern tradition and modern convenience, with classic, colonial furnishings and elegant marble baths alongside high speed Internet access, executive desks and data ports. A fitness center and spa replete with a sauna, Jacuzzi and steam room allow for sumptuous R&R, and a beautiful indoor/outdoor heated pool with retractable roof guarantees year-round enjoyment. From Godiva to Gucci to St. John, upscale shopping is only steps from the lobby, making this a perfect base for travelers who appreciate posh retail therapy.

440 rooms. High-speed Internet access. Two restaurants, two bars. Fitness center, spa. $$$

THE INN AT PALMETTO BLUFF ★ ★ ★ ★

476 Mount Pilla Rd., Bluffton, 843-706-6500, 866-706-6565;
www.palmettobluffresort.com

This Low Country inn, a sister to California's famed Auberge du Soleil, delivers luxury accommodations, fine dining and pure relaxation in a gorgeous riverfront setting. Rooms are loaded with luxury touches such as plasma televisions, wet bars with Sub-Zero refrigerators and deep soaking tubs. Play the Jack Nicklaus-designed golf course or relax at the full-service spa. The River House restaurant serves Southern-influenced recipes like she crab bisque laced with aged sherry or cast iron fried quail with bacon, eggs, arugula and warm ricotta pudding.

50 rooms, all suites. Restaurant, bar. Fitness Center, spa. Pool. $$$$

Summerville

THE DINING ROOM AT WOODLANDS ★ ★ ★ ★ ★

125 Parsons Rd., Summerville, 843-308-2115, 800-774-9999;
www.woodlandsinn.com

This elegant European-style restaurant is accented with cherry wood furnishings, cream-colored walls, a marble fireplace and white linen tables topped with fine crystal and floral-print china. Perfecting the atmosphere of Southern charm, chef Tarver King and his staff offer menus that change daily and feature flavorful, regional American dishes. Standouts include hay-smoked duckling with crispy pomme darphin, or Maine lobster with morels and English pea-acquerello risotto.Wine pairings by sommelier Stephane Peltier and desserts like chocolate napoleon with fleur de sel caramel round out the experience.

American menu. Breakfast, lunch, dinner, Sunday brunch. Bar. Jacket required at dinner. Reservations recommended. Valet parking. Outdoor seating. $$$$

FOUR STAR RESTAURANTS

Charleston

CHARLESTON GRILL ★ ★ ★ ★

224 King St., Charleston, 843-577-4522; www.charlestongrill.com
The Charleston Grill is a clubby spot located in the Charleston Place Hotel. Stained-glass French doors, dark wood-paneled walls and marble floors create a classy, old-world atmosphere. Dishes like shrimp and catfish hoecakes with fried oysters and tartar remoulade provide a hint of the kind of low-country fare served at this sophisticated restaurant. It's worth inquiring about special wines that may not be on the extensive wine list, as the owners make frequent purchases at auctions, and unusual bottles are often nabbed and saved for guests.

American menu. Dinner. Bar. Children's menu. Business casual attire. Reservations recommended. Valet parking. Outdoor seating. $$$$

CIRCA 1886 ★ ★ ★ ★

149 Wentworth St., Charleston, 843-853-7828; www.circa1886.com
Located behind the historic Wentworth Mansion, this restaurant offers classic Charleston charm. The 280-bottle wine list complements the local cuisine on the menu, which is created by chef Marc Collins using regional ingredients. Try the Carolina crabcake soufflé, a cheese course made from Appalachian raw cow's milk cheese, or catfish with lobster and white cheddar grits. Desserts are traditional and rich, from gingerbread pudding with orange blossom honey ice cream to sweet potato butterscotch soufflé. The staff is polished and friendly, and the classic presentation of each dish adds an elegant flourish to the meal.

American menu. Dinner. Closed Sunday. Bar. Business casual attire. Reservations recommended. Valet parking. $$$

PENINSULA GRILL ★ ★ ★ ★

112 N. Market St., Charleston, 843-723-0700; www.peninsulagrill.com
Located in the Planter's Inn, Peninsula Grill is a place where the words fun and fine dining can easily be used in the same sentence. This restaurant has the sophisticated feel of an urban eatery without losing sight of its Southern charm. The menu is inventive, offering boldly flavored dishes

spiced up with low-country accents like collards, hushpuppies, grits and black-eyed peas. Chef Robert Carter's famous coconut layer cake is worth the calories. There's also a Champagne bar menu of decadent little treats like oysters, lobster, foie gras, caviar and duck pâté to pair with glasses of bubbly.

American menu. Dinner. Bar. Business casual attire. Reservations recommended. Outdoor seating. $$$

Kiawah Island

OCEAN ROOM ★ ★ ★ ★

1 Sanctuary Beach Dr., Kiawah Island, 843-768-6253, 877-683-1234; www.thesanctuary.com

The staff at this elegant restaurant charms guests with Southern hospitality and friendly yet unobtrusive service. Offering breathtaking views of the golf course and the ocean, the dining rooms exude sophistication and old-world opulence with rich walnut floors and custom mahogany wine racks. Plates sparkle with New American dishes such as seared Hudson Valley foie gras with sautéed snow peas, sweet soy and snow pea sorbet, or seared rare ahi tuna with crispy shrimp dumplings, wilted wasabi leaves and lavender-scented jasmine rice. If you're feeling especially indulgent, you can order a side of the Iranian ossetra caviar, priced at $220 per ounce.

Seafood menu. Dinner. Bar. Jacket required. Reservations recommended. $$$

FIVE STAR SPAS

Kiawah Island

SPA AT THE SANCTUARY ★ ★ ★ ★ ★

1 Sanctuary Beach Dr., Kiawah Island, 843-768-6340; www.thesanctuary.com

Located inside the Sanctuary at Kiawah Island, the Spa resembles a grand Southern seaside mansion. The hospitable staff greet guests with herbal tea and fresh fruit before leading the way to one of 12 rooms for nature-based treatments, which feature botanical extracts and natural enzymes. The Low Country verbena body polish uses fresh lemon verbena and mild buffing grains of ruby grapefruit and blood orange extracts to hydrate skin. If exercise is on your mind, head downstairs to the fitness center. This ultra-modern facility features the latest cardiovaular and resistance equipment, a 65-foot-long indoor pool and Pilates and yoga studios.

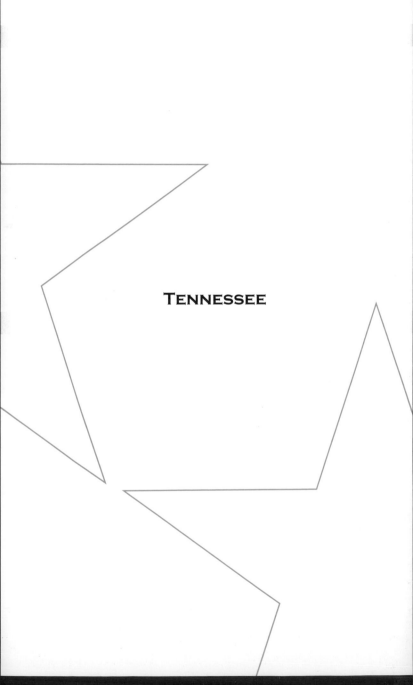

TENNESSEE

TENNESSEE

Nashville

THE HERMITAGE HOTEL ★ ★ ★ ★

231 Sixth Ave. N., Nashville, 615-244-3121, 888-888-9414;
www.thehermitagehotel.com

The Hermitage Hotel is the Grand Dame of Nashville's hotels. Opened in 1910 and renovated in 2003, this glorious downtown hotel offers white-glove service and plenty of opportunities to indulge. Its lobby is magnificent, with vaulted ceilings of stained glass, arches decorated with frescoes and intricate stonework. The spacious guest rooms are filled with elegant traditional furnishings, creating a warm and welcoming atmosphere. On the lower level, you'll find the Capitol Grille, one of Nashville's best restaurants. The adjacent Oak Bar, with its emerald green club chairs and dark wood paneling, is a top spot for relaxing before or after dinner.

122 rooms. Wireless Internet access. Restaurant, bar. Spa. Business center. $$$

Memphis

THE PEABODY MEMPHIS ★ ★ ★ ★

149 Union Ave., Memphis, 901-529-4000, 800-732-2639;
www.peabodymemphis.com

The Peabody is a Memphis landmark that's perhaps best known for the ducks that march twice daily through the lobby to splash in the hotel's fountain. This grand hotel is also well known as a shopping destination and as the home of Lansky's, Elvis's favorite clothing store. The hotel's impressive array of amenities include a comprehensive health club, indoor pool and Gould's Day Spa and Salon. The hotel's popular Capriccio Restaurant, Bar & Café serves delicious Italian dishes, while Chez Philippe adds a twist to traditional French cuisine.

464 rooms. Wireless Internet access. Two restaurants, two bars. Fitness center, spa. Airport transportation available.

Walland

BLACKBERRY FARM ★ ★ ★ ★

1471 W. Millers Cove Rd., Walland, 37886, 865-984-8166;
www.blackberryfarm.com

On a 4,200-acre estate in the foothills of Tennessee's Smoky Mountains, Blackberry Farm is one of the South's most celebrated country inns. Those in the know commend its exquisite location, first-rate service and delicious food. (The inn produces its own cheese, eggs, honey, vegetables and fruit for its guests.). The property's two ponds and stream beckon anglers who travel here solely for the Orvis-endorsed fly fishing. Other diversions include horseback riding, swimming, hiking and tennis. Epicureans savor the regionally inspired haute cuisine. Housed in a charming 1870s farmhouse, the Aveda Concept Spa offers signature treatments using local blackberries to soothe and rejuvenate the body.

44 rooms. Children over 10 years only, excluding holidays. Restaurant. Airport transportation available. $$$

FOUR STAR RESTAURANTS

Memphis

CHEZ PHILIPPE ★ ★ ★ ★

149 Union Ave., Memphis, 901-529-4188, 800-732-2639;
www.peabodymemphis.com

For more than a decade, this sexy, sophisticated restaurant located in the historic Peabody Hotel has been a favorite of foodies, movie stars, celebrity chefs and well-heeled locals. Like clockwork, the crowds show up every evening, filling Chez Philippe's stunning dining room for the opportunity to feast on the culinary artwork on display. The service is efficient and unobtrusive, and the atmosphere is hushed, elegant and refined. Chef Reinaldo Alfonso applies simple, seasonal ingredients to the delicate dishes of French and Asian origin, occasionally accented with regional flair. Leave room for dessert—especially for one of the soufflés.

French menu. Dinner. Closed Sunday-Monday. Business casual attire. Reservations recommended. Valet parking. $$$

Nashville

CAPITOL GRILLE ★ ★ ★ ★

231 Sixth Ave. N., Nashville, 615-345-7116; www.thehermitagehotel.com

Near the state capitol, the Grille hosts power lunches, but it's also a popular spot for theater-goers who want to enjoy a fine meal before a show at the nearby Tennessee Performing Arts Center. Executive Chef Tyler Brown oversees the creation of creative Southern cuisine. The menu is different each week, and includes such dishes as Niman Ranch pork with sweet potato juice and veal loin with root vegetables. Truffle mac and cheese and spicy fried green tomato with spicy pepper relish are just a few of the restaurant's irresistible side dishes, and desserts like flourless chocolate ganache torte end the evening on a perfect note. Located downstairs in the historic Hermitage Hotel, this Southern-influenced restaurant offers a different menu each week.

American, Southern menu. Breakfast, lunch, dinner, late-night, Sunday brunch. Bar. Children's menu. Business casual attire. Reservations recommended. Valet parking. $$$

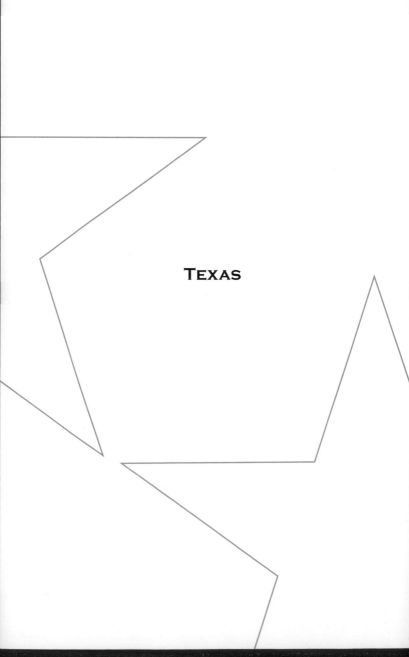

TEXAS

Texas

Dallas

ROSEWOOD MANSION ON TURTLE CREEK ★ ★ ★ ★ ★

2821 Turtle Creek Blvd., Dallas, 214-559-2100, 888-767-3966;
www.mansiononturtlecreek.com

This 1920s Italian-Renaissance mansion, once a private home, retains the ambience of a distinguished residence. Refined accommodations feature French doors that open to private balconies, and some have marble fireplaces. From the business and fitness centers to the salon and outdoor pool, this hotel delivers a comfortable experience. The tradition of a gentlemen's club is alive at the bar, where hunting trophies decorate the hunter green walls, while the Pool Terrace is perfect for light fare. No visit to Dallas is complete without a meal at the Restaurant, where sophisticated Southwestern cuisine is served in a magnificent setting.

143 rooms. Pets accepted, some restrictions; fee. High-speed Internet access. Restaurant, bar. Fitness center, spa. Outdoor pool, whirlpool. Business center. $$$

Austin

FOUR SEASONS HOTEL AUSTIN ★ ★ ★ ★

98 San Jacinto Blvd., Austin, 512-478-4500, 800-819-5053;
www.fourseasons.com/austin

This hotel is located in the rolling hills of Austin overlooking Town Lake. The lobby is decorated with a nod to Texas culture (think cowhide-covered sofas) while the guest rooms feature comfortable beds, plush terry robes and DVD players. Trio restaurant serves creative cuisine influenced by the Texas setting and presented with contemporary flair. Hike or bike the Town Hill Lake trail, adjacent to the property, or hit the fitness center for the yoga classes and outdoor pool.

291 rooms. Restaurant, bar. Fitness center. Outdoor pool, whirlpool. Business center. $$$

Houston

FOUR SEASONS HOTEL HOUSTON ★ ★ ★ ★

1300 Lamar St., Houston, 713-650-1300, 800-332-3442;
www.fourseasons.com

Close to the George R. Brown Convention Center and the Toyota Center, this hotel's downtown location makes it a favorite among business travelers.

The guest rooms are a sophisticated blend of European furniture, Asian decorative objects and Southwestern panache. The outdoor pool, fitness center and spa give the hotel the feel of a resort placed in the middle of the city. Guests can sample tequila, wine and tapas in the Lobby Lounge. Quattro serves delicious Italian cuisine.

404 rooms. Pets accepted, some restrictions. High-speed Internet access. Restaurant, two bars. Fitness center, spa. Outdoor pool, whirlpool. Airport transportation available. Business center. $$$

HOTEL GRANDUCA ★ ★ ★ ★

1080 Uptown Park Blvd., Houston, 713-418-1000, 888-472-6382;
www.granducahouston.com

Staying at the Hotel Granduca is like traveling to Italy without breaking out the passport. From its pastel-colored exterior to its striking interior design, this lovely hotel blends old-world style with new-world amenities. Hotel Granduca may feel like a secluded resort with its quiet sophistication, yet this hotel has a prime location in Houston's Uptown neighborhood. The services—from chauffeurs and personal trainers to a lovely heated outdoor pool—are impressive. Just like a grand private residence, the veranda, conservatory and clubroom are among the many spots to dine.

126 rooms, all suites. Wireless Internet access. Pool. Restaurant. $$$$

ST. REGIS HOTEL, HOUSTON ★ ★ ★ ★

1919 Briar Oaks Lane, Houston, 713-840-7600, 877-787-3447;
www.stregis.com/houston

The St. Regis, located in Houston's tony River Oaks section, has a prime location near the city's best shopping at the Galleria. The guest rooms have rich mahogany furnishings, Pratesi linens, pillowtop beds and Remède bath products. The climate-controlled outdoor pool is ideal for lounging. The quality seafood and steaks at Remington Restaurant make for a memorable dining experience.

232 rooms. Pets accepted, some restrictions; fee. High-speed Internet access. Restaurant, bar. Fitness center, spa. Outdoor pool. Airport transportation available. Business center. $$$

Irving

FOUR SEASONS RESORT AND CLUB DALLAS AT LAS COLINAS ★ ★ ★ ★

4150 N. MacArthur Blvd., Irving, 972-717-0700, 800-332-3442;
www.fourseasons.com

The Four Seasons Resort and Club Dallas at Las Colinas is only moments from downtown Dallas, yet it feels a million miles away. Set on 400 secluded acres, the resort is a sports paradise. Though the Tournament Players Golf Course is undergoing renovations, the resort has several pools, while the Sports Club's spa offers a variety of massages and treatments. The elegant guest rooms are spacious and decorated in soothing, muted tones and feature small balconies or patios that overlook the golf courses or the surrounding Cottonwood Valley.

397 rooms. High-speed Internet access. Three restaurants, bar. Children's activity center. Fitness center, fitness classes available, spa. Indoor pool, outdoor pool, children's pool, whirlpool. Golf, 36 holes. Tennis. Airport transportation available. Business center. Pets accepted, some restrictions. $$$$

San Antonio

THE WATERMARK HOTEL & SPA ★ ★ ★ ★

212 W. Crockett St., San Antonio, 210-396-5800, 866-605-1212;
www.watermarkhotel.com

This property, housed in a building that once served as a saddlery, provides plush accommodations and a world-class spa. Guest rooms and suites are handsomely appointed with iron four-poster beds, colonial furnishings and distinctive local artwork. The rooftop pool is a relaxing spot with great views, and the adjacent café serves breakfast and lunch. Pesca on the River spotlights international seafood in a dazzling contemporary space. The Watermark Spa offers a comprehensive, nature-inspired treatment menu.

98 rooms. Pets accepted, some restrictions; fee. High-speed Internet access. Two restaurants, two bars. Fitness center, fitness classes available, spa. Outdoor pool, whirlpool. Airport transportation available. $$$

FIVE STAR RESTAURANTS

Brenham

INN AT DOS BRISAS ★ ★ ★ ★ ★

604 Brazos St., Brenham, 512-474-5911, 800-252-9367; www.driskillgrill.com

There is definitely rest for the weary at the lovely Inn at Dos Brisas, set in the picturesque Texas countryside. This peaceful place reminds visitors that rustic relaxation doesn't have to come without sophisticated comforts, and gourmet dining at the Dining Room is one of the highlights of a visit. Others come simply for dinner, where the chef prepares masterful creations, many sourced from the inn's own organic gardens. The haute cuisine is a little bit French and a little bit country—poached pheasant with black-eyed pea cassoulet, chilled lobster with Texas Rio-star grapefruit—and there are more than 3,500 different vintages to complement each dish.

American menu. Dinner. Closed Sunday-Monday. Bar. Business casual attire. Reservations recommended. Valet parking. $$$

Dallas

ABACUS ★ ★ ★ ★

4511 McKinney Ave., Dallas, 214-559-3111;www.abacus-restaurant.com

A lively young crowd gathers at Abacus, a modern space that could easily make the top restaurant designers in the country swoon. To match the stylish garnet dining room, the kitchen, led by chef/owner Kent Rathbun, offers a vibrant selection of contemporary global fare that incorporates the flavors of the Mediterranean, Southwest and Pacific Rim. The signature lobster-scallion shooters—small fried lobster dumplings served in sake cups with a red chile and coconut sake sauce—are a memorable treat.

International/Fusion menu. Dinner. Closed Sunday. Bar. Business casual attire. Reservations recommended. Valet parking. $$$

NANA ★ ★ ★ ★

2201 Stemmons Frwy., Dallas, 214-761-7470; www.nanarestaurant.com

Nana, located on the 27th floor of the Hilton Anatole, is one of Dallas's top spots for creative cocktails and inspired modern American cuisine. The chef's whimsical creations include a carrot, pineapple and ginger "float" with foie gras mousse, and oysters with green apple sorbet. Decorated with priceless Asian art from the private collection of Margaret and Trammel Crow, the room feels like a posh art gallery, especially when filled to capacity with its chic crowd of urban regulars. Diners often stick around into the late hours and work off dinner on the dance floor, where live jazz is featured nightly.

American menu. Dinner. Bar. Business casual attire. Reservations recommended. Valet parking. $$$

STEPHAN PYLES ★ ★ ★ ★

1807 Ross Ave., Dallas, 214-580-7000; www.stephanpyles.com

Stephan Pyles has come a long way since his youth when he rolled tamales at his family's truck stop. The chef has created 14 restaurants and garnered numerous accolades for his Southwestern cuisine. Prominently located in the Dallas Arts District, the interior smoothly blends modern architecture with soft regional accents such as warm desert hues and terra-cotta brick. The dinner menu includes dishes such as coriander-cured rack of lamb with Ecuadorian potato cake and cranberry mojo. An imaginative wine list features an extensive selection of imported and domestic wines by the glass and half-bottle.

Southwestern menu. Lunch, dinner. Closed Sunday. Bar. Business casual attire. Reservations recommended. Valet parking. Outdoor seating. $$$

THE FRENCH ROOM ★ ★ ★ ★

1321 Commerce St., Dallas, 214-742-8200; www.hoteladolphus.com

Located in the elegant Hotel Adolphus, the French Room is a charming spot for sophisticated Gallic fare. Softly lit by hand-blown crystal chandeliers, the exquisite mural-clad arched ceiling and gilt moldings create an ambiance of opulent rococo splendor. Executive chef Jason Weaver melds classic French culinary techniques with modern American tastes, and builds three-course prix fixe menus with classics such as rack of lamb with whipped potatoes and roasted garlic mint jam. Desserts range from vanilla and cherry crème brulée to classic tarte tatin of apple and quince.

French menu. Dinner. Closed Sunday-Monday; also first two weeks of July. Bar. Jacket required. Reservations recommended. Valet parking. $$$$

Houston

QUATTRO ★ ★ ★ ★

1300 Lamar St., Houston, 713-650-1300; www.fourseasons.com

Contemporary Italian-American cuisine is the focus at Quattro, the ultramodern restaurant in the Four Seasons Hotel Houston. After a recent makeover, the space now features both lipstick-red, leather-upholstered and vibrant, jewel-toned stained-glass paneled walls. Despite the buzz at the bar, the dining room maintains a sense of calm, and the food remains a top priority. The kitchen focuses on local, seasonal ingredients and the food is as visually alluring as the space.

American, Italian menu. Breakfast, lunch, dinner, late-night, Sunday brunch. Bar. Children's menu. Business casual attire. Reservations recommended. Valet parking. $$$

San Antonio

LE RÊVE ★ ★ ★ ★

152 E. Pecan St., San Antonio, 210-212-2221; www.restaurantlereve.com

Located just above the River Walk, Le Rêve is a charming restaurant that serves innovative French cuisine. It may be tiny, with only 14 tables, but the feel is intimate, not claustrophobic. Chef and owner Andrew Weissman deftly contrasts textures, flavors and spices, always keeping the complete dish in graceful balance. Indulge in the eight-course tasting menu with a wine pairing or choose from the three-, four- or five-course prix fixe menus. The wine list is equally as exciting, with several half bottles, magnums and wine flights available.

French menu. Dinner. Closed Sunday and Monday; also two weeks in January and August. Jacket required. Reservations recommended. Valet parking. $$$$

Austin

THE SPA AT FOUR SEASONS AUSTIN ★★★★

98 San Jacinto Blvd., Austin, 512-685-8300; www.fourseasons.com/austin
Contemporary and colorful, this 5,500-square-foot spa inside the Four
Seasons Austin offers a full range of pampering treatments including
wraps, massages, facials and pedicures. Using the beautiful lakeside setting
as inspiration, a trickling water wall and natural design accents promote
total serenity and relaxation. Signature services include the Yellow Rose
of Texas wrap, which begins with a lavender sea salt scrub, followed by a
lavender-lemongrass body butter wrap and concludes with a head-to-toe
massage. The men's treatment menu includes a natural spice body buff
and a men's manicure with hand massage.

Houston

TRELLIS, THE SPA AT THE HOUSTONIAN ★★★★

111 N. Post Oak Lane, Houston, 713-685-6790, 800-378-4010;
www.trellisspa.com
Popular with hotel guests and locals alike, this Mediterranean-style spa
focuses on beauty and well-being by offering a variety of European-
inspired treatments. The power of water is paramount at the 17,000-
square-foot facility with Vichy showers, hydrotherapy pools and an
indoor float pool extending the width of the first floor. Relax with a
Swedish, stone or aromatic massage. Active contouring helps reduce
unwanted cellulite, while the body bronzing treatment adds a healthy glow
to skin. The Absolute Pearl facial uses real crushed pearl powder, as well
as mulberry and licorice botanical extracts.

Irving

THE SPA & SALON AT THE FOUR SEASONS RESORT AND CLUB DALLAS AT LAS COLINAS ★★★★

4150 N. MacArthur Blvd., Irving, 972-717-0700, 800-332-3442;
www.fourseasons.com
Texas may seem like a place where bigger is always better, but at this spa, it's
the little things that count. During a detoxifying pumpkin enzyme facial,
every detail is thought of as therapists provide a supplementary hand and
arm massage. Cool water and frosty, Texas-appropriate root beers are
offered upon check-in. The spa menu features a thoughtful collection
of therapies designed just for men, including the gentlemen's hot towel
facial and the cowboy shiner soak. The Texas two-step treatment features

a smoothing blue corn body polish followed by stimulating massage with sagebrush to soothe muscle soreness.

San Antonio

WATERMARK SPA @ WATERMARK HOTEL & SPA
★ ★ ★ ★

212 W. Crockett St., San Antonio, 210-396-5840, 800-830-1500;
www.watermarkhotel.com

Feminine without being frilly, this spa has a cool, fresh décor and a menu of treatments that use natural essential oil-based products. Signature body treatments include gentle citrus scrubs, mesquite scrubs and purple sage salt glows, along with mesquite clay body wraps, aloe skin quenchers, and avocado lime blossom scalp and body treatments. The Watermark Restoration massage begins with a Spanish rosemary massage and is followed by the application of yucca, a plant beloved by Native Americans for its healing properties. Men are particularly pampered at the Watermark, with a special menu that includes clarifying back treatments and rescue facials.

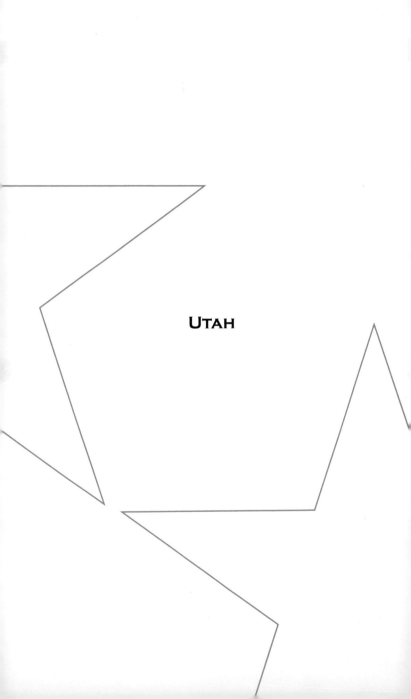

UTAH

Utah

Park City

STEIN ERIKSEN LODGE ★ ★ ★ ★ ★

7700 Stein Way, Park City, 435-649-3700, 800-453-1302;
www.steinlodge.com

Nestled mid-mountain at Utah's Deer Valley ski resort, this Scandinavian masterpiece enjoys a magnificent alpine setting and offers visitors unparalleled levels of service. Heated sidewalks and walkways will keep you toasty, while the ski valet service will take care of all your needs on the slopes. The dining is outstanding, and the Sunday Jazz Brunch and Skiers Lunch Buffet are local sensations. The blazing fireplace and inviting ambience of the Troll Hallen Lounge make it a cozy spot for après-ski or light fare. Guests rest weary muscles at the spa, work out at the well-equipped fitness center or unwind in the year-round outdoor heated pool. Rooms are distinctive but all feature jetted tubs; suites have gourmet kitchens, stone fireplaces and master bedrooms.

175 rooms. Wireless Internet access. Restaurant, bar. Children's activity center. Outdoor pool, whirlpool. Ski in/ski out. Airport transportation available. Fitness center, spa. Business center. $$$$

Salt Lake City

THE GRAND AMERICA HOTEL ★ ★ ★ ★

555 S. Main St., Salt Lake City, 801-258-6000, 800-621-4505;
www.grandamerica.com

Set against the beautiful backdrop of the Wasatch Mountains, the Grand America is a tribute to the glory of old-world Europe. This esteemed hotel is the pinnacle of refinement with thoughtful details at every turn, from hand-sewn English wool carpets to immaculately manicured landscaping in the garden courtyard. Guest rooms are classically French with plush carpets, luxurious fabrics, fine art and Richelieu furniture. The spacious Italian marble bathrooms include cozy robes and lavish soaking tubs. The world-class spa is a sanctuary and provides a full-service salon. Both the indoor and outdoor pools are spectacular.

775 rooms. High-speed Internet access. Restaurant, two bars. Spa. Airport transportation available. $$$

FOUR STAR RESTAURANTS

Park City

RIVERHORSE ON MAIN ★ ★ ★ ★

540 Main St., Park City, 435-649-3536; www.riverhorsegroup.com
Even ski bunnies (and bums) must eat, and when they do, they come to
Riverhorse on Main, a bustling, happening scene. Located in the renovated
historic Masonic Hall on Main Street, this modern restaurant, with dark
woods, soft candlelight and fresh flowers offers lots of scrumptious Asian-
inspired eats such as chicken satay, shrimp potstickers, crispy duck salad,
macadamia-crusted halibut, grilled lobster tail and charred rack of lamb.
American menu. Dinner. Children's menu. Business casual attire.
Reservations recommended. Outdoor seating. $$$

THE GLITRETIND ★ ★ ★ ★

7700 Stein Way, Park City, 435-645-6455;
www.steinlodge.com
The celebrated Stein Ericksen Lodge claims not only the most impressive
views of the Wasatch Mountains, but one of the most lauded restaurants
in Utah as well. Executive chef Zane Holmquist prepares delicious New
American cuisine. Try the scallop and lobster burger or the loin of
organic Utah lamb. The wine selection is also impressive. Managed by
sommelier Cara Schwindt, the selection houses more than 350 types of
wine that total more than 8,000 bottles. The restaurant also provides a
wide selection of dessert and after-dinner drinks, including single malt
scotch, bourbon, Cognac and brandy.
American menu. Breakfast, lunch, dinner, late-night, Sunday brunch.
Bar. Children's menu. Business casual attire. Reservations recommended.
Valet parking. Outdoor seating. $$$

FOUR STAR SPAS

Park City

THE SPA AT STEIN ERIKSON LODGE ★ ★ ★ ★

7700 Stein Way, Park City, 435-649-6475; www.steinlodge.com
The Spa at Stein Eriksen Lodge was designed to appeal to guests
needing remedies for sore and tired muscles after skiing or those affected
by the resort's high altitude. All spa services grant complimentary use of
the fitness center, steam room, sauna, whirlpool and relaxation room.
Vichy showers and kurs are special treats at this European-style spa. The
extensive massage menu includes Swedish, deep tissue, aromatic, stone,
reflexology and a special massage for mothers-to-be. In-room massages
are available for additional privacy.

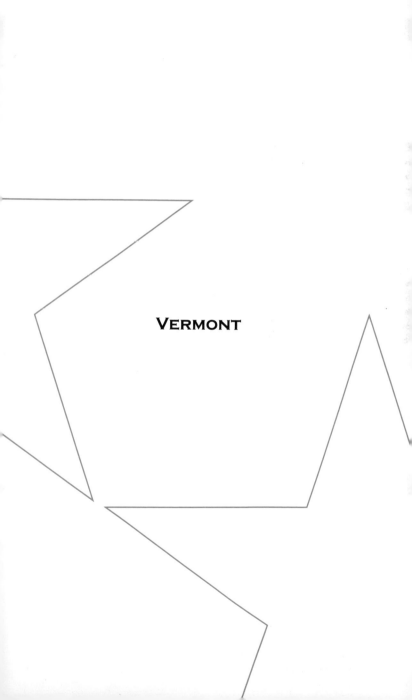

VERMONT

VERMONT

Barnard

TWIN FARMS ★ ★ ★ ★ ★

452 Royalton Turnpike, Barnard, 802-234-9999, 800-894-6327;
www.twinfarms.com

This secluded, exclusive hideaway in central Vermont offers one of the most uniquely sybaritic lodging experiences to be had in America. With 10 private cottages and 10 sumptuous guest rooms, Twin Farms is designed to cater to the individual experience. Meals are made to order and can be taken in the main dining room or the privacy of your cottage. Each was decorated to reflect a different theme by renowned interior designer Jed Johnson. The Moroccan-influenced Meadow has Persian rugs and a mosaic-tiled fireplace while the Scandinavian Barn has bleached pine floors, walls and rafters and crisp white and blue fabrics and upholstery. The cost is all-inclusive.

20 rooms. No children allowed. Complimentary full breakfast. Wireless Internet access. Restaurant (guests only), two bars. Fitness center, spa. Tennis. Ski in/ski out. Airport transportation available. $$$$

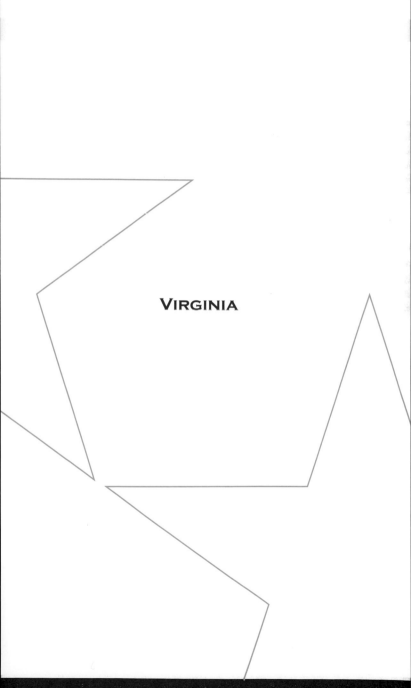

VIRGINIA

VIRGINIA

Richmond

THE JEFFERSON HOTEL ★★★★

101 W. Franklin St., Richmond, 804-788-8000, 800-424-8014;
www.jeffersonhotel.com
The Jefferson Hotel is an institution in the heart of Richmond near
the city's financial district, museums, shopping and the state capitol.
A historic Beaux Arts landmark dating to 1895, the hotel offers elegant
guest rooms furnished in a traditional style with antique reproductions
and fine art. TJ's provides a casual setting for fine dining with local dishes
like oyster chowder and peanut soup, while the hotel's star restaurant,
Lemaire, offers a sparkling ambience and a refined menu. Locals take
afternoon tea here. Complimentary car service transports guests within a
three-mile radius.

264 rooms. Restaurant. Airport transportation available. $$

Washington

THE INN AT LITTLE WASHINGTON ★★★★

309 Main St., Washington, 540-675-3800; www.theinnatlittlewashington.com
Savvy epicureans book a room—and a table—at the Inn at Little Washington.
Tucked away in the foothills of the Blue Ridge Mountains, the lovely inn
offers visitors a taste of the good life, complete with afternoon tea with
scones and tartlets. Tempting as it may be to indulge, guests save their
appetites for the evening's cuisine. Many make special trips just for the
talented chef's award-winning meals. The inn's opulent guest rooms
are filled with rich, custom furnishings and draped in lavish fabrics.
Some suites also showcase balconies and delightful garden views. The
surrounding area provides opportunities for hiking, fly-fishing, hot air
ballooning, antiquing and wine tasting.

18 rooms. Closed Tuesday in January-March and July. Complimentary
continental breakfast. Restaurant. $$$$

FOUR STAR HOTELS

Arlington

THE RITZ-CARLTON, PENTAGON CITY ★ ★ ★ ★

1250 S. Hayes St., Arlington, 703-415-5000, 800-241-3333;
www.ritzcarlton.com

Five minutes from Washington National Airport, the Ritz-Carlton, Pentagon City offers tailored elegance, with feather beds, Egyptian cotton linens, updated technology and luxurious club-level accommodations. Massages and personal fitness assessments are available at the fitness center. Afternoon tea takes on a whimsical edge with the Winnie the Pooh children's tea service in the Lobby Lounge, and the Grill never ceases to delight diners with its all-day dining.

366 rooms. Restaurant. Airport transportation available. $$$

McLean

THE RITZ-CARLTON, TYSONS CORNER ★ ★ ★ ★

1700 Tysons Blvd., McLean, 703-506-4300, 800-241-3333;
www.ritzcarlton.com

Only 15 minutes from Washington, D.C., this northern Virginia hotel is a luxurious retreat from the hustle and bustle of the capital. An inviting fireplace in the lobby lounge welcomes business and leisure travelers alike, and the white-glove service is friendly and refined. Guest rooms feature luxurious fabrics, flat-screen TVs, and down duvet-covered beds. Many also offer spectacular views of the city skyline. The Ritz-Carlton Day Spa showcases unique treatments such as a coffee anti-cellulite wrap or the bamboo lemongrass body scrub. The adjacent Tysons Galleria and Tysons Mall have more than 320 shops and a movie theater.

398 rooms. Pets accepted, restrictions. High-speed Internet access. Two restaurants, bar. Fitness center, spa. Indoor pool, whirlpool. $$$$

Williamsburg

WILLIAMSBURG INN ★ ★ ★ ★

136 E. Francis St., Williamsburg, 757-229-1000, 800-447-8679

Furnished in English Regency style, the guest rooms have just the right amount of sophistication to appeal to adults while keeping children comfortable and satisfied. Blessed with a central location in the heart of this re-created 18th-century village, the inn will take you back in time with a leisurely stroll by the blacksmith's shop, candlemaker and cobbler. Back at your hotel, you can play a round of golf, dive into the spring-fed pool, rally on the clay tennis courts, head to the fitness center to keep in shape, or spoil yourself at the spa or gourmet restaurant.

110 rooms. Fitness center, spa. Tennis Restaurant. Complimentary full breakfast. $$$$

Washington

THE INN AT LITTLE WASHINGTON ★ ★ ★ ★

309 Main St., Washington, 540-675-3800; www.theinnatlittlewashington.com
Chef Patrick O'Connell has amassed almost every culinary award in existence. Diners at the Inn at Little Washington will see why. Seasonal dishes include a crab cake "sandwich" with fried green tomatoes and tomato vinaigrette, sesame-crusted Chilean sea bass with baby shrimp, artichokes and grape tomatoes, rabbit braised in apple cider with wild mushrooms and garlic mashed potatoes, and for dessert, pistachio and white chocolate ice cream terrine with blackberry sauce.

American menu. Dinner. Closed Tuesday (except in May and October). Bar. Business casual attire. Reservations recommended. Valet parking. $$$$

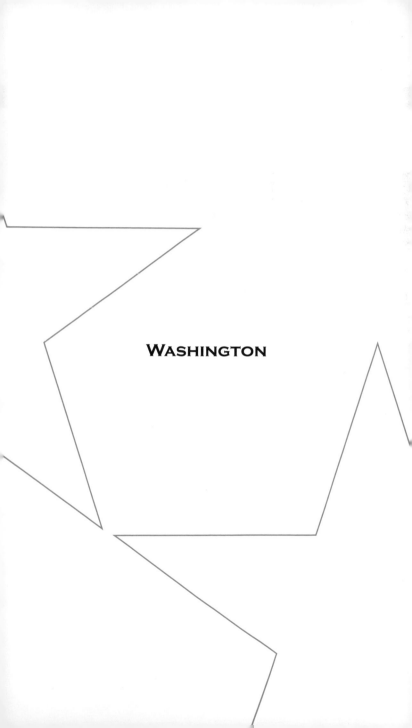

WASHINGTON

WASHINGTON

Seattle

THE FAIRMONT OLYMPIC HOTEL ★ ★ ★ ★

411 University St., Seattle, 206-621-1700, 800-257-7544;
www.fairmont.com

The Fairmont Olympic Hotel brings grand tradition and pampering service to downtown Seattle. Carefully blending its 1920s Italian Renaissance heritage with 21st-century hospitality, The Fairmont is a premier destination. The hotel is conveniently located in Rainier Square, only minutes from the city's top attractions. The guest rooms and suites are tasteful retreats with floral draperies, soft pastel colors and period furnishings. The fresh fruit and flowers make guests feel at home. The Georgian, where pale yellow walls and crystal chandeliers set a refined tone, features Pacific Northwest cuisine, while Shuckers restaurant is a popular oyster bar where you can enjoy Seattle's famous microbrews. Traditional high tea service is a unique treat.

450 rooms. Pets accepted, some restrictions; fee. High-speed Internet access. Three restaurants, two bars. Fitness center, spa. Indoor pool, whirlpool. $$$

Seattle

THE GEORGIAN ★ ★ ★ ★

411 University St., Seattle, 206-621-7889; www.fairmont.com/seattle

The Georgian is perhaps the most acclaimed restaurant in the Pacific Northwest. Chef Gavin Stephenson brings his culinary expertise to the restaurant after honing his skills first at the Savoy Hotel in London and then as personal chef to Saudi Prince Alwaleed Bin Talal Alsaud. While expressing a mastery of all dishes related to seafood, Gavin also excels with dishes such as carpaccio of artichokes and spring asparagus, ashed goat cheese and tomato mousseline, filet of Kobe beef topped with shallot and oxtail braisage and double-chocolate napoleon. The restaurant's elegant décor features crystal chandeliers, arched ceilings and potted palms.

American, French, Northwest menu. Breakfast, lunch, dinner. Bar. Children's menu. Business casual attire. Reservations recommended. Valet parking. $$$

LAMPREIA RESTAURANT ★ ★ ★ ★

2400 First Ave., Seattle, 206-443-3301; www.lampreiarestaurant.com

Gourmands should be prepared to devote a full evening to this edible extravaganza. Not content with serving what many typically identify as Italian food, chef Scott Carsberg is intent on utilizing the highest-quality ingredients in preparations that continue to astound and challenge the palate. The Tomatoes Lampreia, a dish that showcases up to 10 different preparations of the fruit, is a signature. Numerous tableside presentations by the charming staff add a sense of drama and flair.

International menu. Dinner. Closed Sunday-Monday. Business casual attire. Reservations recommended. Valet parking. $$$

ROVER'S ★ ★ ★ ★

2808 E. Madison St., Seattle, 206-325-7442; www.rovers-seattle.com

A small white clapboard cottage located in Madison Park houses Rover's, an intimate restaurant serving innovative and amazing contemporary cuisine. Thierry Rautureau, the chef and owner, stays true to the regional ingredients of the northwest while paying homage to impeccable French technique. The portions are perfect in size, taste and appearance. The restaurant offers five- and eight-course tasting menus, in addition to an á la carte menu. Lunch is served on Friday.

American, Northwest contemporary menu. Dinner. Closed Sunday-Monday. Business casual attire. Reservations recommended. $$$$

Woodinville

THE HERBFARM ★ ★ ★ ★

14590 N.E. 145th St., Woodinville, 425-485-5300;
www.theherbfarm.com, http://willowslodge.com

A four-hour meal of nine courses and five perfectly paired wines. A flamenco guitarist strumming in the half-light of flickering candles in an antique-filled dining room. A sun setting over a gracious, fragrant garden just outside your window. This is a little slice of Herbfarm. Chef (and gentleman gardener) Jerry Traunfeld creates seasonal, themed meals based on the bounty of the restaurant's own gardens and farm, plus produce, meats and artesian cheeses sourced from local growers, producers, ranchers and fishermen.

American menu. Dinner. Closed Monday-Wednesday. Business casual attire. Reservations recommended. $$$$

WEST VIRGINIA

WEST VIRGINIA

White Sulphur Springs

THE GREENBRIER ★ ★ ★ ★

300 W. Main St., White Sulphur Springs, 304-536-1110, 800-453-4858;
www.greenbrier.com

The Greenbrier is one of America's oldest and finest resorts. Located in the Allegheny Mountains, the resort includes rooms, suites, guest and estate houses decorated in lively color schemes and traditional furnishings. Many contain fireplaces, separate dining rooms and kitchens and sizable porches. The resort is home to the highly acclaimed Golf Digest Academy, and three championship courses, tennis courts and fitness and spa facilities. Guests are also invited to partake in unique adventures like falconry, sporting clays and trap and skeet shooting. The new Hemispheres restaurant serves up creative cuisine in a relaxed setting. History buffs get a kick out of the Cold War-era on-site bunker designed for Congress in case of nuclear war.

721 rooms. Fitness center, spa. Golf. Tennis. Children's activity center. Airport transportation available. $$$

White Sulphur Springs

THE GREENBRIER SPA ★ ★ ★ ★

300 W. Main St., *White Sulphur Springs, 800-453-4858*

White Sulphur Springs has long drawn visitors to its waters for their purported healing powers. Modern-day wellness seekers visit the Greenbrier for its state-of-the-art spa facility. The spa's treatment menu draws on the history of the mineral springs, and guests are encouraged to enjoy one of the spa's famous hydrotherapy treatments, from mountain rain showers and sulphur soaks to detoxifying marine baths and mineral mountain baths. Try the mud, rose petal, mineral or marine wraps, or the black walnut and salt glows.

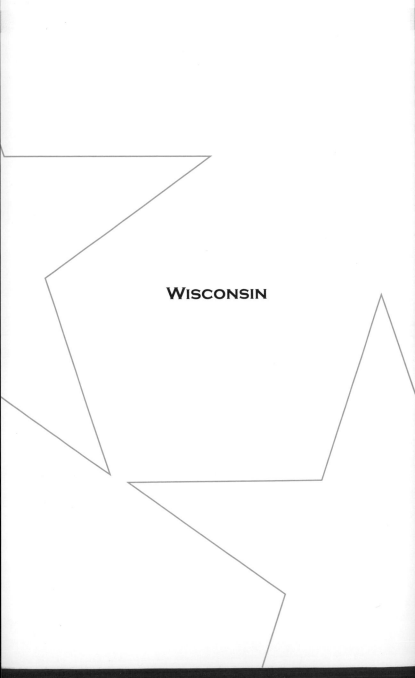

WISCONSIN

WISCONSIN

Kohler

THE AMERICAN CLUB ★ ★ ★ ★

419 Highland Dr., Kohler, 920-457-8000, 800-344-2838;
www.americanclub.com

Located in the charming village of Kohler, the American Club offers a country getaway one hour north of Milwaukee. Travelers stay and play here, and with the wide variety of activities, visitors are never at a loss for something to do. Golfers love the resort's four 18-hole courses sculpted out of the rugged terrain by renowned course architect Pete Dye. Whistling Straits calls to mind the natural beauty of Scotland and Ireland in its design, while Blackwolf Run is considered one of the top public course in America. The Kohler Waters Spa offers a full menu of treatments in a relaxing setting. The 10 distinctive restaurants offer plenty of food options. The guest rooms are tastefully appointed and are a wonderful retreat.

240 rooms. Wireless Internet access. Three restaurants, three bars. Children's activity center. Beach. Spa. Airport transportation available. Golf. Tennis. $$$

Rice Lake

CANOE BAY ★ ★ ★ ★

Off Hogback Rd., Rice Lake, 715-924-4594; www.canoebay.com

Canoe Bay is rather like a luxurious camp for adults, with gourmet dining, an award-winning wine cellar and extensive amenities. Situated on 280 acres in northwestern Wisconsin, the resort's three private, spring-fed lakes are perfect for a multitude of recreational opportunities. The wilderness trails are ideal for hiking in summer months, while snowshoeing and cross-country skiing are popular during the winter. The resort has no telephones or televisions to distract from the peaceful setting. Choose from either well-appointed rooms at the lodge or the inn or cozy private cottages. Linger over dinner in the candlelit Dining Room, where dishes are prepared with organic produce and locally produced ingredients.

19 rooms. No children allowed. Complimentary full breakfast. Restaurant. $$$

Kohler

KOHLER WATERS SPA ★ ★ ★ ★

419 Highland Dr., 920-457-8000, www.destinationkohler.com/spa

Kohler Waters Spa, located adjacent to the American Club, takes full advantage of its namesake's long history in the fixture and bath business. Water plays a part in just about everything at this spa, from the design (waterfalls abound from the relaxation pool to some treatment rooms) to the services (water therapies such as aromatherapy baths are the highlight). A new rooftop deck includes both an outdoor sunning space and an indoor lounge with a fireplace. The spa features a complete menu for couples and specialty treatments for men, including scrubs, baths and a golfer's massage.

WYOMING

Wyoming

Jackson Hole

Four Seasons Resort Jackson Hole ★ ★ ★ ★ ★

7680 Granite Loop Rd., Teton Village, 307-732-5000;
www.fourseasons.com/jacksonhole

Laidback western style is paired with big-city attention to detail at this full-service resort set amid the natural beauty of the Teton Mountains. Rooms are warm and welcoming, with gas fireplaces and décor that hints at the area's Native American heritage. Besides ski in/ski out access to the area's famous trails, the resort boasts a ski concierge, who handles lift tickets, advises skiers on trails and assists with equipment selections. Guests can reward themselves after a day of skiing or fly-fishing with a meal at the cozy Westbank Grill, where local specialties such as mustard and tarragon-crusted Colorado lamb fill the menu. Top off the evening with a soak in one of the outdoor hot pools while you feast on S'mores.

124 rooms. Pets accepted; some restrictions. Wireless Internet access. Three restaurants, two bars. Children's activity center. Fitness center, fitness classes available, spa. Outdoor pool, whirlpool. Ski in-ski out. Airport transportation available. $$$$

Jackson Hole

Amangani ★ ★ ★ ★

1535 N. East Butte Rd., Jackson Hole, 83001, 307-734-7333, 877-734-7333;
www.amanresorts.com

Located outside one of the country's most popular ski resorts, this American outpost of the acclaimed Aman resort group is a welcoming blend of Eastern minimalism and Western style. With only 40 rooms, the atmosphere is one of relaxation and renewal. Rooms are streamlined and contemporary with fireplaces and deep soaking tubs, while the resort's public spaces take advantage of the impressive mountain views. The culinary staff at the Grill keeps the focus on fresh organic ingredients, and the staff at the on-site health center accommodates every whim, from private yoga sessions to soothing spa treatments.

40 rooms. Wireless Internet access. Restaurant, bar. Children's activity center. Fitness center, fitness classes available, spa. Outdoor pool, whirlpool. Airport transportation available. $$$$

FOUR STAR SPAS

THE SPA AT FOUR SEASONS RESORT JACKSON HOLE
★ ★ ★ ★

7680 Granite Loop Rd., Teton Village, 307-732-5200;
www.fourseasons.com/jacksonhole

The Four Seasons Resort Jackson Hole marries the rugged style of the west with international elegance, service and style. Therapies, like the mountain clay body wrap, reflect the resort's alpine location and draw from local ingredients. The massage menu is well rounded, offering everything from aromatherapy and deep tissue treatments to moonlight massages and native stone therapies. Hair and nail care is available in the adjacent salon, while the fitness center and pool complete the well-rounded experience here.

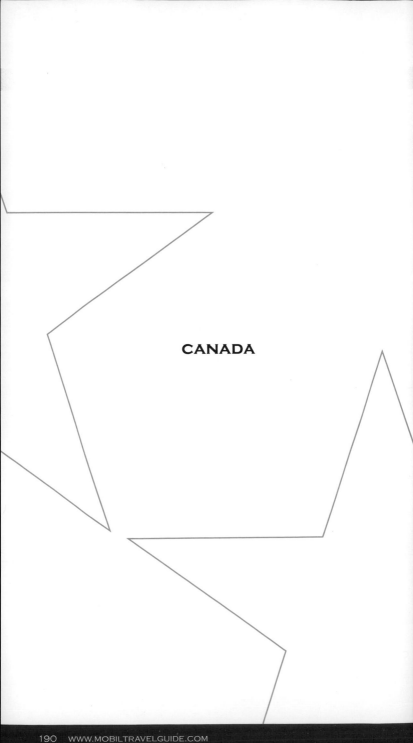

CANADA

ALBERTA

Banff

BANFFSHIRE CLUB ★ ★ ★ ★

405 Spray Ave., Banff, 403-762-6860; www.fairmont.com

After an exhilarating day exploring or skiing the Canadian Rockies, there's no more elegant way to spend the evening than dinner at the Scottish-inspired Banffshire Club. Malcolm tartan plaid and oak panels make the décor stately yet cozy. Warm up with one of many single malt scotches or sample one of the many bottles of wine in the acclaimed cellar. The menu features hearty dishes such as rib-eye with roasted foie gras and truffled potatoes, and roasted date- and pecan-crusted Alberta white-tailed deer loin. Or leave the choices up to the kitchen with the Club Tasting Menu, available with or without wines paired specifically for each course.

American, French menu. Dinner. Closed Sunday-Monday. Reservations recommended. Valet parking. $$$$

Lake Louise

POST HOTEL DINING ROOM ★ ★ ★ ★

200 Pipestone Rd., Lake Louise, 403-522-3989, 800-661-1586;
www.posthotel.com

This gem of a dining experience is tucked into the foothills of the Canadian Rockies and set in one of Banff National Park's remaining historic log lodges. The Post House Hotel Dining Room achieves old-fashioned charm with its rich Canadian pine walls, majestic mountain views and blazing stone fireplace. But it's not only the cozy atmosphere that's made the Post Hotel Dining Room a steady favorite among locals and travelers. Under executive chef Hans Sauter's direction, the kitchen prepares local ingredients like British Columbia caribou and Alberta fallow deer in a modern, global style. The exceptional cuisine is matched by a magnificent wine list; the restaurant's award-winning wine cellar features more than 30,500 bottles.

Canadian menu. Breakfast, lunch, dinner. Closed late October-mid-December. Bar. Children's menu. Casual attire. Reservations recommended. $$$$

Banff

WILLOW STREAM, THE SPA AT THE FAIRMONT BANFF SPRINGS, BANFF ★ ★ ★ ★

405 Spray Ave., Banff, 403-762-6860; www.fairmont.com

Willow Stream Spa is a shining star in the world-class mountain paradise of Banff Springs. This top-rated facility has it all, along with an outdoor whirlpool, an indoor Hungarian mineral pool and three waterfall-style whirlpools. A diverse treatment menu is available, offering therapies customized for reawakening, balancing, rejuvenating, and revitalizing. Sport-specific treatments include massages designed for golfers and skiers, while those who want to enjoy their spa treatments a deux will enjoy massages and other therapies in the specially-designed couples suite. A full-service fitness center offers guided hikes and fitness consultations in addition to its two pools, cardiovascular equipment, and free weights.

BRITISH COLUMBIA

Malahat

THE AERIE RESORT ★ ★ ★ ★

600 Ebedora Lane, Malahat, 250-743-7115, 800-518-1933; www.aerie.bc.ca

Built into the mountains on 85 acres above the southern part of Vancouver island, The Aerie Resort attracts travelers with its casual sophistication and incredible views. Persian and Chinese carpets, goose-down comforters and wood-burning fireplaces make the rooms cozy and comfortable. A multitude of activities, from biking and sailing to hiking and fishing are available. The fantastic Aerie Spa and Wellness Centre offers everything from facials to massages and body wraps. The resort's dining room is a sophisticated spot bathed in tones of cream and white with views of the mountains, and the Asian-influenced cuisine is equally alluring.

29 rooms.Complimentary full breakfast.Restaurant, bar.Indoor pool, whirlpool.$$$

Salt Spring Island

HASTINGS HOUSE ★ ★ ★ ★

160 Upper Ganges Rd., Salt Spring Island, 250-537-2362, 800-661-9255; www.hastingshouse.com

Snuggled on Salt Spring Island, the Tudor-style Hastings House captures the essence of the English countryside. Scattered throughout the lovely grounds, the rooms and suites are housed within ivy-covered garden cottages and the timber-framed barn. High tea and pre-dinner cocktails are served daily in the lounge. Hastings House boasts one of the most accomplished kitchens in British Colombia. Longtime executive chef Marcel Kauer and his brigade have the great fortune to draw on British Columbia's Pacific Northwest bounty. The wine list, although international in scope, features a slate of reds and white from B.C.'s Okanagan Valley.

18 rooms. Closed mid-November-mid-March. Restaurant. $$$$

Tofino

WICKANINNISH INN ★ ★ ★ ★

500 Osprey Lane, Tofino, 250-725-3100, 800-333-4604; www.wickinn.com
Famous for its storm-watching events (the luxurious resort is perched on the edge of a particularly volatile stretch of Pacific Ocean), this three-story cedar inn is a rustic retreat on a remote stretch of Vancouver Island. Wherever the eye glances, floor-to-ceiling windows frame dazzling views of the crashing surf. Furnishings crafted from recycled fir, cedar, and driftwood add a unique touch in the comfortable accommodations, as do fireplaces, oversized tubs and private balconies. Beachcomb with your pet in tow all you want on Chesterman Beach, and then stop by the pet shower station to freshen up Fido. The superb on-site spa takes its cues from botanicals from the nearby ancient rain forest. The sea is the focus at the Pointe Restaurant, where the ocean's bounty is highlighted.

75 rooms. Closed 7-10 days in January. Pets accepted. High-speed Internet access. Restaurant, bar. Fitness center, fitness classes available, spa. Beach. Business center. $$$$

Vancouver

FOUR SEASONS HOTEL VANCOUVER ★ ★ ★ ★

791 W Georgia St., Vancouver, 604-689-9333; www.fourseasons.com/vancouver
Located downtown in the commercial and cultural hub of the city, the Four Seasons Hotel Vancouver is a home-away-from-home for both business and leisure travelers. Families are welcome—children will love the indoor/outdoor pool and the in-room PlayStations. In addition to 24-hour room service, the hotel has three dining options: Chartwell restaurant, headed by executive chef Rafael Gonzalez, The Garden Terrace and the Terrace Bar. Chartwell, named after Chruchill's summer home, is famous for its exemplary service and West Coast cuisine.

376 rooms. Pets accepted, some restrictions. High-speed Internet access. Two restaurants, bar. Fitness center. Pools. Business center. $$$

THE SUTTON PLACE HOTEL - VANCOUVER ★ ★ ★ ★

845 Burrard St., Vancouver, 604-682-5511; www.vancouver.suttonplace.com
Located in the business and shopping core of downtown Vancouver, the hotel offers guest rooms that exude a European flavor, while the dining and lounge areas feature comforting old-world motifs. Business travelers are pampered with the business center that was renovated to provide state-of-the-art technology and efficiency. The hotel offers a serene spa, indoor swimming pool under a big sunroof, and a fitness center

397 rooms. Pets accepted, some restrictions; fee. High-speed Internet access. Two restaurants, bar. Fitness center. Spa. Indoor pool, whirlpool. Business center. $$$

Whistler

FOUR SEASONS RESORT WHISTLER ★ ★ ★ ★

4591 Blackcomb Way, Whistler, 604-935-3400, 800-819-5053;
www.fourseasons.com
This resort is nestled in the foot of the Blackcomb and Whistler mountains and offers a year-round getaway that features signature Four Seasons service and style. Located at the base of Blackcomb Mountain, it is a mere five-minute walk to the ski lifts and a 10-minute stroll to the village center. The guest rooms are spacious, beautifully furnished and decorated. The dining room and lounge, Fifty Two 80, delight with flavorful food and an extensive wine list and specialty cocktails. After a day of activity, retreat to The Spa, where body wraps, hydro-therapy, facials and massages will help you unwind.

273 rooms. Restaurant, bar, children's activity center (winter only). Pets accepted, fee. Exercise center. Pool. Business center. $$$$

FOUR STAR RESTAURANTS

Malahat

AERIE DINING ROOM ★ ★ ★ ★

600 Ebedora Ln., Malahat, 250-743-7115, 800-518-1933; www.aerie.bc.ca
Spectacular views of snowy mountaintops are among the many highlights of an evening at The Aerie Dining Room. The Aerie's kitchen is known for its use of superb local produce, sourcing its ingredients from a network of 60 small farms. The kitchen is loyal to classic French technique but brings plates to modern life with Pacific accents. The result is straightforward, yet innovative and sophisticated, fare. A lengthy wine list features Vancouver's own, in addition to wines of the Pacific Coast.

French menu. Closed 10 days in January. Reservations recommended. Outdoor seating. $$$

Ladner

LA BELLE AUBERGE ★ ★ ★ ★

4856 48th Ave., Ladner, 604-946-7717; www.labelleauberge.com
If you crave the glorious food of France's best kitchens, opt for a 30-minute drive from Vancouver to Ladner and enjoy dinner at La Belle Auberge. Set in a charming 1902 country inn, the restaurant is an intimate, five antique-filled salon-style dining rooms. The kitchen, led by chef/owner Bruno Marti, a masterful culinary technician, offers spectacular, authentic French cuisine.

French menu. Reservations recommended. Outdoor seating. $$$

Vancouver

BISHOP'S ★ ★ ★ ★

2183 W. Fourth Ave, Vancouver, 604-738-2025; www.bishopsonline.com
Intimate, modern and airy, with a loft-like yet upscale feel, this chic duplex restaurant is known for West Coast continental cuisine and has a menu that emphasizes seasonal, organic produce and locally-sourced seafood. It isn't uncommon to spy celebrities and VIPs nibbling on these delicious culinary wares. For those who like to sample lots of different wines with dinner, Bishop's offers a nice selection of wines by the glass and an outstanding range of wines by the half-bottle. In addition to being a visionary chef, owner John Bishop is a gracious host.

International menu. Dinner. Closed December 24-26; also first week in January. Bar. Business casual attire. Reservations recommended. Outdoor seating. $$$

LUMIERE ★ ★ ★ ★

2551 W. Broadway, Vancouver, 604-739-8185; www.lumiere.ca
Lumiere is a stunning and elegant restaurant that offers European-style dining of the most divine order. The inspired and innovative fare is French with Asian accents and displays a respect for regional ingredients. While the eight-course menu could be overkill, each portion is perfectly sized so that you don't finish dinner feeling perilously inflated. Instead, you feel deliciously satiated and utterly pampered by the experience. The global wine list is in sync with the kitchen's style, but attention should also be paid to the classic cocktails served at Lumiere's sexy bar. The bartenders here follow a pre-Prohibition style, where the craft of the cocktail is taken as seriously as the mastery of the plate.

French menu. Dinner. Closed Monday. Bar. Business casual attire. Reservations recommended. Valet parking. Outdoor seating. $$$$

WEST ★ ★ ★ ★

2881 Granville St., Vancouver, 604-738-8938; www.westrestaurant.com
West is one of those sleek, heavenly spots that makes sipping cocktails for hours on end an easy task. It is an ideal choice for gourmets in search of an inventive, eclectic meal, as well as those who crave local flavor and seasonal ingredients. Located in Vancouver's chic South Granville neighborhood, West offers diners the chance to sample the vibrant cuisine of the Pacific Northwest region. Stunning, locally sourced ingredients are on display here thanks to the masterful kitchen.

International menu. Reservations recommended. $$$

Victoria

RESTAURANT MATISSE ★ ★ ★ ★

512 Yates St., Victoria, 250-480-0883; www.restaurantmatisse.com
Right in the heart of downtown Victoria, you'll discover a delightful spot for sampling authentic French fare. Warmed with yellow brick walls, colorful floral arrangements and country charm, Restaurant Matisse is a gem that serves dishes which taste as though they've come straight from a Parisian kitchen. House specialties include duck palette and Marseilles-style bouillabaisse. In addition to the à la carte selections, the chef offers a nine-course prix fixe menu for those who have penciled excess and indulgence into the evening. While French wines dominate the list, a great selection of California bottles is also included.

French menu. Dinner. Closed Monday-Tuesday; also two weeks in spring. Business casual attire. Reservations recommended. $$$

FOUR STAR SPAS

Tofino

ANCIENT CEDARS SPA ★ ★ ★ ★

500 Osprey Lane, Tofino, 250-725-3100
Resting on a rocky promontory jutting into the Pacific Ocean with an old-growth rainforest in the background, this is truly a one-of-a-kind hideaway. The interiors have been designed to bring the outdoors in, with slate tiles, dark colors and cedar decorating this serene space. This treatment menu focuses on relaxation and renewal. Thai, Lomi Lomi and hot stone massage are among the bodywork therapies available or the signature sacred sea treatment, which uses the renowned Bouvier Hydrotherapy tub.

Whistler

SPA AT FOUR SEASONS WHISTLER ★ ★ ★ ★

4591 Blackcomb Way, Whistler, 604-935-3400;
www.fourseasons.com /whistler/spa

This contemporary spa located inside the Four Seasons Whistler offers a full-menu of massages and body treatments designed to sooth and restore sore muscles after a day on the slopes. Chilly feet are wrapped in warm towels while muscles are warmed with hot stones during the après-ski massage. The men's fitness facial restores wind- and sun-burned skin while the BC glacial clay wrap is a great way to warm up at the end of the day. Those who can't pry themselves from the comfort of their rooms can order up an in-room massage.

NEW BRUNSWICK

FOUR STAR HOTELS

St. Andrews

KINGSBRAE ARMS ★ ★ ★ ★

219 King St., St. Andrews, 506-529-1897; www.kingsbrae.com

Fresh sea air and heady fragrances from the garden leave an indelible mark on guests of Kingsbrae Arms. Located in the historic resort of St. Andrews in the Maritime provinces, this winsome 1897 country house hotel has elegant rooms with canopy beds, whirlpools tubs, fireplaces, in-room massage services and balconies with enchanting views of the formal garden and sea beyond. Start the morning with a hearty country breakfast before setting out to sea kayak or whale-watch. Whether it's cocktails and hors d'oeuvres in the library, or a four-course dinner enhanced by fresh herbs and vegetables from the garden, gourmet dining is the centerpiece here.

14 rooms. Closed October-May. Pets accepted, some restrictions. Complimentary full breakfast. Restaurant. Outdoor pool. Business center. $$$$

ONTARIO

Toronto

FOUR SEASONS HOTEL TORONTO ★ ★ ★ ★

21 Avenue Rd., Toronto, 416-964-0411;
www.fourseasons.com/toronto
The Four Seasons Hotel Toronto is in a prime location in the upscale neighborhood of Yorkville. Guest rooms feature elegant colonial décor, plush furnishings and charming views of Yorkville, or stunning views of the city's downtown. Not forgotten are business travels who are pampered with the in-house business center and complimentary limousine service. Guests can relax by the heated indoor and outdoor pools, sauna, whirlpool and fitness center. Dinner should not be missed at with classic French cuisine served in the hotel's restaurant, Truffles.

380 rooms, 32 story. Pets accepted, some restrictions. High-speed Internet access. Two restaurants, two bars. Fitness center. Indoor pool, outdoor pool, whirlpool. Business center. $

PARK HYATT TORONTO ★ ★ ★ ★

4 Avenue Rd., Toronto, 416-925-1234, 800-977-4197;
www.parktoronto.hyatt.com
The Park Hyatt Toronto calls the stylish Yorkville area home. Located at the intersection of Avenue Road and Bloor Street, this hotel has some of the world's leading stores just outside its doors. Public and private spaces have a rich feeling completed with handsome furnishings and a clean, modern look dominates the rooms and suites. The demands of the world dissipate at the Stillwater Spa. International dishes are the specialty at Annona, while the grilled steaks and seafood of Morton's of Chicago are always a treat.

346 rooms. Restaurant, bar. Business center. $$$

Toronto

CANOE ★ ★ ★ ★

66 Wellington St. W., Toronto, 416-364-0054
Canoe is a stunning venue in which to experience creative, satisfying regional Canadian cuisine. While dazzling ingredients tend to be sourced from wonderful local producers, many organic, the kitchen borrows flavors and techniques from the world at large, including Asia, France and

the American South. The end product is inventive food and an equally original room.

Canadian menu. Reservations recommended. $$$

Chiado ★ ★ ★ ★

864 College St., Toronto, 416-538-1910;
www.chiadorestaurant.ca

Paying homage to the old seaside town but updating dishes for a more modern sensibility, Chiado features what might best be described as "nouvelle Portuguese cuisine." The food is first-rate and fabulous, featuring an ocean's worth of fresh fish simply prepared with olive oil and herbs, as well as innovative takes on pheasant, game and poultry. To add to the authenticity of the experience, Chiado has the largest collection of fine Portuguese wines in North America and a superb selection of vintage ports.

Spanish menu. Reservations recommended. $$$

The Fifth ★ ★ ★ ★

225 Richmond St. W., Toronto, 416-979-3005; www.thefifthgrill.com

It takes work to make it to The Fifth. First, an alley entrance leads you to The Easy, an upscale nightclub and former speakeasy. Once inside The Easy, you are directed onto a Persian rug-lined vintage freight elevator. There, an attendant takes you to floor number five. Exit and you have finally arrived at The Fifth, a treasured contemporary French restaurant and supper club. The food is of the delicious updated French variety and the dishes are perfectly prepared, beautifully presented and easily devoured.

French menu. Closed Sunday-Wednesday. Bar. Reservations recommended. Outdoor seating. $$$$

North 44 Degrees ★ ★ ★ ★

2537 Yonge St., Toronto, 416-487-4897; www.north44restaurant.com

Style, serenity and elegance infuse every aspect of North 44 Degrees. From the recently renovated loft-like dining room to the world-class New continental cuisine, North 44 Degrees is a sublime and sexy dining experience. A sophisticated crowd fills the restaurant, named for the city's latitude, on most nights. Chef/owner Mark McEwan expertly blends the bright flavors of Asia with those of Italy, France and Canada. The service is smooth, refined and in perfect harmony with the cool space and stellar cuisine.

International menu. Reservations recommended. $$$$

SCARAMOUCHE ★ ★ ★ ★

1 Benvenuto Pl., Toronto, 416-961-8011; www.scaramoucherestaurant.com
Up on a hillside overlooking the dazzling downtown lights, Scaramouche is the perfect hideaway for falling in love with food or your dining companion. This modern, bi-level space is known for its fantastic contemporary French fare and is often jammed with dressed-up, savvy locals. The restaurant is divided between a formal dining room upstairs and a modestly priced pasta bar downstairs.

French menu. Reservations recommended. $$$$

SPLENDIDO ★ ★ ★ ★

88 Harbord St., Toronto, 416-929-7788; www.splendido.ca
Splendido has hit its stride and has become one of Toronto's best restaurants, with interpretations of international cuisines and a focus on clean, flavorful sauces and local Canadian ingredients. Several charming details like the Champagne cart and the selection of petit fours make this a fun and enjoyable dining experience.

International menu. Closed Monday; July-August: Sunday. Reservations recommended. $$$

TRUFFLES ★ ★ ★ ★

21 Avenue Rd., Toronto, 416-964-0411; www.fourseasons.com
Filled with light, Truffles dining room resembles the parlor room of a fabulous art collector with impeccable taste. Soaring ceilings, rich wood moldings, large bay windows and deep-chocolate velvet seating set a sophisticated but minimalist stage for the works of a talented group of local artisans, sculptors and artists that are on display. Located in the Four Seasons Hotel Toronto, Truffles is known for its distinct, stylized brand of modern Provençal-style cuisine. As the name suggests, the coveted mushrooms do indeed show up on the menu—as in the smoked black cod with truffle poached egg and mustard beurre blanc. Smooth service and an extensive wine list make for a memorable meal.

French menu. Dinner. Closed Sunday. Bar. Jacket required. Reservations recommended. Valet parking. $$$$

Toronto

STILLWATER SPA, PARK HYATT TORONTO ★ ★ ★

4 Avenue Rd, Toronto, 416-926-2389; parktoronto.hyatt.com/hyatt/pure/spas
With its cool, crisp interiors—complete with a fireplace in the Tea Lounge and waterfalls and streams throughout the facility—and fabulous mind and body relaxation therapies, Park Hyatt Toronto's Stillwater Spa offers you an escape. The signature Stillwater massage customizes an aromatherapy blend to accompany a relaxing bodywork combination of Swedish massage, trigger-points pressure and stretching techniques.

QUEBEC

Montreal

HOTEL LE ST. JAMES ★ ★ ★ ★

355 Saint Jacques St., Montreal, 514-841-3111, 866-841-3111;
www.hotellestjames.com
At the majestic Hotel Le St. James, each room and suite is individually decorated with antiques and art. A former bank, the building's imposing facade features ornate moldings and details fully restored to their 1870s grandeur. The convention center, downtown business area, Old Port area and the St. Lawrence River are the main sights of Old Montreal that are just a short stroll away from the hotel. Lunch and dinner feature regional, market-driven fare and afternoon tea is served as well.

61 rooms. Restaurant, bar. Spa. Pets accepted. Fitness ceneter. Business center. $$$$

Adele

L'EAU A LA BOUCHE ★ ★ ★ ★

3003 Ste. Adele Blvd, Ste. Adele, 450- 229-2991; www.leaualabouche.com
Tucked into a forest surrounding the Laurentian Mountains, near the village of Sainte-Adèle, you will find L'eau a la Bouche, a charming little restaurant located on the property of the Hotel L'eau a la Bouche. The gourmet menu is built around local produce, fish, meat and homegrown herbs and vegetables, woven together and dressed up with a perfect dose

of French technique and modern flair. Attentive, thoughtful service and a vast wine list make this luxurious dining experience unforgettable.

French menu. Breakfast, dinner. Bar.$$$

Montreal

TOQUE! ★★★★

900 place Jean-Paul Riopelle, Montreal, 514-499-2084;
www.restaurant-toque.com
Toque! is a graceful, luxurious, contemporary French restaurant located across from the Convention Centre and Jean-Paul Riopelle Park. Plates are garnished with such impeccable attention to detail that you may spend several minutes debating whether or not to ruin it. The talented and hospitable chef, Norman Laprise wields magic with a whisk and uses locally farmed ingredients to create a miraculous menu of sophisticated, avant-garde French fare.

French menu. Closed Sunday-Monday; also two weeks in late December-early January. Reservations recommended. $$$

Quebec City

RESTAURANT INITIALE ★★★★

54 rue Saint-Pierre, Québec City, 418-694-1818;
www.restaurantinitiale.com
This modern French-cuisine restaurant is located in a former bank about one block from the St. Lawrence River in the Old Port district. Country products from local producers result in fresh, pure flavors.

French menu. Closed Sunday-Monday; also first two weeks in January. Reservations recommended. $$$

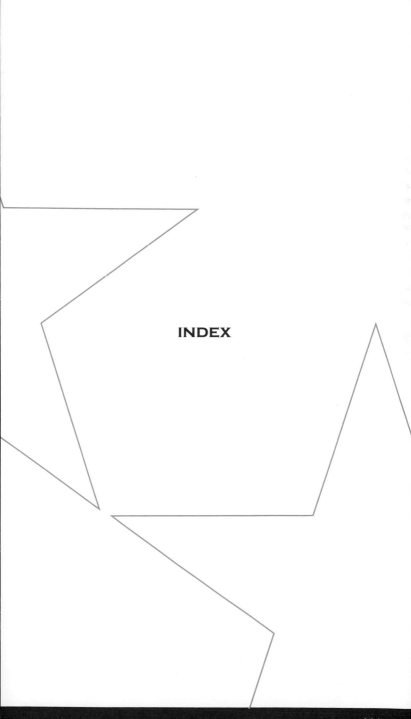

INDEX

INDEX

INDEX

INDEX

INDEX

INDEX

Index